Science and Ceremony

The Dan Danciger Publication Series

Science and Ceremony

The Institutional Economics
of C. E. Ayres
Edited by William Breit and
William Patton Culbertson, Jr.

FOREWORD BY JOHN KENNETH GALBRAITH

University of Texas Press Austin & London

Library of Congress Cataloging in Publication Data
Main entry under title:

Science and ceremony.

(The Dan Danciger publication series)
"Clarence Edwin Ayres: a chronological bibliography": p.
Includes index.
    1. Ayres, Clarence Edwin, 1891–1972—Addresses,
essays, lectures. 2. Institutional economics—
Addresses, essays, lectures. I. Breit, William.
II. Culbertson, William Patton, 1941–
HB119.A9S33   330.1   76–8238
ISBN 0–292–77523–7

Printed in the United States of America

Contents

Foreword

JOHN KENNETH GALBRAITH

Several of the contributors to this volume knew Clarence Ayres over a longer time than I did. All, I think, are better schooled on one or another aspect of his work. My own acquaintance began with his books and articles—I was attracted, like all others, by their independence and solid precision of thought and, above all, by the responsible concern of the author for the world as it is and as it might be.

Then, in later years, as I had occasion to be in Austin, I always called on Ayres, either at the university or at his house. I remember especially the last occasion—a long afternoon visit in the small shady yard back of his dwelling. He was a slight man of kindly expression, in later years a trifle frail, with a sparkling interest in ideas and, as always, in their meaning for practical action. He never said anything that was meant to be fashionable, that was intended to create an impression; he had no interest in the economics that advanced professional position or in-house reputation as distinct from that which advanced knowledge and needed change. I have always found pleasure in enlarging on the errors or absurdities of my professional friends. I don't think Clarence found this line of discussion wholly distasteful. He had much from a lifetime of experience to contribute. But it was not his instinct. He preferred to speak well of people who were useful and who made sense.

He was a liberal in the practical, effective sense—a man, I suppose, of the Roosevelt–New Deal mood as well as vintage. He was also, as numerous comments in this volume attest, a teacher and a leader among scholars. In consequence, during his lifetime he helped make the University of Texas a far more important center for progressive economic discussion than most economists from the parochial east, north, or west have ever quite appreciated. There was a wider range of thought than at more celebrated centers. For a period in the early years of Ayres's tenure there, it was even a place of pilgrimage for Marxists. And all this occurred within a stone's throw of Texas governors and legislators, a category of statesmen that included during Ayres's lifetime some of the most repressive politicians in all the Republic. Most, no doubt, were beyond understanding what Ayres was discussing or urging. But occasionally they did. Sometimes they reacted. Ayres was undeterred.

The essays in this volume are not meant as a monument to Ayres. They are meant to tell what he thought and what he did. They do show his range of interests, his diligence, his originality of mind and method. If, in addition, a man is a good teacher, is the focal point of an important center of professional and scientific discussion, and all this is accomplished in a scholarly cold climate, he can rightly expect to be honored by his colleagues. Alas, in the case of Ayres, it was not so. Professor Breit has given part of the reason; there is, indeed, a marked snobbishness in American professional attitudes combined, oddly enough, with an inferiority complex. Good economic work is done, *pro tanto*, in the universities of established reputation. The institutions make the scholar. And in the past Americans have always thought it better to have made one's scholarly debut in Vienna, Budapest, a German university, or Cambridge or Oxford. And if he has been a critic of neoclassical orthodoxy, if he is called by some an institutionalist, his case is hopeless.

So it was with Ayres. The conventional honors passed him by. A few years ago, not long before his death, I proposed that he be made a Distinguished Fellow, as they are designated, of the American Economic Association. I noted that Ludwig von Mises had recently been elected—a man who, with Friedrich von Hayek, had showed only how, by sufficiently rigorous process of thought, the irrelevant could be converted into the absurd. My case was dismissed without argument.

Later I asked Ayres to join me at the association meetings that winter in New Orleans in honoring Gunnar Myrdal, an economist whom, for his concern for the practical, useful tasks of economics, one groups naturally with Ayres. He readily and generously agreed. It was the occasion for another talk. It was the last time.

Acknowledgments

We are grateful beyond words to Gwendolen Ayres, the widow of Clarence Ayres, for allowing us full access to her late husband's papers and correspondence and for her willingness to be subjected to so many questions (some of them, no doubt, impertinent) in our search for biographical information. This project could not have been completed without her kind patience and cooperation.

In addition we wish to thank the Thomas Jefferson Center Foundation at the University of Virginia for a grant to aid in compiling the bibliography and to acknowledge the financial assistance of the Louisiana State University Foundation. The Louisiana State University's Division of Research provided typing assistance, and we would like to thank Mary Jo Brooks, Brenda Gatlin, and Linda Teekel for typing the final manuscript.

A note of appreciation must be extended to the following persons who at one time or another came to our support in various ways: Calvin P. Blair, Harold Cohen, Margaret Byrd Culbertson, Herman Daly, Ronnie Dugger, Kenneth G. Elzinga, Betty Fitzsimmons, Wendell C. Gordon, Clifton Grubbs, Raja Hassen, Lamar B. Jones, David P. Kimmel, Robert J. Kroner, Stephen L. McDonald, Daniel C. Morgan, Jr., Warren Samuels, and Marvin Vexler.

Clarence Edwin Ayres, 1891–1972

Introduction

These essays were written to provide a long overdue appraisal of the work and influence of Clarence E. Ayres, one of the most original economic philosophers of his time. Although Thorstein Veblen is still the greatest single name to have emerged out of the history of American institutional economics, Clarence Ayres went beyond him in providing the philosophical framework with which to understand the contribution of institutionalism to economic science.

Like earlier institutionalists, Ayres went off in directions that were altogether different from those taken by the establishment economists of his generation. During a period when economic theory was becoming increasingly recondite, abstract, and mathematically formal in its analysis of relative prices, Ayres rejected this approach and argued forcefully and eloquently his proposition that relative prices were merely codes for the deeper submerged forces of technological change interacting with the institutional structure of society; and it was these forces which economic science ignored at its peril and that of industrial society generally.

His arguments were buttressed with brilliant insights into the causes and significance of both the agricultural and industrial revolutions which had brought about what Jacob Bronowski was later to call "the ascent of man." Moreover, he developed a philosophic theory of value and welfare which could be used to judge the progress of society. To Ayres the economists' almost total preoccupation with analytical refinements in theory and statistical techniques involved a kind of twentieth-century scholasticism which would inevitably bring economics into disrepute. For the critical issues of the time and of the calculable future were the full realization of the economic potential of industrial society and the economic development of the underdeveloped world. In his concern with stability, growth, and progress and in his skepticism about the usefulness of much of economic orthodoxy in understanding these issues, Clarence Ayres was at least twenty years ahead of his time.

But Ayres was more than a first-rate thinker on economic and social questions. He was, perhaps first and foremost, a great teacher. From his earliest days in academic life he was interested in educational experimentation and the optimal way to transmit knowledge and a love of learning to the young. A list of his students who were to become luminaries in their own right would include: sociologists

Talcott Parsons, C. Wright Mills, and Marion J. Levy, Jr.; psychiatrist Allen Wheelis; journalist Ronnie Dugger; economists Joseph Dorfman and Carter Goodrich. But one cannot judge a great teacher by counting the noses of his famous students. It is significant that not a single one of those mentioned can be considered a disciple in the usual sense of that word. That is, none of them gave a slavish repetition of his formulations or treated him like an untouchable god. Had they done so, Ayres would have failed in what he considered the main role of a teacher: to teach, to inspire, but never to impair.

The essays that follow analyze Ayres's achievements as economist, social philosopher, and teacher. Apart from the first chapter, which provides a biographical sketch of his career, each study critically treats some aspect of Ayres's work and influence or is a further development of his approach. Aside from the editors, only three of the authors were students of Ayres or knew him beyond the most casual acquaintance. What gives the book coherence is that every essay was written especially for the volume by an author who was assigned his particular topic because of his special expertise. The book does not claim to provide a systematic or complete exposition and critique of Ayres's point of view. Representatives from the fields of anthropology, psychology, philosophy, education, music, art, and many others would have been necessary to make this a definitive work on all the areas of knowledge in which Ayres toiled and had influence. Instead, an editorial decision was imposed which limited the volume mainly to economists who themselves had special competence in the fields of economics in which Ayres devoted his energies. In addition, two outstanding representatives of sociology directly affected by Ayres's thinking and personality were asked to provide personal reflections on Ayres as a teacher.

In the first paper in the volume William Breit, professor of economics at the University of Virginia, and William Patton Culbertson, Jr., associate professor of economics at Louisiana State University, trace the chief events in the making of one of America's foremost institutionalist economists. They show that Ayres's enormous erudition was the product of an inquiring and lively intellect that moved easily from philosophy into educational experimentation, journalism, social theory, and, ultimately, economics. Early in his career his contact with the stimulating environment of the University of Chicago's philosophy and economics departments and, most important, his association with economist Walton Hamilton gave Ayres the inspiration that was to become his central concern: to provide the theoretical formulation for what Veblen had called "the economic life process." During the last forty years of his academic career he taught at the University of Texas, where he became identified with his own brand of institutional economics: a type which avoided the satirical wrappings of Thorstein Veblen, the incomprehensibility of John R. Commons, and the almost purely statistical concerns of the later Wesley Clair Mitchell. Instead, Ayres developed a writing style that was direct, forceful, and highly sophisticated. He fashioned his own set of tools with which to attack the problems of economic order. Soon there was a new regional school of economics alongside those at Wisconsin and Chicago: the Texas school of which Clarence Ayres was the founder and acknowledged leader.

His irreverent attitudes toward the sacred cows of privilege and the status quo eventually embroiled him in controversies with the administration, the Board of Regents, and the Texas legislature. But he survived and was soon recognized as one of the University of Texas's handful of outspoken celebrities of national reputation along with folklorist J. Frank Dobie, historian Walter Prescott Webb, and naturalist Roy Bedichek.

The next three papers in the book provide a trans-Atlantic view of some of Ayres's major themes and ideas. The first of these, by A. W. Coats of the University of Nottingham, an authority on American economic thought, is in some ways the most ambitious in the volume since it gives a detailed summary and critique of Ayres's economic and philosophic contributions. Although Coats does not claim to provide a definitive statement, his essay, more than any other, conveys a sense of the wide range and sweep of Ayres's intellect. He stresses the "Americanness" of Ayres's antecedents, principal interests, and associations. Coats sees Ayres as representing the generation of institutional economists between Veblen, Commons, and Mitchell and today's "neo-institutionalists," that is, the younger members of the Association for Evolutionary Economics. According to Coats, no leading figure in European intellectual circles possesses a similar journalistic background, a comparable list of nonspecialist publications, and equivalent pedagogic charisma and personal influence.

The next essay, by R. M. Hartwell of Nuffield College at the University of Oxford and former editor of the prestigious *Economic History Review*, treats Ayres's contribution to an understanding of the meaning and significance of the industrial revolution. Hartwell is a recognized authority on this topic and his own work was much admired by Ayres. Hartwell shows that Ayres's isolation from other scholars on the topic of the industrial revolution led him to develop original theories which owed little to predecessors or current fash-

ions. In upgrading the role of technology in growth and the role of
the machine in the industrial revolution he anticipated many of the
newer themes in economic history. Since Ayres saw growth not as a
simply induced process but as a social process of overcoming institutional resistances, he came close to the sophisticated views on
economic growth that now prevail. To Hartwell, Ayres's explanation
of Europe's economic leadership is more persuasive than that of Max
Weber, with whom he is compared. Ayres's theory of the permissive-
ness of institutions interacting with advancing technology
is used by Hartwell to explain England's leadership in industrialization in Europe. Hartwell points out that Ayres's one-time lonely
views on the industrial revolution have now become the conventional
wisdom of economic historians.

S. Herbert Frankel, who for many years held the chair in economic
development at Nuffield College in the University of Oxford, takes
as his point of departure the comments of Joan Robinson in her book
Economic Philosophy regarding Ayres's ideas on development. Robinson argued that if Ayres's theory is correct (that in newer civilizations ceremonial patterns put up weaker resistances to new combinations of tools than in older civilizations), then Black Africa, where
modern technology is coming to the attention of peoples little encumbered by ancient traditions, is due to outstrip us all. Frankel, a
specialist on African economic development, challenges Robinson on
this point. He argues that resistance to change in Africa is in fact very
strong and can be explained in terms of the risk and expected costs
to individuals in departing from their customary beliefs. Individuals
cling to the past because of the fear of the trade-off between the
choices of the past and those which can be made now. To Frankel,
Ayres was fully aware of the constraining power of the institutional
structure, but he did not give sufficient weight to the fact that institutions themselves are capable of generating change when opportunities
for doing so are observed to be emerging. Ayres's hostility to the
market mechanism did not allow him to appreciate the power of the
institution of the market to slough off the dead wood of the past. To
Frankel, Ayres was not enough concerned with the value of individual
freedom and its basis in a market economy. Societies that cease to
value the freedom of the individual will find the fruits of the industrial way of life (in which Ayres had so much faith) a snare and a
delusion.

The fifth paper is by W. W. Rostow, professor of economics and
history at the University of Texas at Austin. Since Rostow's name
is itself identified with a highly controversial theory of economic

growth, it is most appropriate that he should be included in this volume. Rostow argues that Ayres anticipated the current dissatisfaction with static equilibrium analysis of prices and that he was correct in insisting that technological change must be brought toward the center stage in any modern theory of economic growth. But Ayres's work shares two weaknesses with the classical tradition which he attacked: a failure to examine the character of the linkages among science, invention, and innovation; and (much as Frankel had argued) a failure to explore the linkages of these three variables to the market mechanism. Nevertheless, in rejecting both the shapeless empirical investigation of other institutionalists and the empty devices of formal elegance of his more orthodox peers, Ayres fashioned a highly powerful and illuminating theory of economic development.

The paper by Joseph J. Spengler of Duke University, a former president of the American Economic Association and an authority on demography, brings up a disturbing issue that has come much to the forefront since Ayres did his work: the limits to growth. Since Ayres's analysis is suffused with tremendous optimism about the future of industrial society and its unlimited potential to give mankind increasingly high standards of living and welfare, it seems particularly pertinent to discuss the question in this volume. In seeing no basis for setting any limits to the magnitude of technological advance, Spengler believes that Ayres underestimated the costs of change. To Spengler, Ayres too cavalierly dismissed the problems posed by Malthus regarding the limited supply of arable land relative to population growth. It may not be possible to surmount the growing problem of depletable resources because of the biospheric constraints on the prospective state of human existence. Limited resources and their dissipation were not given adequate weight in Ayres's analysis, and his easy optimism about the future of industrial civilization may prove to have been unwarranted.

In the paper contributed by Gordon Tullock of Virginia Polytechnic Institute and State University, two of Ayres's earliest books on science are examined. Among his many publications, Tullock is the author of an intriguing book on the philosophy of science, *The Organization of Inquiry* (1967), in which he analyzes the institutional structure within which science is conducted in order to understand the behavior of scientists. Ayres had treated this same subject in his first book, published in 1927, *Science: The False Messiah*. Tullock points out that Ayres had anticipated him by almost forty years in his explanation of how the institutional structure of science, and not the peculiar high-mindedness of its practitioners, generates the honest behavior which scientists typically demonstrate in their work. Tullock shows that Ayres anticipated other developments in modern social science in his first book: Thomas S. Kuhn's paradigm concept (a theme which Ayres neglected to develop) and the possibility of using a Paretian solution in social disputes (specifically, in disposing of the antivivisectionist movement). In Ayres's biography of Thomas H. Huxley, which he published in 1932, he celebrated the triumphant scientific career of one of the nineteenth century's greatest biologists. But, as Tullock perceptively notes, the two books are closely related since the attitude of mind and general approach were the same. In both books, Ayres showed his disdain for the entrenched establishment. Although Ayres seemed to identify with Huxley in the attack on the orthodoxy of his own discipline, in a surprising twist Tullock shows how Ayres's own career more closely resembled that of Bishop Samuel Wilberforce, Huxley's great antagonist. In this essay, Tullock admires Ayres's brilliance as a stylist and social critic.

Alfred F. Chalk, professor of economics at Texas A&M University and an expert on the philosophical background of economic thought, discusses one of the most important themes emerging out of Ayres's later years: the ends-means problem as it relates to the theory of valuation. Ayres argued that moral relativism has led to an impasse in moral theory. To Ayres, if all judgments about what is good and bad are merely relative to the customs of a given community, then the comments of any social scientist concerning the merits or demerits of a given policy are no better than the myth making of savage society. Ayres attempted to find a satisfactory alternative to the moral nihilism of modern social science. But Ayres also rejected a revival of any belief in a final or absolute truth. He acknowledged his indebtedness to John Dewey for the notion of the ends-means continuum as a substitute for the customary ends-means dichotomy. Values must not be derived from metaphysical sources but from the technological process. *Technology*, in Ayres's use of the term, embraces tools *and* human skills. The locus of value is to be found in technology—the continuity of the tool-using function which makes possible all human progress. In so doing, Ayres showed a way out of the modern intellectual paralysis in the sphere of moral theory.

James M. Buchanan, University Professor of Economics at Virginia Polytechnic Institute and State University, is one of the founders of the modern theory of public choice. Moreover, he was a student of Frank H. Knight at the University of Chicago and is one of a handful of economists who are also keen social philosophers in their own right. Since Ayres and Knight were close friends and adversaries throughout their lives, Buchanan seemed the ideal choice to appraise, in the light of modern economics, the Ayres-Knight discussion that took place in the *International Journal of Ethics* in the mid-1930's. Buchanan notes the vivid contrast between the intellectual world of 1935 and of the 1970's. Ayres and Knight concerned themselves with fundamental philosophical issues that emerge naturally from the discipline of economics. But the basic problems they discussed have not been resolved. Buchanan presents the Ayres-Knight dispute in modern form and points out that developments in economics since 1935 have been such as to bring their positions more closely into agreement, although both would continue to be sharply divergent from mainstream economic methodology. He notes that both Ayres and Knight would have become increasingly disturbed at the growing tendency to conceptualize economics as a branch of applied mathematics. Ayres would have been ambivalent toward recent developments in the theory of public goods—the analysis of "market failure." Knight would have been equally ambivalent toward developments in the theory of public choice—the analysis of "government failure." They would have continued to emphasize the limits to the explanatory power of purely economic models of man, and both would have maintained their interests in exploring the moral-ethical requirements for social order.

The last two essays are by two of America's most eminent sociologists who were at one time students of Clarence Ayres, but at widely separated stages in Ayres's career. Talcott Parsons, professor at Harvard University and the dean of American sociologists, was Ayres's student when the latter had first begun his teaching career at Amherst College. Marion J. Levy, Jr., professor at Princeton University and one of the more distinguished members of a younger generation of sociologists, studied under Ayres at the University of Texas. Parsons's paper provides a charming reminiscence of the young Clarence Ayres. Although Parsons later followed his own directions (in which property, authority, and other social categories were to take precedence over Ayres's emphasis on technology in getting an understanding of social structure and development), he gives Clarence Ayres much of the credit for having made him into a social scientist. Levy's paper, on the other hand, is more analytical. He claims that Ayres had the three attributes essential for a good teacher: the ability to preserve knowledge, transmit knowledge, and create new knowledge. Levy stresses the open-mindedness of Ayres, his willingness to allow students to strike out in new directions in their quest for truth. Ayres's insatiable desire for knowledge and love of books was infectious, so that his better students developed a similar enthusiasm for learning.

In looking over the contents of this volume we are impressed most by the lack of any ideological uniformity. Ayres's ideas are seen to be important to scholars representing a wide spectrum of political allegiances. This means that Clarence Ayres's work cut across not only disciplinary but ideological boundaries, and that is perhaps the volume's most eloquent tribute to his genuineness as a scientific inquirer.

Science and Ceremony

Clarence Edwin Ayres:
An Intellectual's Portrait

WILLIAM BREIT AND

WILLIAM PATTON CULBERTSON, JR.

Clarence Edwin Ayres, the leading American institutional economist in the post–World War II era, was born in Lowell, Massachusetts, in 1891. His father, William S. Ayres, was a Baptist minister and a man of erudition. Before her marriage, Emma Young Ayres, his mother, had been a missionary in China, where she started a church school. He was the eldest of three children. His sister, Edith, who was also to become an economist, was born in 1892, and his brother Ernest, born in 1895, died at an early age from complications arising from arthritis.

In the Ayres home prayers began the day and ended the day, and the children were raised in fear of the Lord. But Reverend Ayres also had a keen appreciation for learning to be found beyond the family Bible. Even when the family had barely enough to eat, he found it possible to bring home books. Those books which the young Clarence read were to have an important influence on his development. Although in later years he resisted the typical college professor's urge to amass a large personal library (he considered books to be "excess baggage" if a good library was readily available in the community), throughout his life he kept and treasured a stack of Kipling's works that had so delighted him in childhood. Moreover, he had a sensitive ear for music, and he learned early to play the piano and cello and to enjoy singing. At Brown University, where he took his under-graduate training, he sang in the Glee Club. When he graduated in 1912 he had been a brilliant and spectacular pupil. He was named James Manning Scholar for distinguished excellence in college studies. (The award consisted of a beautifully bound volume of John Hay's poems.)

But he was not all solemnity and seriousness. He had joined a fraternity and learned to enjoy drinking beer with his "brothers." He developed a fondness for Culmbacher beer which persisted until late in life, when he would travel many miles out of his way if he heard some were procurable. One imagines him as a devil of a fellow,

Note: Some passages in this chapter have appeared in the Social Science Quarterly, September 1973. We are indebted to the editor for permission to make use of this material.

carving his name upon the mutilated tables in the fraternity dining room and beerily singing the college favorites of his day.

He was a long and gaunt youth, who, having been raised in an atmosphere of strong faith, soon reacted against the religious beliefs of his home. But, as James Buchanan has remarked, a reaction against religious orthodoxy can be an essential ingredient in one's intellectual development since, having rejected it, the less rigid dogmas encountered in the world of scholarship become easy prey. This was a time when the air was astir with new and shocking discoveries and hypotheses: Freudian psychopathology, Deweyian pragmatism, Veblenian heresies, cultural relativism. Ayres's head was filled with these and other violently novel ideas. Soon he developed a touch of cynicism and enjoyed sneering at the smug beliefs of the elder generation. From Brown, where he had majored in philosophy and minored in economics, he moved to Harvard for a short stay, soon transferring to the University of Chicago, at that time the greatest university in the United States. Dewey had already given birth to the "Chicago School" of philosophy with his *Studies in Logical Theory*.[1] The university was bursting with outstandingly able scholars making pioneer efforts in new research and looking at phenomena in new ways.[2] The economics department could boast of having had men (appointed by J. Laurence Laughlin) like Thorstein Veblen, Robert Hoxie, Wesley C. Mitchell, Alvin Johnson, Walton Hamilton, and J. M. Clark, all heterodox and excellent thinkers. It was natural that Ayres should have been attracted to such an environment in 1916.

He had hoped to study with Robert Hoxie, but unfortunately the latter committed suicide only a few days after Ayres had enrolled in his course. Indeed, Ayres had spent the afternoon previous to Hoxie's death trying to cheer him out of the depressed state of mind which afflicted him.

Switching to philosophy, Ayres formed what became a lifelong intellectual association with a man of similar background. A young instructor in economics, Frank H. Knight had himself started in philosophy while at Cornell, but, because of a disappointment with members of Cornell's philosophy department, had switched into economics. Spurred on by common interests, Ayres and Knight immediately formed an amity-enmity bond and became the closest of friends. They went swimming together nearly everyday, arguing furiously all the time, and, in spite of the violence of the argument, the respect they developed for each other's intellect and integrity persisted throughout their careers. Knight remained undeviatingly neo-Cartesian and antipragmatic, but they admired each other's tough-mindedness and courage to take stands on unpopular issues.

While at Brown, Ayres had met and married a fellow student, Anna Bryan, in 1915. She was to bear him three children, but the marriage ultimately proved unsuccessful.

After leaving Chicago with his Ph.D. in hand (his dissertation was "The Nature of the Relationship Between Ethics and Economics") he joined the faculty at Amherst College. The president of Amherst was Alexander Meiklejohn, who had been dean at Brown in Ayres's undergraduate days. Meiklejohn was a pioneer in educational reform and had assembled, on a smaller scale, a group of unorthodox thinkers similar to that which Ayres had encountered at Chicago. Chief among these was Walton Hamilton, whose famous course was called "Social and Economic Institutions." Hamilton was the economist and legal scholar who was to coin the term *institutionalism* to describe the way of thinking of which Ayres later became the chief exemplar in the United States. Ayres became Hamilton's protégé, and it was under his tutelage that Ayres reacted against the opinions of the economic establishment. The young Ayres was a teacher of philosophy, and Meiklejohn's experiment in liberal education would pay off handsomely with this acquisition. For, as an Amherst observer of those times later reminisced, "Ayres was a most buoyant and resolute soul . . ." The young men continually camped on his doorstep to discuss philosophy out of academic business hours. Meiklejohn conceived of the Amherst experiment as a return to the agora of Athens and the groves of Academe. As Lucien Price was to put it in his admirable memoir, "Just as Athens had its Aristophanes, so Amherst had its Ayres."[3]

Ayres had that elusive quality which enables superior teachers to inspire students. Among his pupils at Amherst was Talcott Parsons, and Ayres played an important role in motivating him to shift from biology into social science.[4]

When Meiklejohn was fired, eight of the most talented instructors resigned, and Ayres was among them. Ayres joined Richard Scholz in educational experimentation at Reed College, where he spent 1923 and 1924. One of his brightest students was Joseph Dorfman, whom Ayres introduced to the ideas of Thorstein Veblen. Ayres's influence was to be seen years later when Dorfman submitted his dissertation to Columbia University. His work became the definitive study of that brooding genius of institutional economics published as *Thorstein Veblen and His America*.

Another pupil in class with Dorfman was Gwendolen Jane, a young British portrait painter who was an ardent admirer of Cézanne and the postimpressionists. "Gwen," as Ayres called her, delighted in the exchanges between Dorfman and Ayres. Soon the mutual interest in music and art drew Clarence and Gwen together. He taught Gwen much of what he knew about music. She in turn talked to him about painting. His deep appreciation of both music and painting and their place in "the technological continuum" were to become familiar themes to his students and readers of later years. When his divorce from Anna was finalized, he and Gwen were married.

The wife of a professor of English who was at Reed College at the time recalled her impressions of the young professor: "Clarence had such a brilliant mind. Everything sparkled when he was around the college. I remember him and Scotty (chemistry) egging each other on from prank to prank. He accompanied us regularly on our hikes usually to the Columbia river gorge. His mind was so alive and brilliant up to the last letter."[5]

When Richard Scholz's policies at Reed were reversed by the choice of Norman Coleman as his successor, Ayres withdrew from the faculty. Heading East, he accepted an offer to become an associate editor of the *New Republic* in 1924. At the time it was perhaps the premier intellectual organ in the country. The editor was Herbert Croly, and, along with Ayres, the small editorial board consisted of such men as John Dewey, Alvin Johnson, and R. H. Tawney. From across the ocean one of its most frequent contributors was John Maynard Keynes. A more formidable posse of intelligentsia would be hard to imagine!

Ayres's contributions from June 18, 1924, when he put in his first appearance, until September 2, 1925, when he resigned to do serious work on his first book, covered a staggering range of topics. He was as at home discussing Freud's theory of the Oedipus complex as he was in describing the essence of Joseph Conrad's literary contributions. The love of Conrad survived Ayres's whole career, and every student of his was infected with a similar enthusiasm for the great literary phenomenon. Ayres's appreciation of Conrad's legacy in 1924 could be taken as a summary statement of one of Ayres's own major themes which came out of his study of economic development: "a sense of the complexity of human life, of the unpredictability of human motives, of the overwhelming significance of the massive impersonal forces of nature and of civilization moving obscurely in the background."[6] Besides belles-lettres, Ayres was an acerbic commentator on theology, sociology, politics, education, and, of course, music. The experience of having to read so much in such a variety of fields gave to Ayres a rare understanding of the significance of man's intellectual endeavors. From his training in philosophy, he was struck by what he conceived to be the essential unity of all knowledge.

But Ayres was unhappy in journalism. The hectic pace, the oppressive deadlines, and the provincialism of New York's intelligentsia caused him to seek a place where he could reflect at leisure on his ideas. A ranch south of Deming, New Mexico, seemed to him and Gwen ideal. The owner agreed that they could live on it for three years for nothing. He had much valuable equipment, and the Ayreses' presence would discourage thieves. In the spring of 1927 they set out for the Long S ranch, stopping off at Ithaca to visit with Ayres's sister, Edith, then married to economist Morris Copeland of the Cornell University faculty. One evening, Copeland invited Herbert Davenport to his home. Davenport had been Veblen's intimate at the University of Missouri and was one of the nation's leading economists. The three talked all evening. Davenport, always the skeptic, pressed Copeland to tell him plainly what was "institutionalism." To Ayres's mind Copeland did not provide a satisfactory answer, and that failing troubled him deeply. He was similarly troubled by Davenport's remarks on institutionalism when the latter visited at the Long S ranch in the spring of 1930. One evening while in front of the ranch house fireplace he suddenly roused and said, "Ayres, I used to think Walton Hamilton was the one who was going to tell us what institutionalism was all about. I've about decided he isn't." Ayres too was afraid. Hamilton had gone to teach at Yale Law School and later wound up a member of the law firm of Arnold, Fortas, and Porter, but none of his writing contained the definitive revelation for which Ayres had fervently hoped. At this time Ayres made up his mind that his own mission would be to "identify the philosophical parameters of Walton Hamilton's Institutionalism."[7]

Life at Long S was little short of idyllic. Ayres became a competent horseman and learned to tie a diamond hitch from the local cowpokes, and from then on Ayres's writing and Gwen's painting were interspersed with adventurous forays into the Black Mountains. A sudden change in this domestic situation followed the unexpected and tragic death of Ayres's former wife in 1929. He went immediately to Springfield, Massachusetts, retrieved his three young children, and returned to New Mexico. With these new responsibilities, Ayres and Gwen realized that the carefree days at Long S were numbered.

His sister, Edith, then a member of the Washington Square branch of New York University's economics department (of which Willard

Atkins was chairman) secured Ayres a summer appointment. Ayres found the department (consisting of Robert Brady, Anton Friedrich, Carl Raushenbush, and Louis Reed) congenial. He collaborated with them on a new edition of their institutionalist textbook, *Economic Behavior*, and contributed the concluding chapter of the volume. Indeed, he might have stayed on had not an offer from the University of Texas come through. The departure of Max Handman, the economic historian, for a year's visit at Ann Arbor, created a temporary opening on the Texas faculty. Ayres's former student, Joseph Dorfman, had a hand in the decision of department chairman E. T. Miller to extend the invitation. Dorfman was a close friend of Corliss Stocking, George Ward Stocking's young brother, and when George, who was at Texas, asked Corliss about Ayres, Dorfman was consulted. Dorfman gave Corliss the high sign and the information reached Austin. Handman's leave of absence gave Ayres and his colleagues a chance to know each other. They found they were compatible both socially and ideologically. When Handman decided not to return from Michigan, a tenured commitment was made. It was to be a long and fruitful association. In later years Ayres liked to tell about E. T. Miller's comment about the Ayres appointment: "'Every economics department ought to be able to entertain *one* philosopher,' with delicate emphasis on the numeral."[8] And so Ayres made a transition from philosophy with economic overtones to economics with philosophical overtones.

When Ayres arrived in Austin as professor of economics, he had two books on social philosophy to his credit. They were, in a sense, companion volumes. Both works demonstrated Ayres's youthful mastery of the vast literature of the history of science, technology, and social institutions. There is much about religion in both of them, and the style is interwoven with abundant biblical quotations and wordplays on scriptural verse. This fascination with religion is indicated by their titles. The first was *Science: The False Messiah*;[9] the second, *Holier Than Thou: The Way of the Righteous*.[10] Ayres was eager to complement these two with a third book, for which the contract had already been signed. As Gwen unpacked, he went straight to the University of Texas Library and began work on *Huxley*, a sprightly yet profound work of scholarship.

Huxley is directly related to the theoretical system that Ayres was to construct for institutional economics. The book was "entertaining" and "racy," as the dust jacket blurb pointed out. The character of Huxley was sketched with painstaking attention to detail and with gripping drama. The high spot of the biography is the historic scene at

Oxford on the momentous occasion before the British Association for the Advancement of Science when Samuel Wilberforce, Bishop of Oxford, debated Thomas Huxley on Darwin's theory of evolution. When the bishop solicitously inquired whether the young scientist supposed himself to be descended from an ape on the side of his grandmother or his grandfather, Ayres tells what ensued with great dramatic effect:

> The audience quivered; but Huxley turned to Sir Benjamin Brodie . . . and emphatically striking his hand upon his knee, exclaimed in a whisper, "The Lord hath delivered him into my hands!" Then, leaving Sir Benjamin in a daze, Huxley slowly and deliberately arose: a slight, tall figure, stern and pale, very quiet and very grave; young, cool, quiet, scientific, he began to speak. He rehearsed the bishop's arguments and riddled them. He examined his facts, exhibiting with perfect lucidity his ignorance and folly. And then he delivered his famous counter-stroke, the upshot of which is that as ancestors apes are preferable to bishops. The science of this point is dubious, but as farce and delivered as Huxley delivered it, there could be no doubt: it spitted Soapy Sam with incomparable éclat. The hostile audience was staggered; a great commotion followed; Lady Brewster fainted.[11]

This is Ayres's writing style at its best. Notwithstanding such excitement and keen wit displayed on almost every page, the royalties on the book were small. Bad luck plagued him. The Great Depression was underway and 1932 was a bad year for best sellers. To make matters worse, the simultaneous appearance of another more widely advertised biography of Huxley received most of the attention.[12] But the book remained Ayres's favorite piece of writing, and he requested that Gwendolen read it to him the year before his death when, his eyesight failing, he was unable to do much reading himself.

After *Huxley*, Ayres turned again to the challenge of developing the definitive statement of institutionalism. He established a disciplined routine, which he followed for the rest of his life. Arising at 6:30 A.M., he breakfasted with the seven o'clock news report and then, leaving orders not to be disturbed, retired to his study and wrote until time for his late morning classes. He rarely lunched with colleagues, preferring instead to return home, where his afternoons were devoted to music and hikes along Shoal Creek. In the evenings he and Gwen read aloud to each other, and it was unusual for him to retire later than 10 P.M. Except for rare occasions, this was his regimen summer and winter. He believed that its discipline made for a calm mind, good health, and steady output.

But if teaching and writing were a job, music was a passion. A portrait by Gwen, painted during this period, shows an enraptured Ayres listening to a favorite recording. High of forehead, with keen eyes beneath overhanging brows, the facial expression shows that music benumbed his senses and soothed his soul. In his later years he made tapes, played records, and listened to Austin's Fine Music Station (KMFA) over FM, hours at a time. Although the "old masters" were dear to his heart, his chief interest was in contemporary works: Bartók, Hindemith, Prokofiev, Vaughan Williams, Copland, and Ives. The only operas he enjoyed were those of Gilbert and Sullivan. Thus, he lived and had his being.

Almost from the moment of his arrival in Austin, Ayres felt comfortable. He liked the people, he liked the town, and he liked the university.[13] His teaching at Texas soon reflected the attempt to orient economic theory along lines consistent with Dewey's instrumentalist philosophy and Veblen's criticism of orthodox economics. His courses in value and welfare, institutional economics, and the technological interpretation of historical change were enthusiastically received and could hold students in their chairs right through the kickoff of Saturday football games. A controversial but popular teacher, he was in steady demand as a speaker to student groups. Though he was never completely satisfied with the term, he could now be earmarked an "institutional economist."

Consistently, however, Ayres proved himself a man hard to categorize. Though a stalwart advocate of economic planning, he found little glory in the New Deal machinations of FDR. At the urging of Walton Hamilton, he agreed to put in an eighteen-day stint at the Consumers Division of the National Recovery Administration (NRA) prior to opening the fall semester in 1935. And again, in early 1936, yielding to a barrage of telegrams from Hamilton, Ayres was pulled back to Washington by the lure of his old mentor. These excursions were hectic for the family, and, in truth, Ayres showed little enthusiasm for them aside from the delight of once more being associated with "Hammy." He wrote, somewhat wryly, of having "just bought a new suit with which to dazzle the nation" and further advised Hamilton, "please don't harbor the idea that I have an unsatisfied passion to join the ring-around-Rosie."[14] Perhaps the Washington experience did little but confirm his earlier prophecy that, "in spite of the celebrated Brain Trust, there is not as yet any monopoly on brains."[15]

A curious posture for one whom the legislature was soon to brand as a "socialist," Ayres's reluctance is perhaps understandable in terms of the very real and personal costs he felt from the New Deal's "brain-drain." The American institutionalist school lost its acknowledged intellectual leader, Walton Hamilton, and, with this loss, the source from which Ayres had always felt the clarifying statement of institutionalist principles would be delivered. The hectic days of the New Deal simply left Hamilton no time to fulfill the institutionalist promise which had begun so brilliantly at Amherst in the twenties.

A second, and in some respects a more significant cost, was Texas's loss of George Ward Stocking to the New Deal's Antitrust Division. Few persons ranked so high in Ayres's estimation as did the young scholar who was destined to become president of the American Economic Association in 1958. Ayres stamped a label of "prime" on Stocking the instant they met and pulled out every stop to get him back to Texas. For in the 1930's, Ayres was a man with a vision when he wrote Stocking, "I have been allowing myself to dream of the possibility of the development in the course of the next few years of a sort of 'Texas school.'"[16]

In 1933 he urged Stocking "to join the 'Back to the College' movement as soon as you can." And again in 1934 he pleaded with Stocking to return to Texas, arguing that: "Roosevelt is on a hot-spot—hotter than anybody has been on since Wilson in 1918. He is going to have to show many times more guts in the immediate future than he has ever showed before, if he isn't to be completely deflated. Unless all you fellows feel very sure about his backing—a hell of a lot surer than anybody has up to now—I should think you would be packing your bags."[17]

Stocking balked, citing "misunderstandings" over his contract and salary prospects at Texas. After repeated entreaties, an exasperated Ayres wrote:

> . . . if you are the man I think you are, all this hubbub about understandings is just an effluvium of the Washington miasma, a sort of occupational disease, or political infection—contracted, perhaps, at the presidential dinner table. (Though if you weren't any nearer the center of the horseshoe than the Hamiltons were, you couldn't have contracted much!) As such, I would argue, it is bound to pass off pretty quickly under the prophylactic Texas sun, and in a very short time you would be the swell guy I know you are, for whom I should be prepared to do everything I could as long as I could . . .[18]

But Stocking did not return to Austin permanently, and it was left mainly to Ayres to shoulder the burden of developing the "Texas school." His warning shot was fired in the pages of the *International Journal of Ethics* with an attack on the linchpin of classical economic theory—the notion of equilibrium. The gauntlet thrown, it was swiftly retrieved by Frank H. Knight with a reply to Ayres in the same issue.[19]

To bring together the inchoate and amorphous ideas that constituted institutional economics and systematize them into a genuine theoretical framework would involve a tour de force. The Ayres-Knight dispute indicated that adherents of neoclassical economics like Knight could make little sense of the loose-jointed doctrines of institutionalism. Ayres admitted the deficiency at the time. Veblen himself had lamented that "there is the economic life process still in great measure awaiting theoretical formulation." Ayres used this statement as the motto of his 1944 volume, *The Theory of Economic Progress.*[20] Glimpses of his system could be found in two earlier essays, "The Gospel of Technology"[21] and "The Significance of Economic Planning,"[22] but the first complete exposition of his views is in *The Theory of Economic Progress.* His one effort between *Huxley* and *The Theory* was a "trial balance," *The Problem of Economic Order*,[23] a small book inspired by the Great Depression and concerned chiefly with the industrial revolution and economic growth combined with some underconsumptionist feelings about the causes and cures of the 1930's stagnation. But it was not the major theoretical work that *The Theory of Economic Progress* was to be, and its best insights were incorporated into the later study.

The Theory of Economic Progress, as its title implies, is a treatment of the forces which have shaped the development of the economy. It is a theoretical work in which a bold and sweeping explanation is given of the economic development of the Western world, isolating those factors which accelerate development and those which impede it. The book is rich in erudition and insight, urbanity and wit, and no short summary can do it justice. In essence, its theme is that human skills and the tools by which they are exercised are logically inseparable; that the term *technology* must be understood to include all human activities involving the use of all sorts of tools; and that our present age of scientific enlightenment and artistic achievement is intelligible only if we see that the simplest striking stones of primeval man, the fire built around a tree to fell it, written language, books, the symbols of mathematics, and the language of poets involve tools and instruments all related to each other by the same developmental process. The tool-using process is thus broadly conceived. It is precisely this surging force growing at an exponential rate which is responsible for the enormous changes in the welfare of the human race over its lifetime. What is really involved in this thesis is a shifting of attention from men to tools—a realization that the key force for increasing benefits to mankind derives not from an increase in human genius but from the fact that the technological process is one of accessible and objective instruments. These instruments are capable of combination. Ayres does not thereby deny that individuals play a role in the process. But the point is that the answer to the conundrum of increasingly rapid progress lies in the tools themselves. All tools are related to each other in the sense that the earlier ones make the later ones possible. The existence of different tools and instruments defines the possibility of their combination into new artifacts. The individual is the agent of combination—it is he who sees the possibility of putting the tools together into new and innovative forms. But the process of change is best understood on the cultural level, since the more plentiful the tools become, the greater is the possibility of recombination. That is why technological advance occurs more rapidly as we go onward.

But there is another side of the story of economic progress. There are forces hostile to development which Ayres summarizes under the rubric "ceremonial" behavior. In his later work, *Toward a Reasonable Society*,[24] Ayres shows that the symbolic process, of which tool using is one manifestation, gives rise to fanciful behavior completely contradictory to the technological process. The ceremonial, myth-and-status aspect of human behavior derives from the same symbolic process that gave rise to technological development. But the authoritarian, taboo-ridden, emotion-fraught aspect of life is static by its very nature. The binding force of any established institution derives from its past and is part of tribal legend.

Ayres was more fully to develop this aspect of his dichotomy in his paper "The Theory of Institutional Adjustment," which he prepared for a conference in his honor in 1965.[25] In this last major contribution he stressed the importance of the Freudian revolution for explaining the intensity with which people hold their various beliefs and adhere to their traditional way of life. The emotional conditioning of the whole community to supernaturalism is what binds together status systems, legends, and ceremonial activities. But this institutional coherence is in the process of destruction, for the Freudian revolution is demythologizing modern culture, and the institutionalizing process is, in consequence, being short-circuited. The root cause of superstition, which is the chief enemy of technological progress, is being shriveled by modern psychopathology with consequences we cannot yet foresee: "This is truly cataclysmic. If it is true . . . that the myths, ceremonies, mores, and status systems which make up the institutional systems of all peoples are themselves welded together and shackled upon their peoples by a community-wide process of emotional conditioning to supernaturalism, then the short-circuiting of that welding current, which is the inevitable consequence of technological progress and its accompaniment of intellectual sophistication, means that the whole institutional complex is coming apart at the seams."[26]

To Ayres, the way out of this total disintegration is to devise new organizational forms, to develop pragmatically organizational arts to match, rather than contradict, our science and technology. For to Ayres the question of whether we should go ever onward is answered by the process itself. Technology, broadly conceived, involves transcultural values altogether different from those beliefs deriving from superstition. Whereas superstitions vary from culture to culture and in all cases are past-binding, the values deriving from technology are progressive and are so recognized by all peoples. A sharp knife is preferred to a dull knife in all cultures in order to perform efficiently the task of cutting, and the values generated by the technological process are shared values, understandable and acceptable to all peoples everywhere. This is Dewey's meaning of the technological value continuum, but never was it put to better use than at Ayres's hands. That is why those who see in Ayres only a disciple of Dewey and Veblen miss the main point. In his articulation of some of their positions and in having the vision to synthesize some of their insights with his own understanding of economic history, Ayres left them miles behind. His Veblen was no longer anyone else's Veblen and his Dewey was no longer the Dewey of pragmatic philosophy. Ayres emphasized those elements in each man's work that best suited his own purpose and temperament, re-creating both of them in his own image.

Ayres's achievements are all the more remarkable when it is realized that they were sandwiched between running battles with the Texas legislature and the university's Board of Regents.[27] The view was growing in the state that something was amiss in the economics department. After all, several members of the faculty had left their positions to join, temporarily or permanently, the New Deal forces which Roosevelt had recruited for combating the Great Depression. Both Ayres and the colorful "Dr. Bob" Montgomery had done short-lived hitches on the Potomac. Each was, in his own way, a reformer. Together, they, along with Professor E. E. Hale, were disturbers of the young. For what they insisted on within their Garrison Hall classrooms was a free and open inquiry into the nature of economic and social relationships. By common admission, Ayres's work formed the philosophical backdrop to this quiet, but persuasive, rebellion.

Battle lines were drawn in 1942 with the regents' preemptive dismissal of three economics instructors—J. Fagg Foster, W. Nelson Peach, and Wendell Gordon—for attempting to defend the forty-hour work week before a public meeting in Dallas. Hale wanted to resign in protest and telephoned Ayres, who was at his Cloudcroft, New Mexico, summer retreat. However, in a letter written the next day to President Homer P. Rainey, Ayres penned a compelling injunction against such academic suicide.

> What should we do about it? Should we march out, as a gesture of disgust, or protest, or an act of self-preservation? I was one of those who resigned from the faculty of Amherst College in protest, or disgust, or self-preservation, on the occasion of the removal of Dr. Meiklejohn from the presidency. I also withdrew from the faculty of Reed College in 1924. . . . But it seems to me that the present situation in the University of Texas is different from those in two important respects. In the first place, in those other situations we of the faculty were not under fire; it was the president and his policies which were under fire and to which others tried to bring support by an act of protest. In the present situation it is we of the economics department who are under fire. You might well feel tempted to resign in protest at the treatment of us. But I wonder if we should resign under fire? I am inclined to think not. I believe we have a good department—an outstanding department—which can well afford to challenge complete and public investigation; and I believe it is our duty to the institution and the people of the state to stand pat and challenge investigation of ourselves and of our treatment.
>
> . . . if you feel able and willing to continue to fight to make the University of Texas what an institution of the first class should be—as I very ardently hope you do and will—I believe that our duty is to stay with you and with the institution and fight that fight with you.[28]

This counsel prevailed, and through the faculty's dogged determination the dismissed instructors were made eligible for reinstatement after the war—a maneuver which secured the return of Wendell

Gordon. Homer Rainey, of course, came under increasing fire for his defense of free academic expression. Several years earlier he had flatly refused a demand by one member of the Board of Regents that he fire Ayres, Hale, Montgomery, and Clarence Wiley. Although Rainey succeeded in retaining the four economists, the conflict intensified, and ultimately Rainey was himself dismissed in an episode which culminated in the "black-listing" of the university by the American Association of University Professors (AAUP).[29]

Some years later, a similar episode very nearly led to Ayres's own dismissal from Texas. The period was the early fifties, and the specter of an invisible but nonetheless sinister communism was all the rage among right-thinking citizens. In 1949 Ayres had appeared before the Texas legislature to talk against a bill requiring all students and employees at the University of Texas to sign a loyalty oath—an oath, according to Ayres, that meant insult to the good citizen and nothing to the bad. Two years later a resolution was introduced calling for the Board of Regents to verify certain statements attributed to Ayres and to advise the House of Representatives if the university proposed to continue his employment. By a vote of 130-to-1, the legislature announced that "we believe that his presence [at UT] can contribute nothing to the culture and progress of this State."[30] The sponsor of the bill labeled Ayres an "educational termite,"[31] and another member suggested that, if the charges proved true, Ayres "should be expelled from the University faculty and action should be taken to deport him from the United States."[32] (The recipient country for this unilateral export of intellectual capital was left unspecified. After all, to where does one deport a nonalien?)

Evidence of the alleged "tendencies toward communism" vested mainly in the content of a couple of talks Ayres had delivered before the University Club and the Upperclass Club. As best as can be determined from newspaper accounts, the burden of Ayres's message was that the currently hostile attitude toward government was an attitude fostered by an uncritical acceptance of the ideology of free enterprise and contributed nothing to an understanding of the development of capitalist society. Consistent with his stubborn advocacy of the proposition that economic depression stemmed from underconsumption, Ayres argued for an all-inclusive social security system coupled with an effective version of progressive taxation. The legislative outcry over these proposals demonstrates that the "radicalism" of one era is likely to become the conventional wisdom of another.

Despite all the smoke, the outcome was almost anticlimactic. A guarded rebuttal of the legislature's charges was prepared through a committee headed by Chancellor James P. Hart and President T. S. Painter. The matter dropped out of the newspapers as abruptly as it had surfaced. Coffee room legend at Texas has it that the decisive factor in the fray was Ayres's friend "Dr. Bob" Montgomery. And while there is no formal record that Dr. Bob acted as a kind of intellectual bail-bondsman in Ayres's behalf, those who know his charm and persuasive power find this a legend hard to resist.

The clarity and vigor with which Clarence Ayres stated his intellectual convictions is expected of, though not often endemic among, social scientists. He pulled no punches in the arena of public debate, and thus he laid his job on the line in the interest of academic freedom. He drew, however, a careful boundary between academic freedom and academic license. Had they taken the trouble to find out, the regents and legislators might have been amazed at Ayres's views regarding communists on the campus.

The *American Mercury* had run a feature entitled "Communism in the Colleges"—a piece which attacked the stand of the American Civil Liberties Union (ACLU), on permitting communists to teach in universities. An alumni organization called President Logan Wilson's attention to the fact that Clarence Ayres was listed as a member of the ACLU Advisory Council. The implication was clear. Wilson replied categorically that the *American Mercury* was resorting to "sensationalism in an effort to bolster a severely limited and dwindling circulation."[33] Upon receiving a copy of this letter, Ayres wrote Logan Wilson to indicate the irony of finding himself identified with a policy he had in fact sought to block. As a member of the Advisory Council, he had argued (in a letter to the chairman of ACLU's Academic Freedom Committee): (1) that the Communist party is a conspiratorial organization; (2) membership in it should be condemned on conspiratorial grounds quite apart from intellectual considerations; and (3) participants in conspiracy, however ignorant and innocent their participation, should not be permitted to occupy positions of public trust nor their right to do so defended.[34]

He had fought much the same battle earlier while a member of the AAUP's National Council, and the outcome was similar—"My counsel didn't prevail but my conscience is clear."[35]

Even as early as 1953, Ayres's stance against permitting avowed members of the Communist party to hold university posts was not a popular one to take *within* the academic community. However, it would have been more popular, though for spurious reasons, *without* the groves of academe. And yet Ayres never publicized, nor sought to have publicized, his position on this issue. He catered to no mob—

academic or otherwise. When, in 1939, Sidney Hook, chairman of the Committee for Cultural Freedom, sought Ayres's support of the antitotalitarianism *Statement* of that group, he declined in characteristic terms.

> . . . a tone of alarm and even panic runs through this statement which I think is not justified by the present situation and is a great mistake in any case. Then too there is a rather fundamental contradiction between the denunciation of propaganda and pressure and calling for the formation of a committee to make propaganda and exert pressure.
>
> I think you folks in New York should take a sedative. Maybe a season in Texas would do the trick. Today for the first time since the "tragic era" a negro sat on a Texas grand jury.[36]

With a consistency that made even friends a bit uncomfortable, Ayres turned up on the "wrong side"—at least by currently fashionable academic standards —of various issues. He supported American involvement in Viet Nam, and his reasoning was spelled out in a letter to Gunnar Myrdal.

> With regard to Viet Nam I'm afraid our perspectives are different. You don't even mention what seem to me to be the two basic issues in that situation—and many others: the issue of total revolution, and the issue of "wars of national liberation." If both of these are approved, then American "intervention" in Viet Nam stands condemned. But if both of these are condemned, then American policy in Viet Nam (and elsewhere) is validated, and the condemnatory attitudes of other countries may be evidence of uneasy consciences. Most especially, of course, France.
>
> There is much to be said for total revolution. I am told that the Maoist revolution in China really has succeeded in breaking down the barriers of the provincial dialects and making Mandarin the *lingua franca* of all China; and when I think of the futility of the efforts of the government of India to unify the country linguistically (not to mention getting rid of the cows and Gurus), I wonder if India too might not profit from total revolution. But the cost is high. In Russia, what? Fourteen million Kulaks, not to mention the less numerous professional classes. What it might be in India, and may be in China before China reaches the stability the USSR now enjoys, I have no guess. But it daunts me. No

doubt Thailand is an only slightly modernized oriental despotism. But Mao's way of fixing things daunts me.

The wars-of-national-liberation doctrine daunts me even more. This seems to be standard doctrine for all the Communist dictatorships; and it seems to me that if it goes unchallenged, it is bound to be eventually disastrous for all others. In effect it means an open season on all democracies, which are condemned to abide by their own rules (the rules of the pre-revolutionary period), while the revolutionary regimes demand to be treated as "peace-loving" non-combatants (since they haven't declared any war), using each others' territories as privileged sanctuaries, and generally chewing up the "capitalist" countries (such as Thailand) while the old fashioned democracies police each other.

In short, to my mind there is a much stronger case for American policy in Viet Nam than any responsible American has dared to make; and the reason no one has dared is that it would indeed place this country in the role of a world policeman—a role most Americans (and everybody else) would vigorously repudiate. Of course, no country should assume such a role. That is the business of World Government, which is impossible as the world is now divided. Indeed, no such role could ever have been assumed by deliberate decision. We have got into it by a long series of short steps. But each of them has been taken in the effort to prevent the deliberate, intended, and astonishingly open advance of the "liberation" process—which begins with the assassination of people like you and me.[37]

Ayres retired from teaching in 1968 after the Board of Regents passed a ruling that persons on modified service should step down on reaching seventy-five, an age Ayres already had passed. He departed gracefully, but, as he wrote to his friend Horace Gray, "I will refuse to stop thinking."

Much of his thought was given to the newly founded Association for Evolutionary Economics (AFEE), of which he was made the first president. He took an almost paternalistic interest in the organ of the association, *The Journal of Economic Issues*. In December 1971, recovering from a serious illness and his eyesight almost gone, he insisted on going to New Orleans for AFEE's annual meeting. The trip was taxing, and he returned exhausted. He looked forward with even more than his usual anticipation to the annual retreat to his Cloudcroft cottage. Perched on the crest of New Mexico's Sacramento Mountains at nine thousand feet, the village afforded him a respite from the sultry Texas summer. Ayres relished the clear dry air and cool temperatures. He hoped to be rejuvenated in the setting he loved most and to which he and Gwen had come each summer without interruption for thirty years.

But it was to be his last visit. On July 24, 1972, with his beloved Gwen at his side, he died in an Alamogordo hospital within a few days of suffering a massive stroke. His body willed to medical science, there exists no epitaph carved in stone. His memory rests instead with that larger audience from whom for over half a century, from Amherst to Austin, he felt he had always drawn his intellectual sustenance: "For without the independent testimony of their bright young eyes—the fact that they too could see something in the direction that I was pointing, and could describe it in language never used by me—I should scarcely have had the courage to go on trying to bring that distant horizon into sharper focus."[38]

NOTES

1. Ayres was later to discuss the importance of this book in bringing him to intellectual awareness in an essay in *Books That Changed Our Minds*, ed. Malcolm Cowley and Bernard Smith (New York: Doubleday, Doran, 1939), pp. 111–126.

2. See the remarks by Milton Friedman at the 54th Annual Board of Trustees' Dinner for the Faculty in *The University of Chicago Record*, January 9, 1974, pp. 3–7. A vivid description of the intellectual environment at Chicago during the period when Robert Hoxie and Ayres were there can be found in Darnell Rucker, *The Chicago Pragmatists* (Minneapolis: University of Minnesota Press, 1969).

3. Lucien Price, *Prophets Unawares* (New York: Century Co., 1924), pp. 11, 122.

4. For the personal impression that Clarence Ayres made on Talcott Parsons at Amherst see Parsons's contribution to this volume. The impression he made on students in later years is described by Marion Levy, Jr., in the latter's contribution to this volume.

5. Letter, Gwendolen Ayres to William Breit, January 2, 1973, citing Mrs. Victor Chittick.

6. *New Republic*, August 27, 1924, p. 391.

7. Letter, C. E. Ayres to Allan Gruchy, February 11, 1968.

8. William Breit, a student of Ayres in the 1950's, remembers Ayres telling this story in class.

9. C. E. Ayres, *Science: The False Messiah* (Indianapolis: Bobbs-Merrill, 1927).

10. C. E. Ayres, *Holier Than Thou: The Way of the Righteous* (Indianapolis: Bobbs-Merrill, 1929).

11. Clarence Ayres, *Huxley* (New York: W. W. Norton and Co., 1932), p. 51. For a contemporary discussion of Ayres's early views on science, see the essay by Gordon Tullock in this volume.

12. The book was Houston Peterson, *Huxley: Prophet of Science* (London: Longmans, Green and Co., 1932).

13. And to his pleasant surprise he could even get Culmbacher beer, his old favorite from his undergraduate days at Brown. Soon after arriving in Austin one hot afternoon he spotted a Culmbacher beer truck passing their home. Like Sherlock Holmes imploring, "Come, Watson, come! The game is afoot," he insisted Gwen join him in tailing the truck to see where the precious beverage was distributed. For a time he and Gwen hosted occasional "Culmbacher" parties for their friends. (Culmbacher, originally brewed by the Moerlin Brewery of Cincinnati, is no longer available in Austin but is still distributed in the Cincinnati area. We are indebted to Kenneth G. Elzinga for kindly supplying us with information regarding the history of Culmbacher.)

14. Letter, C. E. Ayres to Walton Hamilton, August 6, 1935.

15. Letter, C. E. Ayres to Walton Hamilton, January 15, 1934.

16. Letter, C. E. Ayres to George Ward Stocking, April 6, 1934.

17. Ibid.

18. Letter, C. E. Ayres to George Ward Stocking, undated but ca. May 1934. The admiration was mutual. In later years, Stocking told his students that one of his most important achievements was having brought Ayres to Texas.

19. C. E. Ayres, "Moral Confusion in Economics," *International Journal of Ethics* 45 (1934–1935): 170–199. Knight's reply in the same issue is entitled "Intellectual Confusion on Morals and Economics," pp. 200–220. For a recent appraisal of this controversy see the essay by James M. Buchanan in this volume.

20. C. E. Ayres, *The Theory of Economic Progress* (Chapel Hill: University of North Carolina Press, 1944).

21. C. E. Ayres, "The Gospel of Technology," in *American Philosophy Today and Tomorrow*, ed. Horace Kallen and Sidney Hook (New York: Lee Furman, 1935), pp. 24–42.

22. C. E. Ayres, "The Significance of Economic Planning," in *The Development of Collective Enterprise*, ed. Seba Eldridge (Lawrence: University of Kansas Press, 1943), pp. 469–481.

23. C. E. Ayres, *The Problem of Economic Order* (New York: Farrar and Rinehart, 1938).

24. C. E. Ayres, *Toward a Reasonable Society* (Austin: University of Texas Press, 1961).

25. C. E. Ayres, "The Theory of Institutional Adjustment," in *Institutional Adjustment*, ed. Carey C. Thompson (Austin: University of Texas Press, 1967), pp. 3–17.

26. Ibid., p. 11. For reassessments of Ayres's views on the various topics discussed above, see the essays by A. W. Coats, R. M. Hartwell, S. Herbert Frankel, W. W. Rostow, Joseph J. Spengler, and Alfred F. Chalk in this volume.

27. Two other books were published by Ayres between *The Theory of Economic Progress* and *Toward a Reasonable Society*. But one was a "potboiler," *The Divine Right of Capital* (Boston: Houghton Mifflin Co., 1946); the other was an introductory textbook from an institutionalist viewpoint, *The Industrial Economy* (Boston: Houghton Mifflin Co., 1952). The chief significance of these books is that they contained in embryonic form a proposal for income redistribution which later came to be called a "negative income tax."

28. Letter, C. E. Ayres to Homer P. Rainey, June 29, 1942.

29. See Ronnie Dugger, *Our Invaded Universities: Form, Reform, and New Starts* (New York: W. W. Norton and Co., 1974), p. 43. Rainey tells his own story of his battles with the Board of Regents at Texas in *The Tower and the Dome* (Boulder: Pruett Publishing Co., 1971).

30. Texas House of Representatives, 52nd legislature, *House Journal* (1951) 1:904.

31. *Daily Texan*, March 16, 1951, p. 1.

32. Statement of Representative Austin Westbrook, as cited in *Daily Texan*, March 18, 1951, p. 1.

33. Letter, Logan Wilson to the editor of the *Alcalde*, April 16, 1953 (copy to C. E. Ayres).

34. Letter, C. E. Ayres to Logan Wilson, April 20, 1953.

35. Ibid.

36. Letter, C. E. Ayres to Sidney Hook, May 4, 1939.

37. Letter, C. E. Ayres to Gunnar Myrdal, January 26, 1967.

38. Ayres, *The Industrial Economy*, p. x.

Clarence Ayres's Place in the History of American Economics: An Interim Assessment

A. W. COATS

I

A comprehensive scholarly assessment of Clarence Ayres's place in the development of American economics is long overdue, and it is to be hoped that it will soon be forthcoming. Yet it is a task that should not be undertaken lightly, for, in addition to Ayres's voluminous and scattered writings, the author will have to familiarize himself with several major streams of twentieth century American intellectual activity, not only in the social sciences but also in philosophy and politics. And he will find it difficult to avoid partisanship.

Given these circumstances and the proverbial folly of those who rush in, the tentative character of this essay must be stressed. It stems from the belief that a comparatively detached, sympathetic but neutral, transatlantic viewpoint may be of some value in appraising the work of so distinctively American a writer.

Generalizations about national character are often more confusing than helpful. Nevertheless the "Americanness" of Ayres's economics is undeniable, whether one considers his intellectual antecedents and associations, his principal themes and preoccupations, his professional style, or even his academic location and influence. He was, of course, an institutionalist, and institutionalism has generally been regarded as a distinctly, even uniquely American contribution to modern economic thought.[1] Ayres repeatedly and generously acknowledged his personal indebtedness to those characteristically American thinkers Thorstein Veblen and John Dewey; and it is worth noting that all three were decisively shaped, albeit in different ways, by the late nineteenth and early twentieth century Middle West, a region which also nurtured the other two leading cofounders of institutional economics, Wesley C. Mitchell and John R. Commons. By 1917, when Ayres completed his graduate studies at the University of Chicago, Mitchell, Veblen, and Dewey had already left the faculty. But the influence of the last two on Ayres's economics and philosophy teachers was still strong, and the Chicago tradition was still thriving a decade or more later when he published his first book and a shorter statement of his philosophical beliefs.[2]

Ayres has recently been depicted as a member of the post-1945 generation of so-called neo-institutionalists.[3] If there is indeed such a movement, he may legitimately be regarded as its father figure. Yet Ayres himself was manifestly of an intermediate generation, a personification of the intellectual links between the original, *fin de siècle* institutionalist triumvirate and the more dedicated younger adherents of the Association for Evolutionary Economics. To the latter generation Ayres represents a voice from the past, for even a casual perusal of his writings reveals the essential continuity and repetitiveness of his basic themes and concerns. Like Veblen, Ayres took his doctorate in philosophy, and throughout his subsequent career he maintained an essentially philosophical approach to his subject matter. Admittedly neither he nor Veblen was really interested in those pedantic and narrowly technical questions which preoccupy many academic specialists in philosophy and economics. On the contrary, they were concerned with broader issues, such as the preconceptions of established doctrines, especially orthodox economics, and the general nature and processes of economic and cultural change. Both men displayed a sustained interest in matters far beyond the conventional boundaries of the social sciences; and, seeking a broad interdisciplinary synthesis, they aimed to present their findings to intelligent laymen as well as to their academic peers. On policy matters they were usually vague and general, rather than detailed and specific. Yet they undoubtedly sought to influence the course of events as well as the main currents of educated opinion. Like many late nineteenth and early twentieth century American progressives, they were moral and social reformers, preachers as well as teachers, fundamentally optimistic in their conception of American society, its problems and prospects.[4] And, like other reformist intellectuals, they were far less radical in practice than some of their contemporary critics supposed.

In several respects both Veblen and Ayres now seem somewhat old-fashioned—though their admirers will undoubtedly add: so much the worse for current styles! Comparatively unconcerned with conventional academic success in the disciplines they nominally professed, they earned respect and acquired followers largely because they were intellectual mavericks, surviving (sometimes not without difficulty) as generalists in a university environment increasingly dominated by specialists. It has often been noted that Veblen's nearest British counterpart, J. A. Hobson, never obtained an academic appointment and was almost certainly refused permission to undertake university extension lectures in economics on the grounds of his presumed professional incompetence. Difficult and subversive as he was, Veblen nevertheless managed to hold, albeit precariously, a series of academic appointments in leading universities, and his experience may consequently be cited as evidence of the tolerance and heterogeneity of the American academic community.

Somewhat the same is true, *mutatis mutandis*, of Ayres's career.[5] It is surely impossible to find a parallel case among European professors of economics—that is to say, a leading figure in an important university possessing a similar journalistic and disciplinary background, an equally limited technical expertise and interest in his nominal field, a comparable list of nonspecialist publications, and an equivalent combination of pedagogic charisma and personal influence. Admittedly this assessment is somewhat speculative, for the relevant data have not yet been assembled. Nevertheless, Professor John S. Gambs's lighthearted reference to the "Cactus League of Dissenting Economists" should be taken seriously,[6] for a study of regional "schools" of American economics should not be confined to Chicago, Wisconsin, and Harvard. Now that Thomas S. Kuhn and others have sensitized us to the interrelations between the epistemological, social, and institutional dimensions of the scientific process, we must be prepared to examine these matters in detail. And if institutional economics survives as a distinct intellectual movement in America—a matter on which even some of its faithful adherents have expressed reservations—then Ayres's career is of much more than merely biographical interest.

II

In order to understand Ayres's version of institutionalism, some account of his philosophical presuppositions is unavoidable, even though this will take us into an obscure terrain far beyond the conventional boundaries of economics. Most economists prefer to take their metaphysics and values for granted, but Ayres, unlike Veblen, made no attempt to conceal his feelings in satire or convoluted prose. Veblen's basic dichotomies—between science and ceremonialism, technology and institutions, industry and business, workmanship and waste—recur throughout Ayres's writings, though he was constantly reformulating, elaborating, and synthesizing these elements. His conception of socioeconomic development bore marked resemblances to Veblen's, and in later years his acknowledgments to Veblen became more frequent and explicit.[7] Yet he was no mere disciple, largely because his ideas were securely grounded in Dewey's pragmatist/instrumentalist epistemology, a doctrine which Veblen had treated with considerable skepticism around the turn of the century. Moreover, Ayres's commitment to specific values was much more explicit than Veblen's, and his intellectual system was consequently much more coherent and purposeful.

Ayres's critics accused him of preaching technological determinism,[8] and indeed he so strongly emphasized the technological circumstances that "shape and modify and attenuate the institutional heritage" of modern society that the charge is not unreasonable [1951, "The Co-ordinates of Institutionalism," p. 51]. While denying that the technological process was the whole of culture, that technology was an external force, or that machines invent themselves, Ayres nevertheless described technology as the "life process" and "hope" of mankind and declared that machines are "the ultimate reality of modern civilization" [1951, "The Co-ordinates of Institutionalism," p. 51; 1953, "The Role of Technology in Economic Theory," p. 287; 1943, "Capitalism in Retrospect," p. 301].

Yet his concept of technology extended far beyond mere machines: it was essentially epistemological, hence his willingness to view his system as an offspring of Dewey's instrumentalism. As he explained, "I have done my best to state explicitly and repeatedly that I am using the word [technology] in the broadest possible sense to refer to that whole aspect of human experience and activity which some logicians call 'operational,' and to the entire complement of artifacts with which mankind operates. So defined, technology includes mathematical journals and symphonic scores no less than skyscrapers and assembly lines, since all these are equally the product of human hands as well as brains."[9]

Given his later insistence on the value and importance of science and technology, Ayres's treatment of science in some of his earlier writings comes as a considerable surprise. In his first book, *Science: The False Messiah* (1927), he attacked the current worship of pure science as an end in itself, warning that scientists were becoming the high priests of modern society. Strongly contesting the view that popular thought was wholly confused or that science was superior to the "homely ideas" on which civilization turns, Ayres asserted that "from the human point of view science is utterly unsatisfactory . . . science never solves the mysteries of the Forces which rule our lives.

In the field of mystery—and human life is all mystery—religion remains supreme" [1927, S.F.M., p. 154].

Two years later, in a philosophical essay, he reiterated his opinion that science was incapable of dealing with the entire range of human concerns—especially the most important ones. Accepting the Kantian distinction between the *ding an sich*, the philosophical realm, and things as they seem, which he identified with science, he declared that such certainty as science could muster merely stemmed from its "instruments of precision" and its consequent capacity to extend the powers of sensory observation [1927, S.F.M., pp. 47, 156–158]. "No subject matter," he remarked, "can be understood except as derived from a certain type of mental discipline" [1929, "A Critique of Pure Science," p. 178], and, as he offered no criterion by which to compare the validity of one mental discipline with another, his assertion that the study of science and the study of society "have nothing whatever in common except the fact that both are pursued by men" is perplexing [1929, "A Critique of Pure Science," p. 178]. The limitations of science, he continued, "arise from the fact that not all matters of interest and importance to mankind are perceptible to eye and ear. . . . Social behavior is just as real as any behavior, and concepts which arise in social behavior are therefore just as real and sound as concepts which arise in the tinkering of hand and eye."[10]

These passages are of the greatest interest in the light of Ayres's subsequent tendency to adopt a monistic ontology parallel with the monistic epistemology he derived from Dewey. As a loyal instrumentalist, he consistently opposed dualistic disjunctions between body and mind, facts and values, means and ends, knowing and doing. Technology was the only *source* of knowledge and genuine values, for "operational" values derived from tools were uniform and consistent moral values, by contrast with the variability of "false" cultural values.[11] It was the positivistic disassociation of truth and value which defined the moral crisis of the twentieth century, for the crucial issue was not to separate knowledge from values but to distinguish between true and false, both in knowledge and values [1961, T.R.S., pp. 49–50]. As an instrumentalist, Ayres claimed that value judgments could be objectively verified, and he repeatedly referred to technological criteria of value judgments and human welfare [1961, T.R.S., p. 61; 1967, "The Theory of Institutional Adjustment," p. 14].

By contrast with his earlier acknowledgment of the disjunction between science and "the human point of view," Ayres subsequently stressed their fundamental compatibility, for both modern science and "the values of man's achieving" reflected the underlying uniformities of nature [1961, T.R.S., p. 51]. This may explain why at one point he described machines as the "ultimate reality" of modern civilization, while elsewhere he defined reality as "the unique coherence of . . . the non-material culture" [1943, "Capitalism in Retrospect," p. 301; 1967, "The Theory of Institutional Adjustment," p. 7]. In emphasizing the fundamental unity and uniformity of the "mutually intensifying system of concerted values" [1959, "The Industrial Way of Life," p. 9], which he sometimes vaguely referred to as the "life process" (a term to be found in Veblen, Hobson, and Ruskin), he became increasingly critical of the pestilential "moral agnosticism" of those who believed in the relativity of cultural standards [1957, "The Pestilence of Moral Agnosticism," pp. 116–125]. If, as he claimed, culture was an "aspect of nature" like science and technology, presumably the two aspects could not be indefinitely out of phase or at odds with one another, even though he repeatedly referred to the conflict between institutions and technology and declared that institutional and instrumentalist standards were "absolutely opposed" [1935, "The Gospel of Technology," p. 40; 1967, "The Theory of Institutional Adjustment," p. 5].

There was, of course, as Veblen had demonstrated, an institutional lag as society adjusted itself, sometimes slowly and painfully, to the ongoing process of technological advance. But toward the end of his life Ayres appeared to be looking beyond Veblen to a time when the lag would be significantly reduced, if not entirely eliminated. Despite institutional impediments, technology proceeded at an accelerating pace, and twenty years earlier Ayres had acknowledged the "logical and ethical and therefore economic significance of the continuity which is actually present in the technological process and in it alone" [1945, "Addendum to *The Theory of Economic Progress*," p. 939]. Hence, notwithstanding his Veblenian distaste for teleological statements and his reluctance to indulge in prophecies, Ayres's later writings convey an ineradicable impression of the ultimate supremacy of technology. A "de-institutionalization" process was under way, directly parallel to the "de-mythologization of modern culture" which results from the inexorable growth of science and technology [1967, "The Theory of Institutional Adjustment," pp. 8, 16]. But since, in his earliest writings, Ayres maintained that even science was ultimately based on folklore, one wonders what credence can be given to this *Weltanschauung*.

In his first book, Ayres had sneered at the Hegelian dialectic as "a sort of patent Absolute detector" [1927, S.F.M., p. 165]; but sub-

sequently, despite occasional denials, he was preaching his own species of absolutism. This was entailed in his attack on cultural relativism, in which he distinguished between "the fancied values to which
each different culture conditions its community . . . [and] the genuine
values which are common to all" [1959, "The Industrial Way of Life,"
p. 14]. In culture, as in technology, nonoperational norms and prac-
tices were false and irrational, and, although "supernatural fancies"
could be culturally transmitted as readily as "clear and certain knowledge" [1959, "The Industrial Way of Life," p. 15; 1961, T.R.S., p. 289],
in due course the predominant influence of technology would presumably obliterate most, if not all, the spurious variations.[12] Ayres's
warm endorsement of Dewey's famous critique of *The Quest for Certainty* seems curiously at odds with his own confidence in "the progressive certainty of science" and his conviction that true knowledge
and values can be distinguished from false [1946, D.R.C., p. 185]. As
early as 1935 he conceded that "sooner or later any theory of historical
process faces the problem of absolute value," adding that technology
must constitute its ultimate foundation since it "does indeed afford
a basis of judgment which is absolute in the sense that it is in no wise
dependent upon any sort of moral inwardness nor upon any moral
tradition whatever . . . I am therefore, in this sense, a complete mate-
rialist" [1934–1935, "Confusion Thrice Confounded," p. 358]. In his
last book, *Toward a Reasonable Society* (1961), he explicated his set
of interacting, mutually compatible values: freedom, equality, security, abundance, and excellence. Taken together, these constituted
the essence of the "life process" which it was the economist's duty
to promote.

If, as seems likely, the foregoing account of Ayres's philosophy is
somewhat obscure and bewildering, it is at least partly due to his
unwillingness to employ precise philosophical terms and concepts.
This limitation particularly inhibits the effort to understand his conception of the nature of and relationships between institutions, technology, and values. For example, he never precisely specified the
meaning and extension of the term *technology*, although he repeatedly and unambiguously stressed that the development of technology
was continuous, increasingly influential, and compatible with human
values. In later writings he tried to specify the principal values embodied in that compendious expression "the life process," but he
never cleared up certain earlier difficulties arising from his shifting
emphasis on the nature, sources, foundation, and criteria of values.
In the preface to the new edition of his first two books he made a final
attempt to explain his meaning. Whereas the continuity of the tech-

nological process "means that it is *a* locus of value . . . Human life itself is *the* 'locus' of value—not in the animistic sense of totem and taboo, but in the continuously progressive sense of the 'instinct' [or process] of workmanship." Two pages later he went further, almost repudiating his Deweyite insistence on the means-ends continuum, concluding that "human life and well being *depends upon* the furtherance" of the technological process, thereby implying that technology is merely a means to an end rather than an end in itself, since "the values we seek are those of human life and well-being" [1927, S.F.M., first two quotations from p. x, third quotation from p. xii; italics supplied]. Yet if this is the core of his message is it more than a statement of the obvious?

III

Although Ayres was sometimes regarded as a dangerous radical, he was never in fact an extremist, either in political or economic affairs. Consistently hostile to fascism, Marxism, and doctrinaire socialism, he stood squarely in the mainstream of moderate American social and economic reformers alongside the progressives and new dealers. To a transatlantic reader it is noticeable how frequently he cited such British liberal reformers as Hobson, R. H. Tawney, and J. M. Keynes, with whom he was associated in the 1920's during his *New Republic* days; and, when William Beveridge published his *Full Employment in a Free Society* in 1944, Ayres welcomed his social security program as a means of bypassing the traditional controversy between socialism and capitalism.[13] A staunch opponent of laissez-faire, Ayres naturally favored a form of interventionist policy which, he hoped, would produce what he called "limited capitalism." Unlike the first generation of American institutionalists, Ayres developed his economic ideas against the background of the Great Depression of the early thirties and Roosevelt's recovery programs, and contemporary preoccupations influenced his ideas more directly and profoundly than has been generally appreciated. Despite his severe criticisms of business, he wished to extend business principles,[14] and during the New Deal he was advocating regulation of machine industry and some form of social control or guidance of the productive mechanism which would deal with the central problem of idle resources [1933, "The Basis of Economic Statesmanship," p. 215; 1939, "The Principles of Economic Strategy," pp. 460–470]. In the mid-1940's Ayres welcomed the new Keynesian macroeconomics, and,

despite his profound reservations about all forms of economic orthodoxy, he declared, in 1948, that institutionalism, underconsumptionist ideas (which he associated with Hobson and Keynes), and
economic planning were mutually reinforcing [1948, "The New Economics," pp. 226–232].

His conception of planning was no more extreme than his other
policy ideas. He considered that a general economic strategy was
required, not a detailed blueprint, and he opposed planning against
competition and sweeping nationalization or expropriation of industrial property [1939, "The Principles of Economic Strategy"; 1943,
"The Significance of Economic Planning"; 1946, D.R.C., p. 164;
1948, "The New Economics"]. Indeed, considering his advocacy of
piecemeal economic and social reform and his rejection of fears that
increased government activity represented the road to serfdom, it
would not be farfetched to describe him as a typical Fabian.

Another central characteristic Ayres possessed in common with
other American progressives and instrumentalists was his underlying
confidence in the future of American society—and, indeed, of industrial capitalism in general. He was not, of course, a blind optimist.
He repeatedly stated that progress was not inevitable, warning against
the dangers of complacency. He often referred to current "crises,"
and sometimes suggested that capitalism or "society" was in danger
of collapsing [1943, "The Twilight of the Price System," p. 180; 1943,
"The Significance of Economic Planning," p. 470; 1946, D.R.C., p. 80;
1961, T.R.S., pp. 207–208]. Nevertheless, even in periods of the greatest difficulty he never seemed to doubt that some remedy was available, and his pessimistic statements are far outweighed by his fundamentally optimistic views. He vigorously rejected the predictions of
the "prophets of scientific doom" [1943, "The Significance of Economic Planning," p. 479], arguing that "human experience does manifest a developmental pattern of some sort" [1945, "Addendum to the
Theory of Economic Progress," p. 938] and entitling his magnum
opus *The Theory of Economic Progress*.

Underlying this optimism was his belief in the "inner law of progress in technology" [1943, "Technology and Progress," p. 11], and he
had no fear that the growth of science would lead to cultural decay or
a loss of freedom. On the contrary, he anticipated the progressive
replacement of superstition by knowledge, of prejudice by reason
[1961, T.R.S., p. 138]. He claimed that there was an increasing awareness of the importance of machines among the general public, and
even among the economists, after the Great Depression [1944, T.E.P.,
p. 306], and that there was no incompatibility between economic

progress and other values [1952, I.E., p. 403]. In more specifically economic affairs he saw no serious obstacle to sound policies—for example, the need to set farm prices so as to obtain the desired volume of
production [1948, "The New Economics," p. 232]. Nor was there any
economic barrier to the attainment of social security, though there
might be political obstacles [1946, D.R.C., p. 104]. Technological
progress might be checked for a time by institutional impediments,
but this would only be a temporary setback [1952, I.E., p. 402]. And
his comparative lack of concern with the human and environmental
damage caused by industrial technology, a theme which has recently
become almost obsessive, is yet another indication of his membership
in an earlier generation of social commentators.[15] There was no ultimate conflict of values: without being Utopian, Ayres evidently
believed that freedom, equality, security, abundance, and excellence
were all within man's eager grasp.

Like many intellectuals, Ayres possessed a fundamentally optimistic faith in the "power of ideas" [1944, T.E.P., chap. 13], confidently
asserting that "intellectual progress is never destructive" [1948, "The
New Economics," p. 230]. Yet, although he claimed that the power of
propaganda was greatly exaggerated [1944, T.E.P., p. 295], his optimism was by no means unqualified. In the late 1940's, when the
anticommunist phobia was gaining momentum, he warned that
society would collapse if intellectual freedom was suppressed [1947,
"Are Professors Dangerous?"], and in economic and social affairs he
was deeply concerned at the persistence of outworn dogmas and pernicious fallacies. He not only attacked the orthodox tradition of economics as providing ideological support for laissez-faire capitalism,
but he also suggested that, if the ideas of the founding fathers were
not repudiated, disaster would ensue [1956, "The Classical Tradition
Versus Economic Growth," p. 350]. Like other economic dissenters
he thought that the economics profession had great influence over the
general public, arguing that "the consummate fault of the whole
classical theory" was that it prevented the community from recognizing the dangers of "bigness" and its implications for economic
power [1952, I.E., p. 390]. And in his later writings he accused the
economics profession of moral irresponsibility on the grounds of its
persistent failure to warn the public of the pernicious influence of
business power.

Given his background, training, literary skills, and wide-ranging
intellectual interests, it is perhaps surprising that Ayres ever became,
let alone remained, a professor of economics. But once he was situated
within the academic community it was surely inevitable that he

would become a dissenter. When he joined the University of Texas faculty in 1930 the obsequies of institutionalism were already being celebrated in some quarters, and the movement's younger adherents lacked leadership. Of the three cofounders, Veblen was dead; Mitchell had turned from his more heterodox ideas to the statistical study of business cycles; and Commons, though still active in the field, had become increasingly isolated and incomprehensible even to his closest admirers. Although Ayres was obviously a critic of economic orthodoxy, his precise intellectual allegiances remained obscure during the 1930's, probably because he was still feeling his way. During that decade he published much less than in his journalist days of the 1920's, or in the 1940's and 1950's, when he was expounding and elaborating his intellectual system. However, he was neither ignored nor rejected by the professional economic establishment in the 1930's, for he published occasional articles in the *American Economic Review* and became an active and effective member of its editorial board for three years, from 1935 to 1938. This was the closest he ever came to the professional center of American economics. In the mid 1940's his intellectual position became much clearer with the publication of *The Theory of Economic Progress* (1944) and *The Divine Right of Capital* (1946), and it is significant that chapters of these works appeared in general periodicals, such as *The Antioch Review* and the *Southwestern Social Science Quarterly*, rather than in the professional economic journals. He continued this practice in the next two decades, thereby revealing his detachment from the mainstream of American economics and his desire to reach a less specialized readership.

Dissenters and outsiders are often effective and perspicacious critics of established doctrines and opinion leaders, and Ayres was no exception. A brief résumé of his objections to classical and neoclassical economics contains few surprises for those familiar with earlier heterodox effusions.[16] Economic theory, he complained, was comprised of a melange of absurdities, truisms, meaningless tautologies, and circular reasoning. Its philosophical and psychological premises were unsound; its propositions were not merely unrealistic, but false; and as an intellectual system it was devoid of human, moral, or social merit. Despite its positivistic pose, classical economics had never been purely descriptive, and Adam Smith's desire to overthrow the mercantilist economic order merely exemplified the economists' perennial and unavoidable concern with social problems [1918, "The Function and Problems of Economic Theory," pp. 74–78]. Unlike some heterodox writers, Ayres did not regard orthodox economics as static, nor did he entirely reject the concept of equilibrium [1939, "The Principles of Economic Strategy," p. 463]. On the contrary, he insisted that classical political economy was "fundamentally a theory of economic dynamics" and the founding fathers' conception of the equilibrium of institutions and technology was their greatest achievement [1934, "Values: Ethical and Economic," p. 453; 1951, "The Co-ordinates of Institutionalism," p. 50; 1943, "The Twilight of the Price System," p. 163; 1944, T.E.P., pp. 20–21].

Much of his hostility—which, he subsequently admitted, was exaggerated—was directed at the price system. Its importance had been overrated both by its defenders and by the institutionalist opposition. Price theory was the "Freemasonry" of the professional economists [1966, "Nature and Significance of Institutionalism," p. 73], who, for technical reasons, had elaborated it to the point where it became an arcane mystery inaccessible to the layman, and therefore a basis for professional status and recognition [1951, "The Co-ordinates of Institutionalism," p. 49; 1952, I.E., pp. 18–19]. Ayres considered that this analytical apparatus had no meaning or significance once it was detached from its original conception of the harmonious, atomistic, self-regulating socioeconomic order; and he criticized the institutionalists for their failure to provide an alternative theory or to proceed successfully from analysis to policy [1934–1935, "Moral Confusion in Economics," pp. 172–174; 1943, "The Twilight of the Price System," p. 179; 1944, T.E.P., pp. 11–12]. But although the economists were not merely vulgar apologists of the capitalist system [1938, P.E.O., p. 34], as the socialists claimed, price theory had in fact afforded intellectual support for capitalism. Moreover, classical economics had provided a moral justification for the prevailing uneven distribution of wealth [1934, "Values: Ethical and Economic," p. 454; 1944, T.E.P., p. 52], and at times Ayres even accused the economists of perpetrating a confidence trick on the public in claiming that savings and abstinence, rather than technological progress, constituted the main source of capital accumulation [1938, P.E.O., pp. 73–74; 1944, T.E.P., p. 54; 1961, T.R.S., p. 238].

Ayres occasionally adopted a carping and satirical tone when referring to his colleagues in the economics profession,[17] complaining that they had failed to keep pace with the development of Western civilization or to comprehend the existing economic order. Nevertheless, he credited them with sincerity, honesty, and modesty— indeed, they greatly underestimated their influence on the general public [1944, T.E.P., p. 284; 1952, I.E., p. 297; 1966, "Nature and Significance of Institutionalism," p. 78]. Ayres naturally sympathized with outsiders like Hobson, who had been "professionally ostracized" because he had challenged the moral basis of capitalism [1946, D.R.C., p. 195]; and at one point he even referred to the "atmosphere of intimidation" in which economic instruction "commonly proceeds" [1944, T.E.P., p. 54]. He stoutly defended the dissenters against false accusations, denying that "institutionalism is the work of men who are failures and who have therefore in anger and bitterness turned against the economic order they blame for their own failure." Nor was it true, he insisted, that the movement had its origin in "emotional disaffection" or that it led to "social revolution" [1952, I.E., pp. 3, 14].

Throughout the greater part of the 1930's, Ayres remained a detached commentator on institutionalism, as in his first published article, which appeared in 1918. Institutionalism was "bad economics," he declared in 1935; its exponents dismissed orthodox theory too lightly, and they offered no alternative theory—merely "a few stray uncoordinated hints" [1934–1935, "Moral Confusion in Economics," pp. 172, 182, 197–198; 1934–1935, "Confusion Thrice Confounded," p. 357]. Indeed, in 1944 he complained that many of Veblen's followers had displayed "a contempt for theory as such which has led them to eschew 'abstract' thinking and to concentrate their efforts upon empirical studies of actual economic situations . . . with results which are not clearly distinguishable from the work of students who have never strayed from the classical fold, as the latter never tire of pointing out" [1944, T.E.P., pp. 11–12].

In his magnum opus Ayres aimed to set out "a new way of thinking about economic problems," while acknowledging that there was as yet no viable alternative to the orthodox model. "Whatever the defects of the classical design, it still remains the only over-all design we have, and will remain until another conception of the meaning of the economy has taken form" [1944, T.E.P., p. 21]. To provide this alternative design was Ayres's principal aim, for he considered that the primary task of economics was "to elicit the meaning" of the economy, and its proper focus was "the theory of economic order" rather than the narrower range of theoretical, technical, and statistical topics which engaged the attention of most professional economists [1944, T.E.P., p. 85; 1934–1935, "Moral Confusion in Economics," p. 171; 1938, P.E.O.].

By 1952, when he published his textbook *The Industrial Economy: Its Technological Basis and Institutional Destiny*, he had abandoned his detachment and adopted institutionalism (or instrumentalism) as the required "new way of thinking." In so doing he took up a "frankly partisan" standpoint, declaring: "I confess I have no patience with the notion that the business of teachers (and, I presume, writers) is to 'present both sides' of any matter that is in dispute, leaving it to their students (or readers) to 'decide for themselves' where the truth resides . . . the eventual effect of such a practice is likely to be that the teachers and writers gradually acquire indecisiveness as a sort of occupational disease" [1952, I.E., p. ix]. Ayres considered it the teacher's or writer's duty, "seeking all the knowledge and all the wisdom he can manage, to present his understanding of the matter in hand as clearly as he can, together with the clearest possible account of the procedures by which he has arrived at his conclusions, leaving it to others to present similarly sympathetic accounts of alternative interpretations of the matter. There is no reason why anyone who reads this book should not read others that declare otherwise, and every reason why he should" [1952, I.E., pp. ix–x].

Ayres's reasons for declaring his allegiance to institutionalism (or instrumentalism, or technologism, as he would have preferred to call it) were expressed in his earlier writings. Classical economics was a foreign importation which failed to take account of the postindustrial revolution development of technology and post-Darwinian scientific ideas. By contrast, institutionalism was an indigenous American ideology, and its central tenet was the instrumental or technological conception of value, "which takes the place of the 'moral sense' of Adam Smith and the moral nihilism of his present-day successors" [1952, I.E., p. 27]. Following Dewey, Ayres claimed that valuations in terms of instruments and techniques are not irrational, like tribal beliefs and sentiments, for "whereas the institutional values are culture-limited, the instrumental (or technological) values are the same for all cultures" [1952, I.E., p. 26]. This new body of ideas, with its modern conception of human nature as a "social or cultural phenomenon" entirely replaced the erroneous "atomistic Newtonian-Lockean conception of human nature . . . and the whole Hobbesian-Smithian conception of the economy as a natural outgrowth of the natural activities of naturally reasonable beings" [1952, I.E., pp. 12–13].

As the foregoing passages reveal, Ayres's primary aim was to reconstruct the philosophical foundations of economics in accordance with his conception of the economic and cultural development of Western civilization. He admitted in 1935, in response to F. H. Knight, that "any value theory, economic or other, must have a basis which is somehow absolute" and that "technological process does indeed afford a basis of judgment which is absolute in the sense that it is in no wise dependent upon any sort of moral inwardness nor upon any moral tradition whatever" [1934–1935, "Confusion Thrice Confounded," p. 358].

To put the matter differently, he subsequently agreed with Galbraith that mankind "cannot live without an economic theology" [1956, "The Classical Tradition Versus Economic Growth," p. 347], and instrumentalism (or technology) was the central article of his faith. As we shall see, Ayres did not entirely ignore the conventional preoccupations of economists; nor did he endorse Veblen's wholesale and destructive attacks on economic orthodoxy. He was chiefly concerned with other, deeper and more general issues, and it was on this broad philosophical level—where most economists feel uncomfortable—that he functioned most persuasively. He must be answered, if at all, on an equally high level of generality, a plane of discourse on which mere economics may have comparatively little to contribute.

This is especially true of his *Theory of Economic Progress*, where, despite the opening salvoes against conventional economic doctrines, Ayres's main purpose was to develop a comprehensive philosophy of cultural development. With his optimism, his moderation, and his belief in reason, he can be viewed as a latter day exponent of the eighteenth century enlightenment, with its refined taste for *histoire raisonnée*. Like other leading institutionalists, especially Veblen and Commons, he used history selectively to buttress arguments derived from his philosophical preconceptions, not as a source of evidence to be critically examined and tested. Though he frequently spoke of economic history, he did so in terms almost unrecognizable—or at least unacceptable—to most specialist practitioners in the field; and, it seems, few of them have heeded his message. Admittedly there are now some small indications of a revival of interest in large-scale historical growth models,[18] but these owe nothing to Ayres, being largely a reaction against the limitations imposed by mathematical growth models in economics and the new "cliometric" economic history. No doubt, Ayres's conception of economic development has stimulated young dissenting economists—not only in the ranks of the Association for Evolutionary Economics. But although his message is much clearer than Veblen's, it is almost as difficult to follow his lead, for, as Benjamin Higgins has remarked, Ayres tells us virtually nothing about specific programs and policies.[19]

Despite his attachment to Veblen, Ayres took comparatively little notice of the methodological controversies in which his predecessor figured so prominently—with the sole exception of the question of the psychological foundations of economics, a matter he took very seriously. However, this, too, is an issue which now attracts much less attention than it did in the earlier decades of the century—at least if Allan Gruchy's account of neo-institutionalism is accurate.[20]

IV

Orthodox critics claim that when institutionalists turn from polemical attacks on classical and neo-classical economics to constructive work they inevitably draw upon the conventional corpus of economic analysis for the simple reason that they have not yet developed their own alternative theories. It is appropriate to consider how far this observation applies to Ayres, for an examination of his writings suggests that he drew more heavily on orthodox economics than many of his followers have appreciated.

As we have seen, Ayres was a philosopher rather than an economist, and his earlier economic writings mainly represent commentaries on past and present economic doctrines, rather than substantive exercises in economic theory or policy. Indeed, throughout his life he confined himself to the most elementary kinds of economic reasoning, eschewing complex theories, whether mathematical or verbal, and making only the most sparing use of statistical data. He was always more interested in policy problems than in economic analysis. But toward the end of the 1930's his economic ideas began to assume a more definite shape.

A central tenet of Ayres's economics, one that was directly linked to his technological interpretation of history, was his repudiation of the orthodox concept of capital. Classical economics, he maintained, had emerged under conditions where a rapid expansion of the national dividend was accompanied by gross inequality in the distribution of wealth, and this had fostered the misconception that inequality was an essential precondition of economic progress. Orthodox capital theory, he declared in 1938, was responsible for "the greatest confusion in economics." The idea of saving as the source of capital accumulation was a "hoax," perpetrated by those seeking to defend the status quo; and he cited J. M. Keynes in support of his contention.[21] The accumulation of capital was due to the growth of industrial tools, not the expansion of investible funds.[22] Indeed, the growth of financial assets by large business organizations during the 1920's had restricted the expansion of consumers' demand, thereby creating the fundamental economic problem of the 1930's, which the New

Deal administrators had tried to solve by expanding the volume of purchasing power. From this point Ayres proceeded in the 1940's to draw upon Keynes's *General Theory*, with its attack on Say's Law [i.e., the idea that supply creates its own demand], its use of the multiplier concept, and its general endorsement of the underconsumptionist tradition in economic thought. Even in 1935 Ayres had acknowledged the falsity of the supposed conflict between neo-classical economics and institutionalism, and later in life he periodically stressed their compatibility, speaking of the convergence of orthodox and heterodox ideas on the lines of institutionalism, underconsumption, and economic planning.[23] Hence in this respect he was closer to Commons than to Veblen, who had presented his evolutionary economics as being fundamentally incompatible with orthodox economics.[24]

During the 1940's and earlier 1950's Ayres came closer to orthodox economics than at any other time in his career. In his *Divine Right of Capital* (1946)—a book which, he said, bore "a general and pervasive relationship" to *The Theory of Economic Progress* (1944)—and in *The Industrial Economy* (1952) he expounded an elementary form of Keynesianism compatible with his belief that the "full employment" criterion was virtually equivalent to the technological criterion of "full production." Full employment, he maintained, was a good bargain, for the accompanying benefits of increased output could be achieved with little or no additional cost. "What we require, and all we require, to make the industrial economy work is a flow of mass-consumption purchasing power sufficient to absorb the entire product of industry at whatever level of production we may be able to achieve" [1946, D.R.C., p. 95].

He devoted considerable space to a discussion of income flows and what he called the "income diversion" required to achieve this end, giving assurances that this did not entail either confiscation of property or a deliberate campaign to soak the rich. In both volumes he paid some attention to the problems involved in achieving economic stability, such as increased government expenditure, deficit financing, various types of taxation, public works, and the debt burden, and in the 1952 text he even included eleven diagrams and a statistical table—for Ayres, an unprecedented concession to conventional economic pedagogy.[25] It must be admitted that by the standards of orthodox economic theory Ayres's analysis was superficial and lacking in originality. Matters of this kind were simply not his forte; nor was he really interested in them. Moreover, it would be utterly misleading to suggest that Ayres was merely a marginal Keynesian with an idiosyncratic view of economic development and a predilection for encyclopedic sociology. His writings reveal some confusion about the functional relationships between consumption, production, and distribution, for sometimes he stressed their interdependence whereas on other occasions he emphasized the primacy of one over the others.

But his most distinctive theme was his emphasis on physical production, as contrasted with the orthodox concern with exchange values, and in this respect his work is directly reminiscent of Veblen's. During the 1930's he referred to certain essentially quantitative criteria of the success of any society [1935, "The Gospel of Technology," p. 28], and by the end of the decade he advanced the notion that "the first principle of all economic strategy is physical stability" in place of the traditional concept of price stability [1939, "The Principles of Economic Strategy," p. 464]. The key to classical economic strategy was "the idea of natural harmony," and classical price theory was meaningless when detached from that idea. But since the idea of natural harmony was no longer acceptable it must be replaced by the concept of "physical stability," which is "the stability without which civilization is impossible, the reality behind all enlightened social theories" [1939, "The Principles of Economic Strategy," p. 464].

> . . . economic stability can certainly be understood in such physical terms as the relation of food supply to population, the regularity of the working habits of the people, continuity of operation of machines, and so forth. There is nothing esoteric about it, or even complicated. For it must be understood at once that the adoption of the principle of physical stability does not by any means require a set of blue prints showing the place of every man and every tool at every hour of the day to an indefinite future, any more than our past reliance on the principle of price equilibrium presupposed a similarly detailed knowledge of the movements of all prices whatsoever and of all the things of which they were the prices. A principle of strategy undertakes to state in general terms what it is that we are trying to do, and no more. [1939, "The Principles of Economic Strategy," p. 464].

In opposition to the generally accepted view, Ayres maintained that the classical economists had underestimated the importance of production. In considering the general principle of economic strategy, the question "Production of what?" was irrelevant. Here, as elsewhere, he was concerned with society as a whole; not with individual tastes and motivations. "There is no point in saying before you can begin to produce you must know what people want. No society begins to produce. Society is a going concern largely by virtue of the fact that we produce what we can. The effective modification of our habits of consumption does not come about as a result of spiritual revelation made manifest in wants, or by the imposition of some people's ideals on other people. The actual changes come through the adjustment of consumption to the exigencies of production" [1939, "The Principles of Economic Strategy," p. 466].

In his later writings Ayres repeatedly referred to the idea of "full production," which he preferred to the widely accepted notion of "full employment." It was not a new idea in economics, he insisted, but earlier generations had failed to grasp its true significance—which hardly seems surprising when one considers Ayres's comprehensive definition of the concept: "Full production means the sum of human achievement.... We need have no hesitation in committing ourselves to the ideal of full production, conceived as the life process of mankind. No conception on the whole range of human thought is richer in meaning, of surer logical validity or scientific soundness" [1946, D.R.C., p. 187].

Given such a generalized, even metaphysical interpretation, it is hardly surprising that mere economists failed to accept—or even comprehend—Ayres's doctrine, especially when he claimed that it was already unconsciously accepted by more empirically minded economists. Indeed, there was no modesty in his pretensions. "Without being fully aware of its implications (since, after all, most people are not social philosophers), the whole world has come to accept physical production as the criterion of a sound economy. Institutionalism is nothing more, and nothing less, than the intellectual implications of that axiom" [1951, "The Co-ordinates of Institutionalism," p. 55].

As a historian of economics, rather than a metaphysician or social philosopher, the writer is understandably reluctant to accept Ayres's challenge and explore these implications fully. However, it may be appropriate to ask why the notion of "full production" seems bizarre by contrast with the long familiar notion of "full employment." "Keeping the machines running," as Ayres put it, seems intrinsically less interesting and desirable than the objective of keeping men in employment, whether in digging holes in the ground or building pyramids. Idleness of physical plant and idleness of manpower both involve waste; machines, like men, deteriorate if they are not cared for. But the essential difference is surely that the various factors of production are not equally worthy of human concern: as social scientists we necessarily take an anthropocentric view of society, caring more for the sufferings of idle men than for idle machines. It is certainly true, as Ayres repeatedly insisted, that orthodox economics is postulated on the idea of scarcity, while modern technology has revealed possibilities of abundance (subject to the limits of global natural resources) undreamt of by earlier generations. But his preoccupation with technology led Ayres to put machines into a more prominent position in the hierarchy of values than any other economist; and, despite his continual warnings, it is difficult to abandon the traditional notion of consumption as "the sole end and purpose" of production. In Ayres's case, unlike Veblen's, an obsession with full production is understandable, for during the 1930's, when crops and livestock were destroyed in an effort to keep up prices, the spectacle of "poverty in the midst of plenty" was profoundly shocking. In this very real sense, Ayres's technological version of institutionalism, with its key emphasis on physical output, may be regarded as a response to the depression, just as much as was Keynes's *General Theory*. One important difference, however, was that Ayres explicated the underlying epistemological and moral judgments involved and deliberately erected his version of institutionalism upon these foundations.

v

Ayres's relationship to the mainstream of American economics was always that of an outsider, a marginal man, a philosophical critic rather than a practicing economist. His writings contain little or nothing of interest to the historian of economic theory, and at this distance in time his criticisms of orthodox economics seem stale, exaggerated, and often misconceived. For the historian of institutional economics, however, and for all students of the intellectual history of twentieth century America, Ayres has an undeniable fascination. As mentioned earlier, he is a key figure linking the founding fathers of institutionalism to the recent postwar generation of their descendants, for whom he has been an important source of stimulus and encouragement. But is he more than that? Notwithstanding Professor Gruchy's attempt to stake a claim on behalf of a contemporary neo-institutionalist movement, it is still too early to say. Despite widespread and highly miscellaneous dissatisfaction with economic orthodoxy, there is as yet very little evidence of interest in the core of Ayres's system—the instrumental (or technological) theory of value. Nor do many young dissenters seem willing to adopt a "holistic"

philosophy or a cultural interpretation of economics. Much lip service is paid to the ideal of interdisciplinary study, and some genuine
progress has undoubtedly been made. The preoccupation with economic development, both among advanced and backward societies,
has flourished mightily, and this movement, while owing nothing to
Ayres's system as such, has certainly provided an audience for his
views.

Thus, as a system builder, it appears that Ayres has earned few
literal disciples, and his general theory has not as yet been fruitful
in the sense that others have tried to follow his example and elaborate
his central ideas. His work has, therefore, passed into the mainstream
of American economic dissent, and it will take a careful and impartial
scholar to trace and evaluate its influence.

NOTES

In order to avoid the distracting influence of a surfeit of notes, partial
references are used in the text of this paper at many points. For a complete citation, the reader is referred to the bibliography of Ayres's
works as compiled by the editors, which appears at the end of this
book.

1. In the 1957 preface to the Japanese edition of *The Theory of
Economic Progress* (subsequently referred to as T.E.P.), Ayres tried
to define the "Americanness" of institutionalism, describing it as
"a manifestation of the American spirit of impatience with tradition
and dissent from commonly accepted dogma" (not paginated—only
typescript version available). In stressing the importance of the state
of the industrial arts the institutionalists were not concerned with a
uniquely American phenomenon. Nevertheless, he said, owing to "a
medley of historical circumstances," machines had played "a greater
part in the lives of Americans than is true of other peoples." This is
not the place to discuss the parallels and links between American
institutionalists and the European authors who have sometimes been
classified with them. As in the case of Veblen, there have been no
avowed European disciples of Ayres. However, his work has occasionally been warmly praised by leading European economists, for
example Joan Robinson, *Economic Philosophy* (Chicago: Aldine Publishing Co., 1962), pp. 110–113; also, Eric Roll, *A History of Economic
Thought* (London: Faber & Faber, 1973), p. 586, n. 4. Ayres is usually
either completely ignored or merely cited en passant in general his-
tories of economic thought. There is a brief account of his ideas in

Joseph Dorfman, *The Economic Mind in American Civilization* (New York: Viking Press, 1959), 4:126–129.

2. *Science: The False Messiah* (Indianapolis: Bobbs-Merrill, 1927) (subsequently referred to as S.F.M.). The legacy of the University of Chicago and the Middle West region was acknowledged in the editorial introduction to *Essays in Philosophy by Seventeen Doctors of Philosophy in the University of Chicago*, ed. Thomas Vernor Smith and William Kelley Wright (Chicago: Open Court Publishing Co., 1929), p. xi. The volume contained Ayres's essay "A Critique of Pure Science." See also his own acknowledgment in *The Divine Right of Capital* (Boston: Houghton Mifflin Co., 1946), pp. 188–189 (subsequently referred to as D.R.C.).

3. See Allan G. Gruchy, *Contemporary Economic Thought: The Contribution of Neo-Institutional Economics* (Clifton, N.J.: Augustus M. Kelley, Publishers, 1972). For comments on this claim see my review in the *Journal of Economic Issues* 8 (September 1974): 597–605.

4. For an examination of this unduly neglected aspect of Veblen's thought, see, for example, David W. Noble, *The Paradox of Progressive Thought* (Minneapolis: University of Minnesota Press, 1958), chap. 9. On the presuppositions of the pragmatists and instrumentalists see also Louis Hartz, *The Liberal Tradition in America* (New York: Harcourt, Brace and Co., 1955), especially pp. 10, 59. For Ayres's views see below.

5. See, for example, Gruchy, *Contemporary Economic Thought*, chap. 3 and p. 341; also, William Breit, "The Development of Clarence Ayres's Theoretical Institutionalism," *Social Science Quarterly* 53 (September 1973): 244–257. Ayres's personality and life-style were, of course, entirely different from Veblen's. However, his views were bitterly attacked in the Texas legislature and his professorship was sometimes at risk. For one of his public reactions see "Are Professors Dangerous?" *Southwest Review* 32 (Winter 1947): 8–15.

6. John S. Gambs, "What Next for the Association for Evolutionary Economics?" *Journal of Economic Issues* 3 (March 1968): 76.

7. See, for example, his articles "Veblen's Theory of Instincts Reconsidered," in *Thorstein Veblen: A Critical Reappraisal*, ed. Douglas F. Dowd (Ithaca: Cornell University Press, 1958) and "The Legacy of Thorstein Veblen," in *Institutional Economics: Veblen, Commons and Mitchell Reconsidered*, by Joseph Dorfman et al. (Berkeley and Los Angeles: University of California Press, 1963). In the former essay he claimed that Veblen's theory of instincts was "by far his most important scientific contribution," even though "the very notion of

instincts is now scientifically obsolete," and Veblen's account was conspicuous for its "vagueness" (pp. 25, 28). Acknowledgments to Veblen appear very prominently in Ayres's last published item, "Prolegomenon to Institutionalism," Preface to the new edition of *Science: The False Messiah* and *Holier Than Thou: The Way of the Righteous* (New York: Augustus M. Kelley, 1973), pp. iii–xii. (The two volumes are bound together with pagination identical to the originals.)

8. For example, Frank H. Knight, "Intellectual Confusion in Morals and Economics," *International Journal of Ethics* 45 (1935): 208–209. See Ayres's reply, ibid., pp. 356–358.

9. C. E. Ayres, "The Industrial Way of Life," *Texas Quarterly* 2 (Summer 1959): 5. Ayres's definition of technology presents very considerable difficulties, for it is almost indefinitely extensible. Consequently, the relationship between science and technology, on the one hand, and institutions or ceremonialism, on the other, becomes very blurred—possibly because Ayres wished to emphasize the increasing predominance of the former over the latter. As science and technology are indissociable, being respectively the "thinking" and "doing" aspects of technology, it would be helpful to know the precise epistemological boundary between scientific and nonscientific thinking and doing. Unfortunately, Ayres never demarcates these realms.

10. C. E. Ayres, "A Critique of Pure Science," pp. 184, 189. I am indebted to a philosopher colleague, R. K. Black, for drawing attention to a point in this passage which had worried me. The claim that the concepts which arise in social behavior are "just as real and sound" as instrumental concepts seems basically incompatible with Ayres's subsequent distinction between true and false knowledge and values. However, it seems advisable to regard this remark as an isolated aberration.

11. C. E. Ayres, *Toward a Reasonable Society* (Austin: University of Texas Press, 1961), p. 9 (subsequently cited as T.R.S.).

12. There is some residue of ambiguity or inconsistency in Ayres's position, for he made few specific predictions. Thus, although he spoke with conviction of the "progressive abandonment of what might be called the life of fancy and a progressive commitment to the realities of a life of doing and making," he warned against complacency and denied that progress was inevitable (see T.R.S., concluding chapter). Nevertheless, despite these caveats, Ayres exemplifies Max Weber's observation that the claim to a single universal future is an important characteristic of Western civilization. (I owe this point to

Paul Streeten; see his "Some Problems in the Use and Transfer of an Intellectual Technology," in *The Social Sciences and Development* [Washington, D.C.: International Bank for Reconstruction and Development, 1974], p. 21.)

13. D.R.C., p. 176. In Ayres's last five books Adam Smith was by far the most frequently quoted author, followed at some distance by Veblen, Keynes, Marx, Beveridge, and Hobson. Ayres also regarded Edwin Cannan as an ally on the basis of a single article. A somewhat curious bedfellow, indeed!

14. C. E. Ayres, *The Industrial Economy: Its Technological Basis and Institutional Destiny* (Boston: Houghton Mifflin Co., 1952), p. 397 (subsequently referred to as I.E.).

15. Apart from a passing reference to the dangers of the automobile and the possibility of pollution [T.R.S., p. 160], Ayres was remarkably insensitive to the damage caused both to human beings and the environment by twentieth-century urbanization and machine technology. One of his former students, Dorothy Reinders, has suggested to me that his long residence in Texas, amid abundance and close to the "frontier," may have helped to preserve his optimistic view of contemporary reality.

16. C. E. Ayres, *The Problem of Economic Order* (New York: Farrar and Rinehart, 1938), passim (subsequently referred to as P.E.O.). Also, T.E.P. (Chapel Hill: University of North Carolina Press, 1944), chaps. 1 and 2.

17. The economists, he once observed, were a highly skilled profession. "By long practice and by use of a multitude of adroit literary devices, they have been able to bring the art of double-vision and double-talk to a high degree of perfection . . . it might be said that if two things are utterly and completely distinct, but if you nevertheless think of them as being identical, then you have an economic mind" (D.R.C., p. 4). This is an uncharacteristically mocking statement from one of his avowedly popular books. Its journalistic tone resembles that of his earlier books *Science: The False Messiah* and *Holier Than Thou: The Way of the Righteous*.

18. For example, Sir John Hicks, *A Theory of Economic History* (Oxford: Clarendon Press, 1969) and D. C. North and R. P. Thomas, *The Rise of the Western World: A New Economic History* (Cambridge: At the University Press, 1973).

19. Benjamin Higgins, "Some Introductory Remarks on Institutionalism and Economic Development," *Southwestern Social Science Quarterly* 41 (1960–1961): 17.

20. Gruchy, *Contemporary Economic Thought*, passim. For a general background see my Ph.D. thesis, "Methodological Controversy as an Approach to the History of American Economics, 1885–1930," Johns Hopkins University, 1953, chap. 5.

21. P.E.O., pp. 73–75. It is noteworthy that Ayres did not cite the *General Theory* but Keynes's earlier writings—in this instance, *The Economic Consequences of the Peace* (1920) and *Unemployment as a World Problem* (1931). This supports the general impression that Ayres had not yet grasped the underconsumptionist implications of the "new" economics.

22. Ayres argued that the accumulation of funds and the enlargement of industrial tools and equipment were two distinct processes, either of which could occur independently. In a capitalist system the link was the power which the accumulation of funds confers on its possessors ("The Significance of Economic Planning," in *The Development of Collective Enterprise*, ed. Seba Eldridge [Lawrence: University of Kansas Press, 1943], p. 473). Ayres's severe critique of Joseph A. Schumpeter's conception of capitalism is of especial interest in this connection ("Capitalism in Retrospect," *Southern Economic Journal* 9 [April 1943]: 299).

23. The instrumentalist concept of value, he maintained, was just what was needed to make the combination fully effective ("The New Economics," *Southwest Review* 33 [Summer 1948]: 231). His subsequent work was largely devoted to the elaboration of this contention. In his later writings Ayres's conception of the relationship between institutionalism and economic orthodoxy became very blurred. While the institutionalists of the late 1930's had "in part at least . . . become Keynesians," he claimed that by the mid-1960's "most practicing economists have become institutionalists" and the "instrumental, process-oriented conception of value" is present "at least by implication in the thinking of virtually all institutionalists" ("Nature and Significance of Institutionalism," *Antioch Review* 26 [Spring 1966]: 72, 88–89).

24. For Ayres's brief, early, but penetrating attempt to compare his own ideas to Commons's *Institutional Economics*, see "Moral Confusion in Economics," *International Journal of Ethics* 45 (1934–1935): 198–199.

25. It is significant that Ayres's account of demand and supply is relegated to chaps. 13 and 14 (I.E., pp. 320–373). His later essay "Guaranteed Income: An Institutionalist View" represents a development of matters referred to in D.R.C. and I.E. ("Guaranteed Income: An

Institutionalist View," in *The Guaranteed Income: Next Step in Economic Evolution?*, ed. Robert Theobald [Garden City, N.Y.: Doubleday and Co., 1966]).

C. E. Ayres on the Industrial Revolution

R. M. HARTWELL

I

Clarence Ayres was interested in—indeed, spent a great deal of his life pondering about—a problem that also has preoccupied me for a quarter of a century: to determine "just what the forces were which resulted in the appearance of an industrial economy, first in Europe and then in America and so throughout the world."[1] However, when I wrote the article "The Causes of the Industrial Revolution" and edited a book of the same title,[2] in which there was comprehensive discussion of the literature of the industrial revolution, I made no reference to Ayres although he had written extensively on that subject.[3] (And to my knowledge, he is not referred to by other British historians of the industrial revolution.) Even though Ayres reviewed my book in 1968,[4] I did not see the review until recently. Since Oxford is more distant from Texas than is Harvard, my ignorance can be excused more than that of the American economists who ignored Ayres. But it is obvious that there were losses to Ayres because of his geographical, and intellectual, isolation.

Isolation, indeed, cuts both ways. There had to be, in Ayres, much of the autodidact. His general reading ranged widely and self-indulgently but, on any particular subject, often narrowly. Even more important, he gives the impression of having had little contact with other scholars in the fields in which he was interested—for example, the industrial revolution—and thus of not being aware of what was going on outside of Texas.[5] Thus, what is *not* surprising about Ayres is the narrowness rather than the breadth of his reading on any subject. Ayres's books create the impression of a man who early in life had roamed the stacks of a well-equipped library and was clever enough to convert his random readings into a coherent theory of history. Ayres gives the impression, also, of a man who read less as he grew older. His precociousness and confidence led him early to formulate theories which he changed little and apparently did not disturb with further reading. Thus, his industrial revolution is that of an early vintage, of A. Toynbee and J. L. and B. Hammond—not that of J. H. Clapham and T. S. Ashton, the greatest industrial revolution scholars. And Ayres's industrial revolution of *The Problem of Eco-*

nomic Order (1938) is the same as his industrial revolution of *The Industrial Economy* (1952) and the second edition of *The Theory of Economic Progress* (1962), although much new research on the industrial revolution had been published between 1938 and 1962.

Can isolation also explain the most surprising gap in Ayres's reading? Ayres wrote as though he and Veblen had been the first economists to reject classical theory, and as though Veblen had invented the institutional method of explaining economic change. There is nothing in Ayres of the *Methodenstreit*, of the economists and historians of England and Germany in the late nineteenth century, who, with the legal historians from F. C. von Savigny to F. W. Maitland, created the institutionalist school of which the American school was an offshoot.[6] There is a solitary reference to H. Maine in *The Theory of Economic Progress*,[7] but, for example, none to J. E. Thorold Rogers even though he had published the essay "The Conditions of Economic Progress" in 1892.[8] And, although Ayres was preoccupied, above all, with explaining very long-term economic evolution, he drew no support from the historical school which had made such a study the main aim of its historical research.[9] Nor did Ayres use the large literature on the role of institutions in controlling and conditioning economic life which had been developed by the great nineteenth-century legal historians.[10] All this means, of course, that Ayres was genuinely original; except for his dependence on Veblen, his ideas and theories were those of his own making, owing little to predecessors or current fashions. He was, indeed, as W. P. Culbertson, Jr., describes him, a "maverick economist."

II

Ayres, in his analysis of economic history, was concerned mainly with three interrelated problems.

The first was to explain "the tremendous productive efficiency and economy of the industrial system, by virtue of which all of us taken together are as well off as we are."[11] Although "the entire history of civilization is one of grueling restraints,"[12] "the modern Western community is far better off than any other people has ever been."[13] Indeed, Ayres asserted, "No one any longer doubts the physical and technological possibility of a world-wide economy of abundance."[14] But the intellectual problem remains of determining "what social forces are in fact chiefly responsible for the productive achievements of industrial society."[15] Briefly, Ayres's explanation was that modern productivity derives from machine technology, and, in particular, from "the tool-combination principle," "the 'inscrutable' propensity of all technological devices to proliferate."[16]

Second, Ayres wanted to explain why modern machines "made their appearance quite suddenly during the latter part of the eighteenth century"[17]—that is, to explain the industrial revolution, to elucidate "the great mystery of the rise of industrial society."[18] As Ayres disarmingly argued, before dispelling doubts, "We are still unable to state as a matter of scientifically demonstrated fact just what the forces were which resulted in the appearance of an industrial economy, first in Western Europe and then in America and so throughout the world."[19] "Why did the industrial revolution occur in Western Europe and in modern times?"[20] What was it in West European society that provided "the matrix of industrial revolution"?[21] "When and why and how did the first cleavage occur in the development of culture of which industrial society was the end product?"[22] Ayres's explanation of why Western Europe led—because it was "of all the great civilizations of the time incomparably the youngest, the least rigid, less stifled than any other by age-long accumulations of institutional dust, more susceptible by far than any other to change and innovation"[23]—depended on his answer to the third historical problem that he sought to explain.

The third problem was concerned with the determination of chronology. If technology is "progressive" and "inherently developmental,"[24] if "the tool-combination principle is indeed a law of progress,"[25] if technology advances in geometrical progression,[26] what determines the time span between advances? This depended, according to Ayres, on the forces that oppose progress and change, "the imbecile institutions" of society, as Veblen once described them. "The history of the human race," Ayres wrote, "is that of a perpetual opposition of these forces, the dynamic force of technology continually making for change, and the static force of ceremony—status, mores, and legendary belief—opposing change. Most of the time and in most parts of the world status has prevailed. In the whole history of the race there have only been a few technological revolutions."[27] But why should one such revolution, the most important, have occurred in Europe? Western Europe had not been one of the centers of ancient civilization; it had been, rather, "the frontier region of Mediterranean civilization."[28] But in this fact was the answer; as a frontier region it was much less prone to "institutional rigidity and cultural ancestor-worship."[29] The cleavage which led to industrialization came in the Middle Ages. European feudalism, as it developed, was institutionally inhibiting, but the medieval towns became "technological concentration points . . . semi-detached from the institutional structure of feudal society."[30] "From this point onward," Ayres argued, "the character of the industrial revolution is unmistakable. Modern European society is an outgrowth of the process which was going on in the medieval towns."[31]

The essential characteristic of all societies, according to Ayres, was technology, and that of modern society was machinery, but he distinguished in modern society, as he did in all societies, two aspects, a *technological*—machine technology—and an *institutional*—market economy. He argued that the economists' preoccupation with economic organization, with the mechanism of market economy, had blinded them to the essential characteristic of modern society, its machine basis. Modern society was industrial and mechanical, in present form and in origins, and industrial technology had imposed a pattern upon "the whole structure of society and every department of life."[32] "No other social revolution has embraced changes more sweeping or more profound."[33]

But if Ayres's first preoccupation was with modern industrial society, he quickly developed a long view, indeed, a very long view. He saw his historical inquiry as part of "the effort to view modern Western civilization in the perspective of present knowledge of the whole five-hundred-thousand-years-long history of the race."[34] "Modern European society is an outgrowth of the process which was going on in the medieval towns."[35] "Not only is the continuity of the ancient civilizations of the Mediterranean region much more fully known today than half a century ago, primitive culture also is far better understood, including the continuity of ancient civilization with neolithic culture."[36] "To a far greater extent than ever before, anthropological studies enable us to see why and how later civilization is conditioned by earlier civilization, how the industrial revolution itself extends back to include even primeval man."[37] Thus Ayres was able to explain both "industrial evolution" and "industrial revolution." In seeking an explanation of modern society and economy, he was led to consider the major, but neglected, problem of economic history, the history of economic progress, mankind's long haul from cave to skyscraper. Theories of very long-term growth, or progress, have fallen into disfavor in the twentieth century, whether advanced by a Toynbee or a Rostow. Historians and economists have shortened their time span, and not only have they avoided problems of the very long run but they have also criticized, indeed despised, the occasional long-run theorist.

III

In upgrading the role of technology in growth, and the role of machine technology in the industrial revolution, Ayres was reviving old and anticipating new themes in both economic history and economics. Nineteenth-century historians had the same belief as Ayres—that technology was not only a powerful but also an autonomous force for progress. A. Ure in *The Philosophy of Manufactures* had made factories and machinery the dominating forces in modern society;[38] S. Smiles had depicted the engineers as "the makers of modern civilization;"[39] J. James had seen the factory as "containing within itself powers for its own direction."[40] Other historians, by defining man as "a tool-making animal," were able to reduce history to a series of stages, differentiated according to the type of artifact used. Technology offered an explanation not only for the industrial revolution but also for the whole of history. Thus, since the mid-nineteenth century, partly as a response to the obvious technical achievements and socioeconomic consequences of the industrial revolution, a persistent theme in history has been the power of technology and its impact on society and economy.

In the meantime, postclassical economics was ignoring technology. After David Ricardo, technology was relegated to *ceteris paribus* clauses, or to that bag of exogenous tricks that were to explain anything that could not be explained by endogenous variables. And even with the development of growth theory, the measurement and explanation of growth was at first in terms of simple production function theory, which related outputs to inputs, *given* the state of technology. Only recently have the economists reluctantly learned that growth is not a process automatically induced by capital accumulation, that increasing output cannot be explained by measured inputs of capital and labor, and that improved capital (physical and human) is a main source of increasing productivity. With recognition by the economists of technological change as a main ingredient in "the residual," technology is at least where it should be, among the important variables of growth. But this recognition owed nothing to Ayres, whose insistence that technology had always been the force that had shaped society and economy was ignored, or, probably, unread.

But Ayres had the same difficulty as modern economists in determining the causes of technological change itself. Was technology an exogenous factor—a windfall gain from the autonomous growth of scientific knowledge—or was it an endogenous factor—the product of social forces, particularly market forces? Was it "heroic"—the unprompted act of genius—or "systematic"—the product of social forces that could be analyzed economically?[41] It is difficult to say how much Ayres drew on the literature of the history of technology, but to him technological change was largely autonomous, certainly automatic, and potentially continuous. "Technology is organized skill," he wrote. "All skill is organized, of course, and all behavior skilled in some sense or other."[42] If there is a human propensity to be technologically skilled in this sense, technology itself has "the peculiar characteristic" of being "progressive." "It is inherently developmental."[43] It is developmental because of "the tool-combination principle." "Granted that tools are always tools of men who have the capacity to use tools and therefore the capacity to use them together, combinations are bound to occur. Furthermore it follows that the more tools there are, the greater is the number of potential combinations."[44]

But how then to explain the differences between societies? And differences in the rate of growth of technology over time in the same society? If technological change had been continuous and progressive, should not all societies have been on the same path of progress, traveling at the same pace? But, as Ayres admitted, technological change was more progressive at some times than at others. "There is no community," he admitted, "whose history does not reveal periods in which technology has been virtually stationary for long periods of time."[45] The continuous, cumulative, and progressive process of technological change was delayed, or arrested, according to Ayres, by institutional opposition, by "ceremonial patterns" of behavior which inhibited change. The explanation for the timing and rate of progress was to be sought in the analysis of social institutions. Ayres saw the human agency, not in the advance of technology, and hence of progress, but in its delay.

Ayres, in one sense, came close to the more sophisticated views of economic growth that now prevail, views that see growth not as any simply induced economic process, but as a social process of overcoming institutional obstacles to growth, of freeing enterprise rather than of creating it. But his emphasis on technology led him to a position as untenable as that once held by the economists whom he attacked. He uncompromisingly denied the relevance of any factor in economic progress except technology. "Obviously the tremendous physical efficiency of modern industrial society stems from the use of machinery. The land has not changed. Men have not changed. What has changed is our physical complement of apparatus and equipment."[46]

If Ayres anticipated the economists in his emphasis on technology, he failed completely to anticipate their interest in human capital as a factor in growth.

His insistence on a theory of progress that depended on the automatic development of technology, inhibited only by institutional rigidities, therefore, is difficult to accept. It has the advantage of being long-term; it covers the whole of history, transcending periods and revolutions. It does highlight a continuing characteristic of human societies—technological change—and it emphasizes the cumulative character of technological knowledge. It has the attraction of being simple: technology has been the force of progress in all societies; only its form has changed. But as a theory of progress it has serious disadvantages. Man and his institutions appear almost as negative factors, the opponents of progress, rather than the initiators of change; little allowance is made for the creative abilities of man. The theory still leaves invention as a mystery; not all new knowledge is a combination of previous knowledge. The theory, also, is deterministic; it has about it an air of "fatalistic transcendentalism," as A. P. Lerner has pointed out.[47] But, most of all, it lacks precision and explanatory power; it is too general to be operationally useful. Ayres could not explain spurts and lags in progress, revolutions and stagnations, differences in performance between societies, except in very general terms. And there have been at all times in history other forces than technology making for change—like the growth of population—which Ayres all but ignored.

IV

Perhaps the most interesting question that Ayres addressed to himself, however, was about the timing and location of the industrial revolution. "Why did the industrial revolution occur in western Europe and in modern times? Why not in China, or in ancient Greece? What forces were operative in the modern European situation which were not operative elsewhere and at other times? Granted that inventions occurred which altered the material framework of society, why did they so occur?"[48] It is curious, at least to a parochially minded Britisher, that Ayres was not equally interested in the question: "Within Europe, why in England? Why not in France or in medieval Italy?" But Ayres was interested in continuity of civilization rather than in regional variations within civilizations. He wanted to know why industrial society evolved out of only one of the great civilizations of the world, not why the industrial revolution came first in one country, England, within one civilization, Europe.

Ayres's explanation was geographical and institutional. The great civilizations—in the Nile and Mesopotamian valleys, the Indus and Ganges valleys, the Yangtze and Hwang Ho valleys, and the valleys of Central America and the Andes—had all been agricultural, culturally advanced, well-developed technologically, but institutionally different. As Ayres wrote, "There is no one line of cultural evolution along which all peoples are moving."[49] But Ayres did not explain why Chinese civilization was so different from that of Egypt and, in particular, why civilizations varied in degrees of "ceremonial dominance"—that is, in the degree to which ceremony (which to Ayres was, broadly speaking, tradition reinforced by custom, religion, and law) determined social status, mores, and beliefs. Certainly these ancient civilizations had accumulated similar "technological accretions" from thousands of years of agriculture, but they also had different "agelong accumulations of institutional dust," which inhibited progress.[50]

Western Europe, however, as Ayres pointed out, was able to inherit the technology of the Mediterranean civilizations, and not their institutions—this, because of geography. "The actual experience of the European people was that of a frontier community endowed with a full complement of tools and materials derived from a parent culture and then almost completely severed from the institutional power system of its parents. The result was unique. It is doubtful if history affords another instance of comparable area and population so richly endowed and so completely severed."[51] The American analogy is obvious and explicitly acknowledged;[52] the idea of "frontier Europe" came naturally to Ayres, who grew up during the dominance of American history by Frederick Jackson Turner and before its eclipse. Medieval Europe was like nineteenth-century America, "an old world," but it did not have to inherit the old world's conservative institutions.

Ayres can be compared with Max Weber in his search for an explanation of Europe's economic leadership. But whereas Max Weber used religion—Christianity, contrasted with the religions of Asia—to explain the economic rationality and individualism of Europe, he also used religion—Protestantism, contrasted with Catholicism—to explain the economic leadership of England in Europe.[53] Weber's thesis has been subjected to damaging criticism,[54] and Ayres had the advantage in at least two ways: first, the broader institutional basis, ceremonial conservatism, allowed for a more convincing range of growth-inhibiting factors; second, it gave a convincing explanation for perhaps the most striking characteristic of European medieval society, its technological receptiveness. Much of European economic advance occurred because of the European capacity to absorb technology that had originated elsewhere but had not been developed there. "Flowing into Europe from all directions, paper, compass, Arabic numerals, astronomical instruments, dyes, ships, printing blocks . . . were eagerly received, put to work, combined with one another and with old familiar things; and the result was a great cultural explosion and the beginning of industrial society."[55]

And, although Ayres did not do so, his analysis could have been extended to explain England's leadership in industrialization within Europe. There was in England, before it occurred in Europe generally, a significant freeing from the bonds of custom and command, from the inhibiting restrictions of feudalism and mercantilism, of man's creative and innovating powers. And it was not just economic freedom; it was the establishment of a society in which there was much greater freedom in all directions. On the political level, the Whig revolution finally destroyed the centralizing tendencies of a king-dominated national state and effectively dispersed political power. At the economic level, both statute and court law led to the increased use of the market as a mechanism for the allocation of resources and the distribution of income. Increasing freedom took the form of removing the state's restraints on individual action and of allowing greater personal freedom in religion, intellectual inquiry, and expression, political action and economic enterprise.[56] The power of ceremony was reduced; the progressive force of technology was released. So Ayres could have argued for England, as he did for Europe.

v

Ayres in his academic work, unfortunately, was not as much concerned with explaining economic history as with persuading contemporaneous economists that they were preoccupied with the wrong problems, the problems of market economy. Shortly before his death Ayres affirmed what he had written in the 1930's in *The Problem of Economic Order*: "I would deny flatly that ours is a market economy. Ours is an industrial economy. That is what distinguishes it from the manorial economy of the middle ages, the village economy of India, the tribal economies of Africa, and primitive economies of all sorts."[57] The forces for progress over history have not been those of the market. "The dynamism of the scientific-technological process has been the guiding principle that has raised man above all other animals and modern industrial society above all the previous efforts of mankind."[58] But much of *The Theory of Economic Progress* is concerned with the failings of neoclassical economics, rather than with "the lesson of the industrial revolution," which Ayres had already declared to be "the transformation of Western civilization by the machine" and "the continuity and pervasiveness of the whole process."[59] Ayres's "neurotic phobia for price analysis"[60] obscured this lesson and diverted attention from his more important contributions to economic history.

Had Ayres looked more to the large literature on economic growth, both theoretical and empirical, he would not have felt so out-of-tune with his contemporaries. What Ayres said about technology in the 1930's, Simon Kuznets was saying, with a different emphasis, in the 1960's. "The epochal innovation that distinguishes the modern economic epoch," Kuznets has written, "is the extended application of science to problems of economic production. We may call this long period 'the scientific epoch'—although this may be too broad a term if the cumulative application of science results in some further revolutionary breakthroughs. . . . Since the second half of the nineteenth century, the major source of economic growth has been science-based technology."[61] Similarly, in the most ambitious attempt yet written to interpret "technological change and industrial development in Western Europe from 1750 to the present," D. S. Landes argued, "It was the Industrial Revolution that initiated a cumulative, self-sustaining advance in technology whose repercussions would be felt in all aspects of economic life."[62] This sentence could have been written by Ayres himself. His ideas were becoming the conventional wisdom.

Ayres's economic history was very long-term in perspective, and he returned to the nineteenth-century tradition of trying to provide a general theory of history, all history, in operational terms. By adopting the Veblen dichotomy, which distinguished technological and institutional behavior, and by showing that the former was progressive and the latter conservative, and that technological culture and institutional culture did not necessarily move at the same pace, Ayres had a dynamic and a pacesetter for economic change. Given this perspective he was certainly out-of-step with his fellow economists, not so much because of differences in opinion about price theory but because of the time perspective deemed appropriate for the study of economics. Economists since Ricardo have not been interested in the long run, and even the revival of interest in economic growth has not lengthened views to Ayres-like proportions. Above all, Ayres resembled the historical economists of the late nineteenth century, who, similarly, in their various stages theories, tried to explain man's long-term economic evolution.

Ayres also differed from contemporaneous economists in his emphasis on institutions, particularly on what he and Veblen called the ceremonial functions of institutions, including property. It is on institutional analysis that Ayres was most interesting and most original and provided a useful tool of analysis for the economic historian. He may not have been able to explain the fall of Rome, or the industrial revolution in England—except in very general terms of the clash of progress and conservatism—but he did make clear, and prove, the importance of institutions for economic change. He may not have provided a historical theory of operational power, but he did provide a framework within which the right sort of questions could be asked, and from which the beginnings of answers could evolve. He was not a Clapham or Keynes, but he was original, provocative, productive of problems and ideas, and very readable. It is a reproach to the profession that his work was not more critically evaluated during his lifetime, so that his ideas on the industrial revolution could have evolved and not have remained, as they did, essentially static from the writing of *The Problem of Economic Order*.

NOTES

1. C. E. Ayres, *The Theory of Economic Progress* (Chapel Hill: University of North Carolina Press, 1944), p. 126.

2. R. M. Hartwell, "The Causes of the Industrial Revolution: An Essay on Methodology," *Economic History Review*, 2nd series, 18, no. 1 (August 1965): 164–182; R. M. Hartwell, *The Causes of the Industrial Revolution in England* (London: Methuen, 1967).

3. Specifically on the industrial revolution see C. E. Ayres, *The Problem of Economic Order* (New York: Farrar and Rinehart, 1938), sec. 1 ("The Rise of Modern Industry"); Ayres, *The Theory of Economic Progress*, chap. 7 ("Industrial Evolution"); *The Industrial Economy: Its Technological Basis and Institutional Destiny* (Boston: Houghton Mifflin Co., 1952), chap. 3 ("How the Industrial Economy Evolved").

4. C. E. Ayres, Review of *The Causes of the Industrial Revolution in England*, by R. M. Hartwell, *Journal of Economic Issues* 2 (June 1968): 252–254.

5. This took the form, sometimes, of attacking a nonexistent ortho-

doxy. For example, see the article by Jack E. Robertson ("Folklore of Institutional Economics," *Southwestern Social Science Quarterly* 41 [June 1960]: 22–31) in which he argues of the institutionalist school that "its principal criticism of orthodoxy is directed at a theoretical position not generally held in orthodox thought to-day." *The Problem of Economic Order* (1938) and *The Theory of Economic Progress* (1944) are not well documented; in the latter, Clapham, Tawney, and Toynbee are quoted, but only Toynbee is used as a prime source. *The Industrial Economy* (1952) has a section entitled "Suggestions for Further Reading," and on the industrial revolution only Toynbee, the Hammonds, and S. Lilley are mentioned. There is no evidence that Ayres had read or took notice of the mass of industrial revolution literature that had appeared in England between, say, 1918 and 1952 (see, for example, the essay "The Causes of the Industrial Revolution: An Essay on Methodology," in *The Industrial Revolution and Economic Growth*, by R. M. Hartwell [London: Methuen, 1971]). It is interesting to note, also, that Ayres's idea of imperialism, stressing underconsumption, came from Hobson and seemed to ignore later work, for example, the three volumes published in the thirties by W. K. Hancock.

6. See R. M. Hartwell, "Good Old Economic History," *Journal of Economic History* 33, no. 1 (March 1973): 28, for an account of the work and importance of "the historical school" in economics.

7. Ayres, *The Theory of Economic Progress*, p. 161.

8. J. E. Thorold Rogers, *The Industrial and Commercial History of England* (London: Fisher Unwin, 1892), chap. 2.

9. As W. J. Ashley wrote, "The historical school . . . hold that it is no longer worthwhile framing general formulas as to the relations between individuals in a given society . . . and that . . . they must attempt to discover . . . the laws of social development—that is to say generalizations as to the stages through which the economic life of society has actually moved" (W. J. Ashley, *An Introduction to English Economic History and Theory* [London: Longmans, Green and Co., 1888], p. xii).

10. See, for example, W. E. Johnson, "Method in Political Economy," in *Dictionary of Political Economy*, ed. R. H. Inglis Palgrave (London: Macmillan and Co., 1894), 2:746: "Individual action is controlled by certain legalized institutions with regard to property, and . . . individuals are forced to act according to their own will within certain limits." On law and institutions, generally, see the work of Sir H. Maine.

11. Ayres, *The Industrial Economy*, p. 62.

12. Ayres, *The Theory of Economic Progress*, p. 103.

13. Ayres, *The Industrial Economy*, p. 92.

14. Ayres, *The Theory of Economic Progress*, p. 232.

15. Ibid., p. 261.

16. Ibid., p. 119.

17. Ayres, *The Industrial Economy*, p. 62.

18. Ayres, *The Problem of Economic Order*, p. 13. See also, Ayres, *The Theory of Economic Progress*, p. 128: "The Mystery of Industrial Revolution."

19. Ayres, *The Theory of Economic Progress*, p. 126.

20. Ibid., p. 129.

21. Ibid.

22. Ibid.

23. Ibid., p. 137.

24. Ibid., p. 111.

25. Ibid., p. 119.

26. Ibid., p. 120.

27. Ibid., p. 176.

28. Ibid., p. 133.

29. Ibid., p. 145.

30. Ibid., p. 148.

31. Ibid.

32. Ayres, *The Problem of Economic Order*, p. 8.

33. Ibid., p. 7.

34. Ayres, *The Industrial Economy*, p. vii.

35. Ayres, *The Theory of Economic Progress*, p. 148.

36. Ibid., p. 128.

37. Ibid.

38. A. Ure, *Philosophy of Manufacturers*, rev. ed. (London: P. L. Simmonds, 1861).

39. S. Smiles, *Lives of the Engineers: Early Engineering* (London: John Murray, 1904), p. xxiii.

40. J. James, *History of the Worsted Manufacture in England* (London: Longmans, Green and Co., 1857), p. 333.

41. The distinction made by A. P. Usher in *The History of Mechanical Inventions* (New York: McGraw-Hill, 1929), chaps. 1 and 2.

42. Ayres, *The Theory of Economic Progress*, p. 105.

43. Ibid., p. 111.

44. Ibid., p. 119.

45. Ibid., p. 121.

46. Ayres, *The Problem of Economic Order*, p. 35.

47. A. P. Lerner, Review of *The Theory of Economic Progress*, by

C. E. Ayres, *American Economic Review* 35, no. 1 (March 1945): 164.

48. Ayres, *The Theory of Economic Progress*, p. 129.

49. Ibid., p. 130.

50. Ibid., pp. 136–137.

51. Ibid., p. 137.

52. "Just as frontier America later became the melting pot of Europe, so frontier Europe became the cultural melting pot of the medieval world" (Ayres, *The Problem of Economic Order*, p. 17).

53. See Max Weber, *The Protestant Ethic and the Spirit of Capitalism* (London: Allen and Unwin, 1930).

54. See, for example, Kurt Samuelsson, *Religion and Economic Action*, trans. E. G. French (London: Heinemann, 1961).

55. Ayres, *The Problem of Economic Order*, p. 17.

56. See, for example, R. M. Hartwell, *The Industrial Revolution and Economic Growth*, chap. 11.

57. C. E. Ayres, "Beyond the Market Economy: Building Institutions That Work," *Social Science Quarterly* 50 (March 1970): 1055.

58. Ibid., p. 1057.

59. *The Problem of Economic Order*, p. 9.

60. A. P. Lerner, Review of *The Theory of Economic Progress*, p. 161.

61. Simon Kuznets, *Modern Economic Growth: Rate, Structure, and Spread* (New Haven, Conn.: Yale University Press, 1966), pp. 9–10.

62. D. S. Landes, *The Unbound Prometheus* (Cambridge: At the University Press, 1969), p. 3.

Clarence Ayres and
the Roots of Economic Progress

S. HERBERT FRANKEL

In her book *Economic Philosophy* Professor Joan Robinson quotes an intriguing question Ayres once posed: "Why did the industrial revolution occur in Western Europe and in modern times? Why not in China, or in Ancient Greece?" She interprets Ayres as finding the answer in the fact that Western Europe was the "frontier region of the Mediterranean civilization." She states that Ayres attributed technological progressiveness to the weak hold over society of religion. The great inventions that lead to technical revolutions are, she says, in Ayres's view essentially new combinations of tools devised for different purposes. The preconditions for the industrial revolution were generated by an accumulation of such combinations. According to Robinson, "The special characteristic of Western Europe was not that such combinations occurred there, for they happen everywhere, but that 'ceremonial patterns' of behavior put up a weaker resistance there, than in the older civilizations, to the spread of new inventions." This conception, she believes, "throws light on what from some points of view is the outstanding problem of the present day—*the relatively slow economic development of India under institutions imitated from parliamentary democracy contrasted with that of China under the direction of the Communist Party.* Western liberalism has only warmed the surface of the deep waters of Indian tradition, while in China a violent reversal of ideas has opened the way for rapid changes in technology and in the social forms appropriate to exploiting them" (italics added). Joan Robinson continued, "The closest analogy, however, to the departure of the legions from Britain and Gaul is in Black Africa. Here the most modern technology is coming to the notice of people very little encumbered by ancient traditions; if Professor Ayres's theory is correct, they are destined, in due course, to outstrip us all."[1]

These comments seem to me to express the very essence of a fallacy in much economic writing on economic development in the last twenty-five years.

Let me in expanding upon this assertion say at the outset that whether or not the African peoples will indeed "outstrip us all" (whatever that prediction may mean) the reasoning—indeed the mythology —which lies behind it is both historically and logically untenable.

It cannot be denied that in a few passages in his book *The Theory of Economic Progress* Ayres seems to depart from his general thesis that economic progress is socially and institutionally determined by ascribing to technology an almost mechanistic role in economic development.[2] This might lead the unwary reader to believe that he would have accepted Robinson's interpretation—but this would be a travesty of his views.[3]

In the passage quoted from Robinson, development is pictured as a process of displacement which can be expected to work best when there is nothing at all to displace. The peoples of Africa are consequently, in this view, particularly fortunate because, according to Robinson, they have such fragile ties with the past that they can be more easily molded to our or to Robinson's or Mao Tse-tung's desires.

Unfortunately for this theory, there is no evidence to show that the traditions and forms of organization governing tribal Africa are any less strong than those of other peoples. African tribes often fear changing the forms and content of their social heritage as much as other societies did in the past, and as much as most of the peoples of the world still do now. The main factor which arrested change was not merely the prevalence of customary beliefs but the risk and expected cost to individuals, and societies, in departing from them.

To an African tribe with little or only costly access to new markets, the close dependence on its immediate environment, without economically meaningful opportunities for diversification, made communal control over ownership of land, and over many economic activities, extremely difficult to change. A wrong step by any one group of persons along the road of innovation could easily endanger the whole community. How else could one explain the fact that even in the colonial era provincial administrators still clung to the belief that it was best to prevent agricultural diversification (though apparently profitable) because, should the customary grain crop fail, the population might starve owing to its inability to purchase grain from neighboring territories, or from farther abroad, with the money earned from the newly introduced export crops.

There are no societies without strong traditions for the simple reason that it is owing to those traditions that they have survived. Traditions incorporate the experience—often the quite unconscious experience—of the past. If individuals or societies cling to the ways of the past it is because of fear of making or inability to make the trade-off between the choices of the past and those which can be made now—particularly those which depend for their fulfillment on the unknown and unknowable future. For example, for a community living largely on the basis of localized subsistence agriculture to shift to the production of export crops means becoming dependent on others —a risk which the society's elders, or leaders, may fear to take because of memories of past disasters.

I can see in my mind's eye a smile flitting across the face of the reader, as if to say how irrelevant all this is to the modern world with its vast industrial technology and scientific knowledge, which so greatly impressed Ayres and led to his optimistic view of the consequence of technology itself. But I would ask the reader to hesitate before so readily dismissing the analogy I have drawn. It was only a few years ago that an eminent economist suggested in a closely reasoned book that Europe could afford to close most of its coal mines and purchase oil from abroad, and that it would even pay to pension off all the coal miners to achieve the economies which oil would provide. Can the reader imagine the smile that would spread over the face of a black tribesman who persists in the old ways of subsistence farming when he hears about Europe's, Japan's, and even the United States' recent shocks over oil supplies?

It is very easy for an *observer* to express views as to what risks should be taken by individuals or societies that he happens to be observing—or desires to improve. It is a very different matter for those who may have to suffer the costs thereof.

In this connection I am reminded of the suggestion so glibly made by J. M. Keynes—with that artistic élan of his accomplished writing— that "something—there is just a chance—might come out. And even a chance gives to what is happening in Russia more importance than what is happening (let us say) in the United States of America."[4] One is tempted to ask just exactly what is meant by such a seemingly innocuous phrase. How is such a chance to be measured or evaluated? Would, for example, the millions who died of starvation or who were purged by Stalin and others to give Russia "her chance" have been regarded by Keynes as a measure of the cost? Or should the fact that after fifty years Russia has not yet been able to organize her agriculture effectively (and that even as I write vast quantities of wheat have to be imported from the United States) mean that she had her "chance" but has not yet been able to make use of it?

I have often been astonished in Africa, and in other underdeveloped regions, and even nearer home in the Western Hemisphere by the glib manner with which the bearers of the gifts of new scientific techniques or discoveries assume that those who do not immediately adopt them do so out of sheer ignorance or cussedness since clearly they cannot know better than their scientific mentors. I am reminded of an occasion when an agricultural experiment station in East Africa had put out a new strain of cotton. The African peasants, however, could not be got to switch over from their planting schedules with the old strains of the plant. The most intensive propaganda failed to move what to those in charge of the operation appeared to be nothing but the obstinacy of the "natives." But one curious inquirer discovered something very different. By patient discussions with the elders of the community he found that they had noted that the new variety would be harvested earlier than the old—just at a time when there was usually in *their* experience a serious infestation of a weevil. So much for science which ignores experience.

Billions upon billions of dollars of aid to developing countries have been, and continue to be, wasted because of the fallacy that the other fellow's social heritage is buncombe. I have only to remind you of the fantastic African groundnut scheme in which modern science, technology, capital, and enthusiasm were to prove that science could do anything anywhere—and therefore also even in the drought-stricken wilderness of Kongwa in the heart of Tanzania. This area, incidentally, was shunned by the African tribesman whose experience was, of course, regarded as of no consequence.

After an expenditure of near fifty million of preinflation pounds sterling, not a ton of groundnuts had been produced with the machinery gathered from the four corners of the world. In the end African women had to be brought in to harvest the remnants of a crop which machinery, stuck in the unanticipated mud of Africa, could not handle after the rains—just as other machinery had previously unanticipatedly failed to cope with ploughing the granite-hard earth before the rains fell. All these attempts to beat Africa were vividly, wisely, and quite unconsciously summed up for me by an African whom I found making a garden for one of the managers at his home. To my query whether he liked working for him he replied, "Yes, Bwana—you see he at least will *stay* in Africa because he is planting something that will last." By this he meant that at any rate his master was making the attempt to become a permanent part of Africa and of its past. Lest anyone should accidentally mistake my meaning let me add, before I pass on, that the moral of this little digression is *not* that technology or science or modern discovery is to be despised or in any way shunned; but that it is fallacious to believe that it can be applied hurriedly or mechanically, like writing on a slate. That is only possible on the blackboards of our classrooms! The slate of reality is very old and heavy with the encrustations of ages; we have not yet even scratched its surface.

The fact is that change has been resisted in Africa and is still resisted there, as it is the world over, not because of outworn tradition,
or ceremonials as Ayres called them, but because better alternative
modes of action were not, or were not observed to be available, or did
not prove, or were not expected or thought likely to prove more successful.

This complex situation can be summed up in the phrase "the dilemma of security"—a dilemma which is met with not only in "frontier" situations but also whenever security is threatened, and it involves the forging of new economic and social bonds. These bonds
imply the creation of, and dependence on, new structural relationships. In terms of the conditions prevailing in Africa in the 1950's, the
dilemma of security was described by the East African Royal Commission as follows: "The economic security which can be achieved
by individuals engaged either as wage-earners or as producers for the
market differs fundamentally from the security which can be attained
in a tribal subsistence economy . . . purely subsistence economies can
find no method of satisfying the wants of the people other than that
of adjusting these wants to what the environment will permit and to
what the land or stock will yield with the minimum of improvement
for the future. There is little margin . . . which will enable the community to escape from its complete dependence upon the particular
area of land which it occupies."[5]

It is significant that British colonial governments were anxious to
preserve for the African people such past forms of security. They
assumed that somehow these African tribal societies could and would
evolve under their guidance to modern forms of economic organization.

This view, of course, proved to be false precisely because it was not
possible to break out of the vicious circle of the constraints on production within tribal society without transforming tribal rights,
which are status rights, into the functional values determined by the
market.

The commission's report vividly described the resulting situation
as follows: "In whatever direction he turns, the African, whether he
wishes to become a peasant, a farmer, a businessman, a permanent
wage-earner in the towns or a modern tenant on the land, is hampered
by the requirements of his tribal society with its obligations and restraints. As a farmer, in many areas, he cannot buy or lease land or
obtain a fully defensible title thereto. In consequence he cannot easily
specialize in particular forms of agricultural production for export or
home markets."[6]

These rigidities brought about a situation of increasing tension, the basis of which was fear. In the words of the report:

> Those who occupy land fear that they may lose it or be deprived of it, without proper compensation and with no opportunity to purchase other land in its place. Those who have no land fear that they will never be able to acquire it. Thus those who occupy land cling to it irrespective of their ability to use it properly. Those who have too little land for proper economic production on modern methods cannot easily extend their holdings, while those who have too much are not permitted to dispose of it for economic purposes at its appropriate price without consulting authorities, whose decision will not be made on the basis of economic considerations but on the basis of the old conceptions of tribal, clan or family security.[7]

So much for Africa.

I have referred to these matters to illustrate what I believe to be a fundamental error in thinking of technology as the main agent of progress, and of "ceremonial" or existing institutions as obstacles thereto. That error rests on a mistake in categorizing. It consists in regarding technology as an *extra* member of the class of which the other units or factors, which are regarded as constituting a progressive society, are composed. Technology is not something extraneous to society—it is just one part or aspect of it. To regard it as *causing* the progress of society is as mistaken as to suggest that the growth of a university is caused by the growth of its buildings. The buildings, without the other members of the class of things of which a university is composed, would have no significance at all.

In the same way, a new technology introduced into a society without the markets at home or abroad to absorb its products, or without the labor or specialized legal or economic or financial systems on which production and distribution depend, would have no meaning.

The error involved in thinking of technology as the main agent of progress, and of existing institutions as obstacles thereto, finally rests on what, in a scientific logical context, Sir Karl Popper has called "the bucket theory of science (or the bucket theory of mind.)" "The starting point of this theory," he writes, "is the persuasive doctrine that before we can know or say anything about the world, we must first have had perceptions—sense experiences. . . . According to this view, then, our mind resembles a container—a kind of bucket—in which perceptions and knowledge accumulate. (Bacon speaks of perceptions as 'grapes, ripe and in season' which have to be gathered, patiently and industriously, and from which, if pressed, the pure wine of knowledge will flow.)"[8]

As against this view he contends that: "In science it is *observation* rather than perception which plays the decisive part. But observation is a process in which we play an intensely *active* part. An observation is a perception, but one which is planned and prepared. We do not 'have' an observation (as we may 'have' a sense experience) but we 'make' an observation. . . . An observation is always preceded by a particular interest, a question, or a problem—in short, by something theoretical."[9] The error, in other words, consists in thinking of the agents of progress as something given—as a stock of knowledge or capital or techniques which can somehow simply be transferred from one situation to another to achieve similar known results.

To fall into this error is to overlook that every situation differs from every other because it raises new problems depending on time, place, and circumstance. Each problem has to be solved anew by observation and by a new hypothesis as to the best approach to solving it. This involves a process of trial and error to bring the ultimate solution nearer. In turn, every such tentative "solution" brings with it new problems which will present the need for further theorizing, hypothesizing, and trial and error for their solution. Technology is like capital, which, as I expressed in a paper read to the first round table discussion of the International Economic Association in 1950,

> . . . is apart from the symbolism of accounting, always "concrete" in the sense that it is embedded in, and attuned to, the particular purposes and state of knowledge which led to its "creation." It is but temporarily incorporated in ever changing forms and patterns suited to the evanescent ends for which it is designed. It is a social heritage dependent upon the institutions and habit-patterns of thought and action of individuals in society. In the last resort it dissolves always into its basic element: the action of man's labour upon the natural environment. That is why capital cannot be "stored-up" for long; nor can it be "transferred" from one situation to another without the individuals who will re-adapt and "re-fashion" it for use in a new pattern of activity. For no two situations, no two societies, no two problems of choice, in time, or place, are alike. In this sense capital is like technical "know-how," which also does not exist in the abstract ready to be applied to any new situation. To transfer "know-how" is not

to apply something which is known. It is to apply new ways of thinking to find out what is not known: as when research is undertaken to develop new crops; discover the nature of soils; prospect for minerals; adapt old aptitudes to new skills; and perfect machines for new tasks. It is because existing forms in which knowledge i.e. capital, is incorporated are no longer suitable that the old has constantly to be re-fashioned anew in attempts to meet the future. Capital is, as has been said repeatedly, a means of saving time; but it is only possible to save time if one can discover the purpose to which one will devote it.[10]

The fallacy that progress—and not only progress but survival itself —can be ensured by possessing a stock of knowledge—available like a computer printout to answer any question—has undoubtedly had a very deleterious influence. It has probably contributed in no small degree to the decline of many empires. These empires, resting on the mistaken belief that they "possessed" the most developed and the most advanced body of culture, regarded themselves as superior to others for all foreseeable time—if not for ever.

Europeans of my generation have reasons enough to remember the consequence of such mistaken and arrogant beliefs: their disenchantments are probably similar to those of the Spaniards and the Portuguese when witnessing the decline of their empires and the waning supremacy of their cultures.

At the root of the matter surely lies what has recently been so well formulated in the inaugural lecture by Professor Jerome S. Bruner at the University of Oxford, who needs no introduction to American readers as an eminent scholar in the field of psychology and pedagogy. Speaking of what for him is central to an understanding of the growth of human behavior, he said: "Growth is organized around the acquisition of skill, skill in carrying out one's intentions. Skill implies knowledge that makes action flexible, foresightful, and open to new learning. To cultivate growth humanely is to provide conditions in which human beings can become alert and skilful in pursuit of their goals. All of this requires a communal setting, a social meshing of intentions and their pursuit. Human intentions are obviously not 'natural,' though constrained by natural or biological factors."

He draws attention to the fact that the pattern of *looking* and *attending* becomes stereotyped by social habit, and that "human culture can then be said to regulate and 'socialize' the means-end activities of its members. Desirable ends are specified implicitly or explicitly, and the culture legitimizes certain means to their attainment while tabooing others. Man's goals and the paths to their attainment are then an uncertain mix of social convention and human biology." He conceives of culture "as a limited body of *generative* rules which once learned permits one to act, to anticipate, to predict in a wide variety of situations" (italics added).[11]

In my view Ayres, although fully aware of the constraining power of institutional structures, did not give sufficient weight to the fact that they are capable of generating change when the opportunities for change emerge and are *observed* to be emerging. It is precisely here that the functioning of the market mechanism is so important. It makes possible the exercise of freedom in testing new ways of observing and solving the problems which change involves.

Ayres, I believe, did not appreciate the power of the market mechanism to slough off the encrustations, and the dead wood, of the past. Nevertheless, while he was almost obsessed by their constraining influence, he did not, as Robinson and so many others do today, fly to the other extreme. He did not support the notion that all that was needed in regard to the social heritage from the past was to abolish it.[12] Thus he emphasized: "The tenacity of institutional traditions is likewise a generally admitted fact. But it is one thing to reach the logical conclusion that institutional atavisms are the seat of all our trouble and quite another to determine methodologically what to do about it. The immediate and complete abrogation of the institutional structure is both impossible and inconceivable. We may deplore the organization of society along the lines of coercive power with its penumbra of legend and mysticism; but the immediate alternative would be a void."[13]

That is why he placed his faith so greatly in the beneficent effects of technological progress. That optimism was based on faith in the universal values which he thought were engendered in the technological process itself. As late as 1962 he wrote:

> . . . the values which are engendered in the technological process are universal values. Science, the intellectual aspect of technology, assumes and requires a commitment to the discovery of truth, and science prescribes its own conception of truth. It is a processual, or operational, or instrumental—tool-defined—conception of truth.
>
> This conception of truth and of human values generally is at variance with all tribal legends and all tribal authority; and since the technological revolution is itself irresistible, the arbitrary

authority and irrational values of pre-scientific, pre-industrial
cultures are doomed. . . . The only remaining alternative is that
of intelligent, voluntary acceptance of the industrial way of life
and all the values that go with it.[14]

But this argument rests on the same mistake in categorizing as that
to which I have referred previously. It lies in confusing the *methods*
of science and technology with the *values* of the industrial way of
life, of which they are only a part. The methods of science and technology are the objective methods of *solving* problems; but they do not
determine which problems are to be solved.

Problem solving by trial and error has been characteristic of man
in society since time immemorial. In recent centuries it has blos-
somed into scientific achievements of amazing complexity.

However, let us beware of hubris. The concluding passage of the
1962 Foreword by Ayres, from which I have already quoted, reads as
follows:

> We need make no apology for recommending such a course.
> Industrial society is the most successful way of life mankind has
> ever known. Not only do our people eat better, sleep better, live
> in more comfortable dwellings, get around more and in far greater
> comfort, and—notwithstanding all the manifold dangers of the
> industrial way of life—live longer than men have ever done
> before. Our people are also better informed than ever before. In
> addition to listening to radio and watching television, they read
> more books, see more pictures, and hear more music than any
> previous generation or any other people ever has. At the height
> of the technological revolution we are now living in a golden
> age of scientific enlightenment and artistic achievement.

Who would recognize in this the authoritarian tyrannies and the
mass demagogy which now threaten us? Millions of the peoples of
the world now fear more than anything else that they should be accused of "thinking new thoughts" at all, quite apart from even the
possibility of daring to apply them.

On this situation all experience from the past is emphatically clear.
It is that in societies which cease to value, and protect, the freedom
of the individual, even the expected fruits from the industrial way of
life will prove a snare and a delusion: for the path-breaking forces
of science and technology will then inevitably be arrested by the very
lack of freedom which society no longer can, or cares to, guarantee—
but on which they are so inescapably dependent.

NOTES

1. Joan Robinson, *Economic Philosophy* (London: C. A. Watts and Co., 1962), pp. 110, 113.

2. C. E. Ayres, *The Theory of Economic Progress* (Chapel Hill: University of North Carolina Press, 1944).

3. I am greatly indebted to Professors William Breit and W. P. Culbertson, Jr., for elucidating many of Ayres's views for me, and to Professor Breit's penetrating article "The Development of Clarence Ayres's Theoretical Institutionalism," *Social Science Quarterly* 54 (September 1973): 244–257.

4. John Maynard Keynes, *A Short View of Russia* (1925; reprinted in *Essays in Persuasion* [London: Macmillan and Co., 1931]), p. 311.

5. *East Africa Royal Commission Report, 1953–1955* (London: Her Majesty's Stationery Office, Cmd. 9475, 1955), chap. 5, p. 48. This chapter was drafted by Professor D. T. Jack and the author.

6. Ibid., p. 51.

7. Ibid.

8. Karl R. Popper, *Objective Knowledge: An Evolutionary Approach* (Oxford: Oxford University Press, 1972), pp. 341–342.

9. Ibid., p. 342.

10. S. Herbert Frankel, "Some Aspects of International Economic Development of Underdeveloped Territories." Reprinted in my book *The Economic Impact on Under-developed Societies: Essays on International and Social Change* (Cambridge, Mass.: Harvard University Press; Oxford: Blackwell, 1953), p. 69.

11. Jerome S. Bruner, *Patterns of Growth* (London: Oxford University Press, 1974), pp. 4, 17.

12. He was, however, well aware of it. Thus he wrote in the 1962 Foreword to the new edition of *The Theory of Economic Progress*:

> In this matter of institutional resistance the practitioners of total revolution enjoy a tremendous advantage. During the colonial period Europeans made it a matter of deliberate policy not to "interfere" with "native" cultures. They did so partly as a matter of snobbery by holding themselves aloof from the indigenous population, and partly out of respect for the human rights of the "subject" peoples as a matter of humanitarian conviction. Revolutionists scorn both these motives, and so make the extirpation of the indigenous culture their first order of business, following which the introduction of industrial technology is relatively easy. This is the secret of the astonishing rapidity with which the

Soviet Union has been catching up with the West. To be sure, revolutionaries may be afflicted with traditions of their own which act as a brake on the developmental process. The compulsive collectivization of agriculture may be such an institutional liability. (P. xx)

Clearly here once again the *cost* of the introduction of industrial technology is ignored by the innocent-looking phrase "following which the introduction of industrial technology is relatively easy"— as easy as it was made to appear in the passage I quoted previously from J. M. Keynes.

13. Ibid., p. 251.

14. Ibid., p. xxiv.

Technology and the Price System

W. W. ROSTOW

I

As he made scrupulously clear, Clarence Ayres drew upon the insight of many of his contemporaries: Dewey and Veblen, above all, but also Sumner, Freud, Durkheim, Pareto in his phase of sociology, and Keynes of the *General Theory*, among others. But no one can study Ayres without knowing that he constructed out of his environment a private vision of man in society, informed by deeply held private values. Ayres read widely in history as well as the social sciences. He rejected that branch of institutionalism which retreated into shapeless empirical investigations. He sought a general theory which would embrace it all—from the elements of human nature to how the economy really worked. In the phrases of Alfred Marshall, to which we shall return, Ayres addressed himself directly to "the high theme of economic progress" in the context of "society as an organism."[1]

Technically, Ayres was an economist in revolt against classical theory. In *Toward a Reasonable Society* he describes vividly how he "felt the heavens falling" when, at Amherst, Walton Hamilton responded to his question about when he would get around in his undergraduate course to some ideas about marginal utility with the reply: "I'd do so at once if only I understood them myself."[2] And soon Ayres followed Hamilton as a disciple of Veblen. But he did more than protest against "the dogma of the classical tradition." He was both a general theorist of society and a pamphleteer on behalf of the future of man and Western civilization.

In theory, he rejected the legitimacy of demand curves and the concept of the unique individual with private values. Tastes and income distribution were, in his view, the arbitrary product of culture and mores. He believed Darwin had erased the notion (Ayres attributed to Descartes and Kant) that scientists could be scientists and still be men. But, paradoxically, he built his synthesis and projected his view of its meaning as a unique scientist and a quite particular man of a special integrity.

Ayres hammered out his system with such intense clarity that it is not difficult to summarize.

Man acts in terms of his culture: there is no meaning to individuality outside this frame of reference.

How man gets his living is simply a part of his culture: the economy must be put in its full cultural context.

The economic aspect of a culture is shaped, in turn, by the tools man has and those he develops: the tools determine both how man gets his living and the social structure and mores (ceremonies) he elaborates.

There is an eternal clash between the introduction of new tools and the existing ceremonial structure of society.

What distinguishes Western culture is the process of progressive development of new tools, a process Ayres attributed (following Pirenne) to the fact that Western Europe was a frontier area which received the cumulative scientific and technological achievement of the ancient and Eastern worlds but where the mother culture was incompletely installed. Therefore, the inhibitions to technical change were less than in the older civilizations, where the power of ceremony was greater and more stifling.

Technical change has been the motor of Western civilization; progress and value can only be defined as the continuity of technical development permitting a more effective organization of the whole life process. Technical progress has been real, reducing humbug, cruelty, and squalor; further progress will overcome war and poverty, yielding abundance and a world state.

From this perspective, the price system is not central to the economic system. The price system is a moving picture of a deeper process conventional economics fails to analyze. Equilibrium analysis is a misleading technique in this dynamic setting and is also shot through with implicit but wrong moral values. Capitalism (and the commercial revolution) is a product, not the parent, of the technological revolution. The holding of private financial claims on physical capital assets (and the right to inherit them) is the product of ceremony rather than a legitimate function in modern societies. The institutions of property (like the nation state) require, therefore, profound modification.

When he came to specific prescription, Ayres's proposals were relatively moderate: a Naderesque consumerism and income redistribution, justified on both ethical and Keynesian grounds. But his analysis was radical.

I would agree with parts of this vision and creed and disagree with others. Here I shall deal only with a limited but fundamental segment of Ayres's system; that is, the place of technology in economic theory —the place it has occupied and something of the place it should occupy.

II

In a curious way, Ayres's analysis shares two fundamental weaknesses of the classical tradition, stretching from *The Wealth of Nations* to Nicholas Kaldor's "The Irrelevance of Equilibrium Economics." The first is a failure to examine satisfactorily the character of the linkages among science, invention, and innovation.[3] The second is a failure to explore satisfactorily the linkage of these three variables to the price system.

In Ayres the development of technology is an autonomous aspect of Western culture unfolding more or less at a geometric rate, as tools multiply and are combined in new ways. He spends little time on the relation of science to invention and virtually none on innovation. The three activities are lumped together. He places the total process of technological advance at the center of his system; he sets it in motion with his analysis of the peculiar historical nature of medieval western Europe. But, once the creative explosion of the fifteenth century occurs (notably, printing), technological change, as it were, looks after itself. Ayres was not particularly interested in the coming in of particular technologies and did not explore the extent to which necessity, as reflected in the price system or the demands of the state, was the mother of invention.

Classical theory is equally casual about the relations among science, invention, and innovation. And the process of technological change is mainly dealt with in either of three ways: first, by exclusion, as in Marshallian short-period partial equilibrium analysis and Walrasian general equilibrium analysis; second, by assuming it is a simple function of an expanding overall level of demand or of investment, as in Adam Smith and Kaldor; or, third, by assuming it is an exogenous variable, as in Harrod-Domar growth models. Thus Ayres and the classical economists of the nineteenth and twentieth centuries were asserting a similar if not identical proposition. Ayres pounded the table in demanding that the automatic process of technological change built into Western culture be recognized as the heart of the economic as well as the social and political process; classical price and production theory and Keynesian income analysis said, in effect: "Why, of course. But it is an automatic long-run function of increasing demand; let us, therefore, concentrate on how things unfold from day to day, and on maintaining steady high levels of employment."

Links of technology to the price system do emerge in classical economics, primarily in the theoretically troublesome partial equilibrium case of increasing returns; and these we shall examine. Moreover, from Adam Smith to the present, classical analysis also included the recurrent, haunting theme of long-run diminishing returns to land, natural resources, and, perhaps, to capital itself. And the notion of diminishing returns continues to underlie many of the most important propositions in contemporary economic theory. But in the past it was left mainly to economic historians, a narrow group of specialists on the absorption of technology, and occasional bold exercises (like Schumpeter's treatment of the Kondratieff ["long wave"] in his *Business Cycles*) to try to relate the unfolding of technology to the economic process, including the price system. In recent times, as we shall see, theorists of development planning have begun to address themselves head-on to some of the difficult issues involved.

III

But economists come to the task with an awkward heritage. The trouble started with Adam Smith's assertion that "the division of labor is limited by the extent of the market." If this famous dictum is taken to mean that the widening of the market is a sufficient condition for major technological change, the proposition is false. It is simply not the case, in eighteenth-century Britain—before or since—that commercial expansion led on automatically to regular and substantial technological innovation.[4] Certainly, the emergence of modern experimental science, interweaving in complex ways with the processes of invention and innovation, is what distinguishes the early modern history of Europe from the many prior periods of economic expansion, when agricultural, commercial, and industrial activity increased without significant technological change. Put another way, without the scientific revolution and all its complex, ramified consequences, the great expansion of trade in Asian and American groceries and bullion that we call the commercial revolution would have yielded not an industrial revolution but, as in the past, a long cycle. Students of the vital ancient empires would agree with Dwight H. Perkins's dictum: "There is no natural or irresistible movement from commercial development to industrialization. The experience of China is alone testimony to this."[5] And, one can add, so is the experience of the southern half of the world in the nineteenth and a good part of the twentieth centuries, where commercial expansion proceeded for long periods without generating sustained industrialization. Ayres was notably emphatic on this point in his Foreword to the 1962 edition of *The Theory of Economic Progress*, perhaps overdoing it a bit by making the commercial revolution of the sixteenth to the eighteenth century a simple function of the technological revolution.[6]

Smith was, indeed, a historian, philosopher, analyst, and pamphleteer of the commercial rather than the industrial process. *The Wealth of Nations* was published in precisely the interval between the acceleration of British inventive effort, after the end of the Seven Years' War, and the first phase of rapid innovation in textiles, iron, and steam power, after the end of the American War of Independence. Smith exhibited no awareness of the momentous changes germinating around him: "There was not a line in his book anticipating such transformations as were to take place."[7] He did perceive that specialization of function could increase the productivity of labor with, essentially, constant or marginally improved technology; and he also perceived, in the case of the woolen industry, that three "capital improvements" had taken place since the end of the fifteenth century.[8] But there is no inkling of how rapid, discontinuous technological change fitted his system; nothing about the new textile machines, the new developments in iron and the steam engine; and not even a reference to the concurrent wave of English canal building.

Koebner finds Smith's myopia about technological change a result of the timing of his work and, especially, its main purpose—that is, an attack on the mercantile system. In this view, the economics of technological change would have been an excessive diversion from his main theme. But it may be that, like his successors, Smith perceived that the introduction of discontinuous technological change would have disrupted the elegance of the price system, which emerged on the basis of competition, and the incremental technical improvements a widening of the market under competitive assumptions might yield. It would also have led him into the inevitable elements of monopoly, involved both directly in a patent system and, indirectly, in the real if transient advantage of early innovators. Smith was in no mood in *The Wealth of Nations* to suggest that private monopoly might serve constructive purposes.

In any case, Smith's successors, living in times when technological change was an inescapable, massive, and central fact in the world economy, have generally followed his lead: they made technological change a function of expanding demand (or a widening of the market); they viewed it as a diffuse, incremental process that could be assumed rather than examined; and they did not explore the interactions among science, invention, and innovation and their place in a general theory of production and prices.

Smith's most significant successor, Alfred Marshall, was, to a degree, an exception, for Marshall understood better than any economist
in the classical tradition the depth of the problem posed by technological change for equilibrium price theory. In a passage that Ayres
might have written (or, at least, applauded) Marshall said this:

> The theory of stable equilibrium of normal demand and supply
> helps indeed to give definiteness to our ideas; and in its elemen-
> tary stages it does not diverge from the actual facts of life, so far
> as to prevent its giving a fairly trustworthy picture of the chief
> methods of action of the strongest and most persistent group of
> economic forces. But when pushed to its more remote and intri-
> cate logical consequences, it slips away from the conditions of
> real life. In fact we are here verging on the high theme of eco-
> nomic progress; and here therefore it is especially needful to
> remember that economic problems are imperfectly presented
> when they are treated as problems of statical equilibrium, and
> not of organic growth. For though the statical treatment alone
> can give us definiteness and precision of thought, and is there-
> fore a necessary introduction to a more philosophic treatment
> of society as an organism; it is yet only an introduction.
>
> The Statical theory of equilibrium is only an introduction to
> economic studies; and it is barely even an introduction to the
> study of the progress and development of industries which show
> a tendency to increasing return. Its limitations are so constantly
> overlooked, especially by those who approach it from an abstract
> point of view, that there is a danger in throwing it into definite
> form at all.[9]

Marshall then refers the reader to Appendix H, where the case of
increasing returns is formally examined.[10]

In dealing with increasing returns Marshall is, of course, posing
the question of the relation between demand and supply over substantial periods of time. He distinguishes four concepts of supply,
each related to different time intervals:

> As regards *market* prices, Supply is taken to mean the stock of
> the commodity in question which is on hand, or at all events
> "in sight." As regards *normal* prices, when the term Normal is
> taken to relate to *short* periods of a few months or a year, Supply
> means broadly what can be produced for the price in question
> with the existing stock of plant, personal and impersonal, in the
> given time. As regards *normal* prices, when the term Normal is

to refer to *long* periods of several years, Supply means what can be produced by plant, which itself can be remuneratively produced and applied within the given time; while lastly, there are very gradual or *Secular* movements of normal price, caused by the gradual growth of knowledge, of population and of capital, and the changing conditions of demand and supply from one generation to another.[11]

In his fourth time interval, and in other observations on the case of increasing returns, Marshall argues that a shift in demand and a short-period rise in price will yield in time an increase in efficiency as well as in scale of production, granting a price lower than that which preceded the initial shift in demand. (Here Marshall evokes a sudden fashion for watch-shaped aneroids.) There is some implication that technological change is induced by the initial outward shift in demand and increase in price. But this insight—linking the course of technology to the price system—is not systematically pursued. It is in an institutional section of the *Principles of Economics* devoted to industrial organization (bk. 4, chap. 9) that Marshall deals with machinery; and there we are out of the price system and back with Adam Smith, the widening of the market, and the division of labor. In fact, there is no index reference to invention in Marshall's *Principles*; and inventions are considered in *Money, Credit, and Commerce* only in the context of their disruptive effect on employment and how to cushion it (pp. 244–245, 260).

Despite his sensitivity to the problem posed by increasing returns, his distinction between internal and external economies, and his appendixes and diagrams, Marshall never addresses himself satisfactorily to "the high theme of economic progress," "organic growth," or "society as an organism." Like *The Wealth of Nations*, Marshall's work contains long discursive passages on history and institutions, labor, and even education. Appendix A in the *Principles* is an essay entitled "The Growth of Free Industry and Enterprise," but Marshall's greatest admirers would agree that it is an indifferent account of how the industrial revolution came about. This is the case not only because of its curious racial cast but also because Marshall had no firm grasp on the relation between the market process and the emergence and application of new technologies. Indeed, in creating his celebrated device of "the representative firm," reconciling declining long-period marginal costs with a gradual increase in demand, Marshall explicitly excluded from view "any economies that may result from substantive new inventions."[12] Thus, as in Adam Smith, technical change in

Marshall is a matter of incremental adjustment: to use his own language, changes "which may be expected to arise naturally out of adaptations of existing ideas."[13] He never asked nor answered the questions: where did the "existing ideas" come from; what was the impact on the economy of their introduction? Thus, although he was acutely aware of the limits of short-period partial equilibrium analysis, there is a rude justice in the fact that his refinements in this branch of economics were his major residual contribution. Marshall had, in the end, little fruitful to say about the process of economic growth.

Allyn Young took a quite serious crack at the unresolved problems left by Marshall in his famous presidential address of September 10, 1928, "Increasing Returns and Economic Progress."[14] Building on Adam Smith, as well as Marshall, Young advanced the analysis by challenging the notion that increasing returns could be analyzed or understood in terms of a single industry with its representative firm. He argued that economic progress took the form of specialization, which created new industries rather than merely new, narrow tasks within an industry. (His illustration is the transformation of the old printing trade to a complex of industries embracing pulp and paper, inks, type metal and type, presses, etc.) He argued, also, that progress within an industry involved increasingly roundabout methods of production, which led to specialized plants, "which, taken together, constitute a new industry"; and, thus, the concept of the representative firm "dissolves." Finally, like Ayres he perceived that new technology could lead to a widening of the market, as well as vice versa.

Aside from these specific conclusions, there was a distinctive general thrust in Young's paper toward the creation of a dynamic general theory of production and prices:

> . . . the counter forces which are continually defeating the forces which make for economic equilibrium are more pervasive and more deeply rooted in the constitution of the modern economic system than we commonly realize. Not only new or adventitious elements, coming in from the outside, but elements which are permanent characteristics of the ways in which goods are produced make continuously for change. Every important advance in the organization of production, regardless of whether it is based upon anything which, in a narrow or technical sense, would be called a new "invention," or involves a fresh application of the fruits of scientific progress to industry, alters the conditions of industrial activity and initiates responses elsewhere in the industrial structure which in turn have a further unsettling

effect. Thus change becomes progressive and propagates itself in a cumulative way.

The apparatus which economists have built up for the analysis of supply and demand in their relations to prices does not seem to be particularly helpful for the purposes of an inquiry into these broader aspects of increasing returns.[15]

And Young throws out, at one point, the evocative observation that "the appropriate conception is that of a *moving* equilibrium."[16] But Young did not try to grapple with major discontinuous technological breakthroughs. Like Marshall, he confined himself to "such new ways of organizing production and such new 'inventions' as are merely adaptations of known ways of doing things, made practicable and economical by an enlarged scale of production."[17] This is the confining assumption built into Young's much-quoted dictum: "Even with a stationary population and in the absence of new discoveries in pure or applied science there are no limits to the process of expansion except the limits beyond which demand is not elastic and returns do not increase."[18] Young was aware that there was more to technological progress and increasing returns than this. In assessing the influences which make for increasing returns, he observed: "The discovery of new natural resources and of new uses for them and the growth of scientific knowledge are probably the most potent of such factors. The causal connections between the growth of industry and the progress of science run in both directions, but on which side the preponderant influence lies no one can say."[19] But this fundamental question Young did not pursue. On balance, he held to the view that the commercial revolution yielded the industrial revolution; and, subsequently, the expansion of the market (or its potential expansion) was the engine that drove forward the refinement of technology and business organization.

Young's effort to reconcile classical partial equilibrium price and production theory with the dynamics of economic progress was not pursued by others. The Great Depression came; the Keynesian revolution; the war; and postwar European reconstruction and growth. The center of the stage was taken over by the study of short-period fluctuations in national income and employment. The refinement of aggregative income analysis did, however, involve two problems which brought back the question of invention, innovation, and economic progress. First, there was the analysis of business cycles in terms of the interaction of the multiplier and the accelerator. This exercise required a distinction among investment which expanded capacity with existing techniques (motivated by expected increases in output), investment incorporating new technology, and investment motivated by profit possibilities looking beyond the current rate of increase in output.[20] Formally, the problem was solved by introducing the concept of "autonomous investment," organized in some mysterious and irregular way by innovators, coming along from time to time to set the multiplier-accelerator machine into motion. But, as Richard M. Goodwin observed: "No analytic solution can be given if ϕ (t) [autonomous investment] is taken, as it must, to be an arbitrary, historically given function."[21]

Harrod-Domar models of growth also posed the question of how to deal with technological change and innovation, as well as population increase. Again, the formal problem was solved by arbitrary assumption: in Harrod's model, by taking as given, population growth, the flow of inventions into the production process, their productivity, and their neutrality with respect to the saving of labor and capital.[22] Such models contributed little to our understanding of growth, although they may have added something to the case for public policy addressed to the task of maintaining relatively full employment.

To see where we had come by the late 1960's it is instructive, by way of example, to examine the references to increasing returns, invention, and innovation in Professor Paul A. Samuelson's textbook *Economics* (page references are to the seventh edition):

—A simplified version of the multiplier-accelerator model is presented on pages 248–251, with a casual reference to "technical progress" in the last paragraph.

—On pages 369–370, supply under three of Marshall's four time periods is illustrated, the case of decreasing cost dealt with in an appendix (pp. 386–387) along Marshallian lines (of demand-supply interaction) but diagrammed in terms of a downward shift in cost curves rather than movement along a downward sloping cost curve.

—On page 446 it is noted that internal decreasing costs for a firm lead to monopoly, and that external economies, notably social overhead capital, can shift downward a firm's cost curves, a point elaborated on pages 450–451.

—On page 579 it is noted that new inventions and discoveries "are constantly being made"; and these have thus far offset diminishing returns to capital and maintained the rate of interest, a point made again on pages 716–718 in dealing with productivity and real wage trends in advanced, growing economies and in demonstrating how the capital-output ratio has remained low. Labor and capital-saving inventions are explored on pages 720–722, after which an appendix discusses various development theories, including the Schumpeter and Harrod-Domar models.

—On page 743 it is noted that, in dealing with developing nations, "the phenomenon of increasing returns can make it possible for dramatic spurts and accelerations to occur in economic development"; but this possibility is solely illustrated by the impact of external economies induced by enlarged social overhead capital.

—On pages 751–754, there are a few paragraphs dealing with the transfer of existing technology to developing nations, the possible embodiment of technology in capital investment and replacement, and an admonition on the importance of creative innovation.[23]

These are all, essentially, peripheral references. What we have here is a lucid and faithful summary of neo-Marshallian value theory and neo-Keynesian income analysis. (Walrasian general static equilibrium is well but briefly summarized on pages 606–608.) The strengths and ambiguities of these cumulative achievements are all there. Nowhere are the relations among science, technology, and innovation dealt with fully or as a working part of a modern economic system. Major technological change remains exogenous, in both value and growth theory, dealt with in the case of the former by ad hoc illustration; in the latter, by means of highly aggregated flows whose average productivity offsets diminishing returns to land and capital. Problems of development are treated as an afterthought, in no way linked structurally to the corpus of received economic theory.

In the past several years this way of looking at the economic system has come under increasing attack. The mood is well summed up by the title of Janos Kornai's study, *Anti-Equilibrium*, which, after examining the weaknesses in the received tradition of theory, calls for "a broader synthesis."[24] One effort in revisionism is Kaldor's article "The Irrelevance of Equilibrium Economics."[25] Kaldor takes as his platform a mixture of Adam Smith on the division of labor, Allyn Young on increasing returns, Keynesian income analysis, and Kornai's specification of the arbitrary and unrealistic assumptions underlying Walrasian general equilibrium theory. His mood is almost Ayresian: ". . . without a major act of demolition—without destroying the basic conceptual framework—it is impossible to make any real progress."[26] He believes economics went wrong in the middle of the fourth chapter of book one of *The Wealth of Nations*, when Smith abandons his examination of the relation between the extent of the market and the division of labor and becomes fascinated with money and price theory. From that point on the theory of value took over the center of the stage, with its constraining and unrealistic assumptions about production functions.

Kaldor believes that Young's treatment of increasing returns rendered incremental technological change endogenous. Young's consequent judgment about the elasticity of supply, combined with his assumption that demand curves were adequately elastic, yields a chain reaction "between demand increases which have been induced by increases in supply, and increases in supply which have been evoked by increases in demand."[27] Kaldor indicates his respect for this intuitive pre–*General Theory* insight, but believes that, without Keynesian assumptions about the course of total expenditure (as opposed to increased expenditure on a particular commodity subject to increasing returns), Young's system does not guarantee steady overall economic progress. He turns, therefore, to a specification of the conditions required for Young's demand-supply interaction to yield self-sustained growth.

His conditions are these:

—With respect to primary commodities (subject to diminishing returns), merchants' expectations about future price prospects must be sufficiently inelastic so that they will increase the value of their stocks in the face of a phase of excess supply and falling prices.

—With respect to manufactured commodities (subject to increasing returns), entrepreneurs' expectations about the future volume of sales must be sufficiently elastic so that an increase in demand yields increased investment in both working and fixed capital.

—The monetary and banking system must be sufficiently permissive (or passive) to respond to these inducements to expand investment, generating the required savings out of the consequent increment to production and income.

At the close of an appendix to his paper Kaldor observes that the task before us is to replace "the 'equilibrium approach' with some, as yet unexplored, alternative that makes use of a different conceptual framework."[28] His initial contribution to that objective does not, in my view, take us very far. It is wholesome that, like Kornai (and Marshall, Robertson, and Young), he underlines the arbitrary and unrealistic assumptions underlying partial and general equilibrium theory and the explosive meaning of increasing returns. But when he turns to self-sustained growth, his treatment of technological change suffers from the same weakness as his predecessors. In Kaldor it is a diffuse incremental process, related to (and encouraging) a Smithian widening of the market, governed by no defined principles except a linkage to the scale of industrial investment. In his analysis, investment induces increasing returns in three ways: by an enlargement in the scale of plants; by the simplification and specialization of production methods, yielding "embodied technical progress"; and by cumulative improvements resulting from the number of plants constructed per year. There is no more in Kaldor than in Smith or Marshall about the interplay of science, invention, and innovation. There is not even Marshall's awareness that his treatment of increasing returns excluded "any economies that may result from substantive new inventions" or G. T. Jones's awareness that it was necessary to exclude from the Marshallian case the "epoch-making discoveries" that created "new industries rather than economies reaped from the growth of the old."

In the end, as in Harrod-Domar growth models, Kaldor is simply trying to refine marginally our knowledge of what is required on the demand side to guarantee growth under conditions of full employment. He evades the critical historical question with a bland projection backward of Youngian supply-demand interaction: "It is a hen-and-egg question whether historically it was the growth of commerce which continually enlarged 'the size of the market' and thereby enabled increasing returns to be realized, or whether it was the improvement of techniques of production and the improvement in communication which led to the growth of commerce. In the process of the development of capitalism the two operated side by side."[29] That is not an adequate answer for a serious historian. More important, the treatment of technology by Kaldor—and his predecessors back to Smith—is an inadequate basis on which to build the dynamic theory of production and prices required to supersede Walrasian and other static equilibrium formulations.

IV

Well, then, how should we proceed if we are to build a dynamic theory of production and prices, embracing the flow of technology as an endogenous variable and facing up to the complexities of increasing returns? I believe we face four distinct but related tasks. First, we must bring science, invention, and innovation within the bounds of economic analysis, as forms of investment. Second, we must expand the concept of increasing returns to embrace the case of "substantive new inventions" and "epoch-making discoveries"; third, we must construct a concept of dynamic sectoral equilibrium embracing not only the dynamic cases of increasing returns but also older sectors where progress is slow and incremental, nil, or where diminishing returns may apply; and, finally, we must relate this dynamic map (from which flows the concept of an optimum pattern of investment) to aggregative income analysis, the foreign balance, and to the lags and frictions of the real world.

I can only suggest here—and briefly—how these objectives can be accomplished. But if I am right, it is possible to salvage more of traditional price and production theory than Ayres's (and Kaldor's) analysis would suggest, while meeting the thrust of Ayres's argument by moving technological change toward the center of the stage, without quite dominating it.

v

First, then, the connections among science, invention, and innovation.[30]

Science and invention represent forms of investment within a society. Men devote time and current resources to produce new knowledge or new, more efficient ways of doing things. A decision is required to forego some other activity and accept the risk of failing to achieve a result valued by the market or public authorities or sought by the scientist or inventor in personal fulfillment.

Viewed in this way, the volume of resources (including human talent) devoted to fundamental science and to invention in a given society at a particular period of time can be symbolized by quite conventional supply and demand curves. A demand curve would exhibit the expected yield to be derived from the application of additional resources to the pursuit of fundamental science, with the existing scientific stock given. Since the results of pure science do not enter directly into the private economy (except in certain contemporary sophisticated industries with great laboratories), the demand for scientific achievement may reflect the premium in prestige and academic status a given society attaches to such achievement or public subsidy. A supply curve would exhibit the volume of resources actually offered by a given society to the pursuit of fundamental science. Some men are driven to search for new knowledge by inner compulsions not closely related to external reward; but for substantial numbers of human beings one can expect that talent would be responsive in degree to the rewards, financial and otherwise, a society offers for scientific achievement.

A similar pair of curves would exhibit the demand for inventions and the supply of talent and resources offered in response to the expected yields. Here we are closer to the market place. Therefore, for invention, one can probably presume somewhat greater elasticity of supply in relation to expected yields. But, we are also dealing with men with an instinct to express a creative talent, and the shape of the supply curve for inventors may also reflect nonmaterial rewards.

The purpose of viewing science and invention in these static supply and demand terms is extremely limited. It is to suggest that the actual volume of talent devoted to these enterprises within a society at any given time is the result, on the side of demand, of the premium, economic and/or otherwise, that the private market and the public authorities attach to these activities; and, on the side of supply, of the extent to which the system of education, social opportunity, and values within a society lead men of potential scientific and inventive gift to offer their talents in these directions—for achievements in science and invention are cumulative, and the numbers engaged matter. The simple point here is that the numbers can be increased if the demand curve shifts to the right, since some elasticity in supply is likely; but the numbers can also be increased if the supply curve shifts to the right, under the impact of a change in social circumstances, social values, or the intellectual and philosophical environment.

So much for a simple, static picture. Over a period of time, the demand curves and supply curves lose their independence and interact: a demand curve that shifts steadily to the right can shift the whole supply curve to a new position. It can induce a substantial increase in the numbers of talented men devoting themselves to science and invention; and, in turn, the achievements of such men can stimulate an interest in and awareness of their potentialities which increase the effective demand for their efforts; that is, it can shift the position of the demand curve.

How do science and invention evolve if, in fact, increased numbers of talented men devote themselves to these activities?

We assume that progress in science is cumulative and is a function of the volume of talent and resources applied to the solution of particular problems. Therefore, the development of a particular branch of science through time might be shown as a curve exhibiting, after an episodic start, with low yields, a period of gradually increasing returns; a rather dramatic breakthrough, bringing together in a new and striking way the insights previously accumulated; then a period of refinement, framed by the new paradigm, ultimately subject to diminishing returns to additional applications of talent and resources, as in figure 1.[31]

Talent and Resources Applied to a Given Branch of Science

FIG. 1. Marginal Yield in a Branch of Science

For fundamental science as a whole, the experience of the past three centuries does not permit us to predict diminishing returns. Its overall course (like that of production in growing economies) would sum up movements in numerous sectors, some in a phase of increasing returns, others in a phase of diminishing returns; some expanding rapidly, others less so, or even stagnating or declining. The marginal yield from fundamental science would exhibit a gradual rise (with breakthroughs averaged out), leveling off, at some point, when fundamental science (on a world basis) became a sufficiently massive effort to exploit economies of scale and when, in a rough-and-ready way, marginal returns were equated as among science, invention, and other forms of investment of talent and resources. Figure 2 exhibits these characteristics.

Talent and Resources Applied to Fundamental Science as a Whole

FIG. 2. Marginal Yield from Science as a Whole

Curves of similar general shape to figure 1, reflecting phases of increasing and diminishing returns, would characterize the yield from the application of talent and resources to particular lines of invention, where dramatic breakthroughs generally occurred against the background of much cumulative effort by many hands; and a curve like that in figure 2 would show the yield from invention as a whole.

We can regard, then, the pursuit of science and invention as a form of investment by societies or, as knowledge moved more freely across international boundaries, an international society. Like other forms of investment, they appear to have been subject to certain general patterns which decreed in the modern era phases of increasing and diminishing returns in particular sectors and relative overall stability in the profit rate, when the quantum of resources applied reached a certain point.

Now, how are science and invention related? The simplest assumption would be that invention in a given sector is the application to practical matters of a particular branch of fundamental science. In that case the productivity of talent cumulatively applied to invention in a given field would rise, with an appropriate time lag, as the stock of fundamental scientific knowledge was built up in the related field. Science and invention would then be closely linked in a straightforward way, with each following, suitably lagged, a pattern like that in figure 1. This close, automatic linkage of science and invention is precisely what cannot be assumed either in the early phase of the scientific revolution (from the sixteenth to the eighteenth centuries) or at present. And we shall return to this point. For present purposes, however, we can continue to assume they are closely, positively, and functionally connected, without specifying the nature of the connection.

If we take that view, what determines the areas of science and invention to which talent and resources are applied? The answer, in simple economic terms, would be that men devote their creative scientific and inventive talent to solving the problems whose solution will yield the greatest profit, as determined in the market place or by public authorities. In short, we can assume, formally, that necessity, as reflected in profitability or public policy, is the mother of science and of invention, in the sense that it determines the areas of science and the kinds of inventions developed at particular periods of time, with suitable lags required for the creative processes to work their way to solutions.

With respect to invention, there is an important element of truth in this proposition which has long been recognized,[32] although necessity (or profit) is, in itself, no guarantee that human knowledge and

ingenuity will always provide a fruitful response. The link of necessity to fundamental science is less clear. The sequence in which modern science developed (mathematics, astronomy, physics, botany,
chemistry, etc.) is related to ease of observation and tools for experiment and measurement.[33] Moreover, fields of science have an inner
life of their own, in which the participants carry forward their work,
debating and probing contrapuntally, relatively insulated from the
demands of the active world. At different times and places external
demands have played their part in shaping the lives and activities of
scientists and, to a degree, affected their work. But we are dealing with
a linkage less powerful, more remote than that which shapes the pattern of invention.

I have examined elsewhere the links between science and invention
in the critical period from Copernicus to the great innovative breakthroughs at the end of the eighteenth century.[34]

I conclude that there were three powerful but oblique linkages:
philosophical ties, the ties of scientists to toolmakers, and os-
motic ties (like those of James Watt to Professor Joseph Black) which
strengthened the inventor's hand in significant but indirect ways.
Jacob Schmookler arrived at similar conclusions about the linkage in
twentieth-century America:

> The negligible effect of individual scientific discoveries on
> individual inventions is doubtless due to the orientation of the
> typical inventor, even those well trained in science and engineer-
> ing, to the affairs of daily life in the home and industry rather
> than to the life of the intellect. The result, however, does not
> mean that science is unimportant to invention, particularly in
> recent times. Rather it suggests that, in the analysis of the effect
> of science on invention, the conceptual framework of the Gestalt
> school of psychology is perhaps more appropriate than is that of
> the mechanistic, stimulus-response school. The growth of the
> *body* of science conditions the course of invention more than
> does each separate increment. It does this by making inventors
> see things differently and by enabling them to imagine different
> solutions than would otherwise be the case. The effect of the
> growth of science is thus normally felt more from generation to
> generation than from one issue of a scientific journal to the
> next.[35]

In the end, then, the growth of the stock of scientific knowledge
does relate to the productivity of inventive activity; although the con-

nection is not the simple one postulated on page 91 above, for purposes of stylized exposition. Despite the quasi independence of science and the limitations on the proposition that necessity is the mother of invention, the pool of scientific knowledge and the pool of inventions can be regarded as a productive stock on which a society can draw. But until the innovating entrepreneur acts, science and invention represent potential, not actual, increases in the productivity of the economy.

The number of existing inventions actually incorporated in the current volume of investment at any period of time can be presented in various ways. Perhaps the most useful is to modify the familiar Keynesian marginal efficiency of capital curve by drawing above it a theoretical optimum curve in which the current demand for investment would contain within it all existing profitable inventions. The gap between the actual and optimum curves would exhibit for any society, at a particular period of time, the propensity to innovate or the quality of entrepreneurship. The level of investment (and the degree to which inventions were incorporated in the capital stock) would be determined, in the Keynesian world, by the intersection of the rate of interest (as set by the intersection of a liquidity preference curve and the supply of money) and the actual marginal efficiency of capital curve. The point to be made here is, simply, that with a given stock of inventions available, the quality of entrepreneurship—the number of entrepreneurs willing to take the risks of innovation—will help determine the productivity of actual investment outlays and the progress of the economy. This factor, like the numbers engaged in science and invention, can be influenced by noneconomic as well as economic factors at work in a given society at a particular period of time; and it may be subject to significant sectoral (as well as interregional and international) variation.

We conclude, then, that the scale of scientific activity in the world economy is a function of a recognizable investment process, although its sectoral composition is related in only a partial and dilute way to current demand; the cumulative stock of science is obliquely but significantly related to the productivity of current invention; the scale and sectoral composition of inventive activity is, like other forms of investment, significantly related to profit possibilities signaled by the price system; the innovative zeal of entrepreneurs cannot be assumed automatically to exhaust all potentially profitable inventions: the quality of innovative entrepreneurship must be specified by sectors.

VI

Now, what happens if an innovation in a particular sector is pursued over a period of time? How does the notion of rising and then declining yields from a particular inventive breakthrough (figure 1) translate itself into economics? Here there are two familiar and closely related formulations: the case of increasing returns if we are prepared to apply it to a major change in production functions, and the concept of a leading sector complex in the growth process.

Breaking from the now hoary tradition of segregating major innovations from incremental technical change (or external economies), I. D. Burnet has applied the concept to a leading sector in takeoff. Using the diagram in figure 3, Burnet describes the outcome as follows: "Contrary to one's first impression, [figure 3] is representative of an explosion rather than an equilibrium. Starting, for example, from P_1Q_1 in period T_1, industry decides to expand production in period T_2 to Q_2, which reduces costs to P_2, which inspires industry to expand production to Q_3 . . . and so on. The only constraints to the explosion are the time lags involved in accumulating capital, refining technology, acquiring tastes, training the work force and so on."[36]

After citing some famous cases of explosive growth in particular sections (from the Model T Ford to ball-point pens), he asserts: "The entrepreneur lucky enough to discover a virgin field of consumer demand can look forward to a golden age of self-generating growth."[37]

In fact, Burnet's falling supply curve must level off for any given breakthrough which lowers costs with an increase in output. Ultimately, constant or diminishing returns will set in; for trees do not grow to the sky and deceleration is inevitable, as his reference to a succession of innovations implies.

Translated from Burnet's world of the lucky entrepreneur to the path of an industry which has seized on a major technological innovation, we find that, after a possible phase of acceleration, deceleration becomes the normal path of increases in output and decreases in price. This was the powerful insight of Simon Kuznets in his *Secular Movements in Production and Prices* as he concluded: "As we observe the various industries within a given nation system, we see that the lead in development shifts from one branch to another. The main reason for this shift seems to be that a rapidly developing industry does not continue its vigorous growth indefinitely, but slackens its pace after a time, and is overtaken by industries whose period of rapid development comes later. Within any country we observe a succession of different branches of activity leading the process of develop-

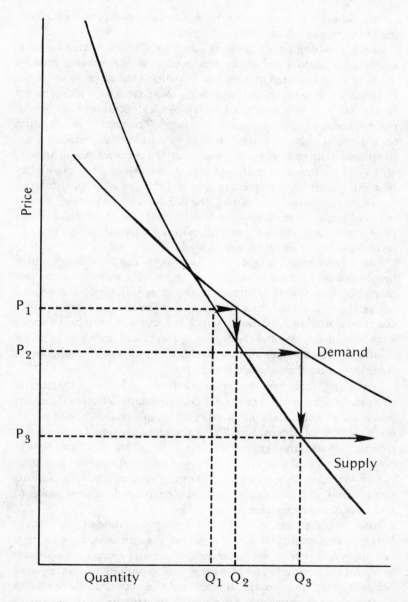

FIG. 3. The Case of Increasing Returns. (Reprinted, by permission, from I. D. Burnet, "An Interpretation of Take-Off," *Economic Record: Journal of the Economic Society of Australia and New Zealand* [September 1972], p. 425.)

ment, and in each mature industry we notice a conspicuous slackening in the rate of increase."[38]

At any period of time a growing economy is characterized by a few accelerating sectors and many decelerating sectors moving forward (or declining) at different trend rates, when cleared of short-period fluctuations. In a rough-and-ready way, these rates tend to be related to the time of the last major technological breakthrough which granted them a phase of increasing returns. The pace of deceleration for a national industry can be affected by a wide range of factors: the likelihood that technological change, after an initial breakthrough, will yield diminishing marginal reductions in cost; the possibility that the quality of entrepreneurship will decline after an industry's heroic generation of innovation; the diffusion of technology abroad may reduce a given national industry's share of the world market; price and income elasticity of demand may diminish with expanded consumption and incomes; and so forth.

The sectors enjoying high rates of growth and increasing returns link backward to those which supply them with machinery and raw materials; laterally, they stimulate the growth of cities and regions where they take hold; and they link forward through externalities and the creation of bottlenecks which it becomes profitable to widen with new inventions and innovations. The multiple impact of a new leading sector thus requires one to think in terms of a leading sector complex, rather than a single sector.

In the end, then, one economic result of the bringing together of sustained scientific, inventive, and entrepreneurial effort is the emergence of a powerful case (or cases) of increasing returns and of a leading sector complex capable of lifting the economy into a new stage of growth. Self-sustained growth requires, *inter alia*, a continued flow of creative effort in these three domains—science, invention, and innovation—yielding new cases of increasing returns and new leading sector complexes as the older impulses inevitably lose their power to lower costs and expand total production.

From its beginnings, modern economics has contained another case of increasing returns. It was recognized that, in opening up a new agricultural region or source of raw materials, a certain minimum quantum of effort and scale of acreage or of exploitation were required before the maximum marginal yield could be obtained. There was, in short, a phase of increasing returns before classic diminishing returns set in. This process, too, has its place in a dynamic theory of production.

VII

With these concepts and tools we turn now to the outline of a dynamic, disaggregated general theory of production and prices. At this stage, we shall assume that full employment is steadily maintained and that the rate of population increase and its composition (as it affects the size of the working force) are given, and the consumption function, as well.

In accordance with the previous analysis we shall assume that the available stock of scientific knowledge is being steadily built up. The sectoral composition of current scientific effort is determined partially in response to potential profit signals from the market place and the political process and partially on an autonomous basis, but it is constrained and shaped in both cases by what we might call the Rosenberg reservation; that is, the limits and possibilities of scientific advance are set and opened up by available tools and devices for experiment. The rate of buildup of the scientific stock is determined by the numbers at work in the various fields of science on a global basis (assuming scientific knowledge is fully communicated); and the numbers, in turn, are determined by a recognizable market process, including public as well as private incentives (as above, pages 94–96). By oblique routes the stock of scientific knowledge helps determine the productivity of the flow of inventions.

The scale of the flow of inventions is determined by the numbers engaged in the inventive process, again on a global basis, although the availability of inventions is more inhibited (and costly) than the transmission of scientific knowledge. The composition of the flow of inventions is a function of profitability (necessity) as determined by the private market system, supplemented by public incentives (e.g., aerospace requirements).

The path of sectoral evolution in both science and invention is assumed to follow that set out in figure 1, and we assume the scale of total effort in both domains has reached the yield plateau in figure 2.

The economic system is assumed to equate net marginal value product in all uses of resources (including fundamental science and invention) and to equate relative marginal utility in the disposition of private income (with income distribution given). Corrections for major elements of private monopoly must be made, and for the functions of public policy: in helping determine full employment; income distribution via the tax system; direct and indirect subsidy to science, invention, and other sectors; and provision of social overhead capital.

Where relevant, direct government operation of productive segments of the economic system must be specified.

The quality of entrepreneurship, as it determines the proportion of inventions actually incorporated in the current flow of investment, must also be specified; and this variable must be assumed to vary by sectors.

On the side of demand, tastes are given, as well as the income elasticity of demand.

A system of this type yields not only an aggregate level of GNP and its overall rate of increase but also optimum sectoral paths for each sector and, therefore, an optimum pattern of current investment, when both the market process (with all its imperfections) and the political process (with all its imperfections) are granted legitimacy.[39] In concept, this is a formidably complex system: in effect, a fully dynamic multisector economic model, sufficiently disaggregated to catch all changes in production functions actually introduced into the economic system, including external economy effects, other spreading effects, organizational changes, and so forth.

In fact, however, it permits in a manageable way some critically important aspects of economic progress to be isolated which are impossible to grip with either static equilibrium models or overaggregated models of the Solow-Dennison type.

First, leading sector complexes. The grand sequence of major inventive breakthroughs becomes a part of the system—that is, factory-manufactured textiles; the steam engine; modern iron metallurgy; the railroads; steel; electricity; the various major branches of chemicals; the automobile; the aerospace complex; the postautomobile age service sectors which are expanding rapidly in real terms; and so forth. In partial equilibrium analysis, we no longer need to exclude major inventive breakthroughs from the case of increasing returns. They become induced phenomena, brought about by the sustained effort of many hands, focused on the task by incentives set up by the economic system, supplemented in some cases by incentives created by public policy.

Second, the technologically older, slower-growing sectors. As Kuznets noted, the major technological changes tend to be bunched in the early years after a great inventive breakthrough.[40] This, along with other factors which decree deceleration as the normal path of a given sector, provides a significant element of shapeliness and order to a dynamic theory of production, as Kuznets's logistic curves for a wide variety of sectors demonstrated.

Third, declining sectors. Major inventive breakthroughs can significantly displace older vital sectors, as the automobile displaced the railroad, since the broad categories of final and intermediate demands (food, shelter, clothing, transport, power, etc.) can be satisfied in a variety of ways. Moreover, for a given economy, the international diffusion of inventions can shift the locus of production, sending a vital national sector into decline, when the pace of technological change fails to compensate for lower wage rates abroad. Such declines in production are usually accompanied by a decline in the quality of entrepreneurship, including a failure to introduce new technology becoming available. This process may open up at some stage the possibility of new entrepreneurs moving in to exploit profitably the gap between current costs and potentially lower costs. This happened, for example, in the British railroads and in the coal industry, with government as entrepreneur. In theoretical terms, this case illustrates the requirement of specifying by sectors the quality of entrepreneurship.

Fourth, the inputs of foodstuffs and raw materials. In general, the evidence suggests, as we are all brought up to believe, that the production of foodstuffs and raw materials is less subject to productive technological change than manufactures.[41] On the other hand, these input sectors are by no means subject to a simple, protracted operation of Ricardian diminishing returns. Indeed, major breakthroughs can occur not only through the opening up of new acreage and mineral discoveries but also from the application of new technology—for example, the application of chemical fertilizers, pesticides, new seeds, and new methods of organization in agriculture.

Fifth, social overhead capital. As we all know, a very high proportion of investment in all modernizing societies goes into housing, other forms of construction, transport, and electric power. Housing has been, historically, a sector of low productivity increase; transport has experienced a series of great inventive breakthroughs subject to retardation; electric power has followed a similar course, with significant incremental productivity improvements in the use of fuels.

From the perspective of a dynamic theory of prices, production, and investment, the point to make here is that a great deal of economic history (and, indeed, current economic activity and policy) is centered on the forces set in motion by increasing population, incomes, and urbanization, as they affect the demand and prices for foodstuffs, housing, transport, and a portion of power requirements; and by increased industrialization, as it affects the demand for raw materials, transport, and the balance of power requirements. In theory and in practice the composition of investment (including investment in inventions and exploration) cannot be understood without taking into account the incentives set up through the price system by these derived demands for the basic inputs to an advancing industrial system.

At one point, in discussing increasing returns, Dennis H. Robertson put a cogent question and gave his long-considered reply: "Can we really, even if we are careful to correct for the effect of major inventions which clearly did not depend on the scale of the industry, ever hope to get beyond what is really simply an historical record of the way costs have fallen as output has risen? . . . after a period of revolt, I am now of the opinion that the concept of a true falling long-period supply curve is one which we cannot do without, though we must handle it carefully."[42]

I am asserting a similar but not identical proposition. The structure outlined here would embrace major inventions (and leading sector complexes) within the system, and it would shift the treatment of increasing returns from firms to sectors. But, like Robertson, I conclude that we need to deal formally with the dynamic case of increasing returns (in the wide sense used here) if we are to have a serious theory of production and prices; for in a modern dynamic economy, all sectors are, in fact or potentially, subject to increasing returns.

I would go further. It is precisely the kind of dynamic sectoral map outlined here—with implicit or explicit notions of optimum sectoral paths—which intelligent economic planners carry in their heads in both socialist and mixed economies. As planners set their sectoral targets and formulate their investment programs, what else are they doing but seeking to define optimum sectoral paths and to guide the economy along them? And, if they are wise, they initiate action (sometimes by inducing private capital imports, but by other means as well) to improve the quality of entrepreneurship in critical sectors, including the introduction of major new technologies. A good development planner knows the leading sector complexes appropriate to his nation's stage of growth and nurtures them; is concerned to avoid a falling off in the quality of entrepreneurship in older, slower-growing or declining sectors; and provides for the requisite foundation of supporting inputs from agriculture, raw material sources, and social overhead capital, seeking always greater efficiency in these sectors where productivity increases are harder to come by. In mixed economies he is also concerned that elements of monopoly in the private sector (including those induced by excessive protectionism) do not distort the price system and frustrate the full utilization of capacity and the optimum flow of innovation. He will also be using the government's influence over the flows of credit and capital to back not only the sectors which require expansion but also, within them, the entrepreneurs of greatest quality. In command economies, burdened with trying to plan the whole, he will be struggling to create the equivalent of a competitive pricing system (in part as the basis for an optimum allocation of capital to the sectors) and to establish a system of incentives and rewards to elevate the quality of entrepreneurship.

In advanced economies like those of the United States and Western Europe (after postwar reconstruction), the planners have mainly (not wholly) confined their attention to the environment of aggregate demand, the rate of inflation, and the foreign balance. And we shall comment on these familiar matters at a later point. The implicit assumption was that optimum dynamic sectoral paths (including the optimum scale and composition of invention) would be generated by the competitive private sectors within this framework. And in the stage of high mass-consumption, where the diffusion of the automobile, a suburban house, and a standard package of durable consumers goods to a large proportion of the population constituted the leading sector complex, this was a tolerably realistic way to proceed, leaving for the state the primary task of providing the requisite roads, schools, and public utilities, as well as the other social services decreed by the political process. But as we move into a time when the inputs of food, energy, air, water, and, perhaps, basic raw materials are in question, we shall face—and, indeed, already are facing—the need for more explicit sectoral planning on a national and international basis.

In short, we have been talking prose for some time; that is, while the main body of formal economic theory has gone its way in terms of essentially static micro- and macro-theory, plus overaggregated growth models of limited relevance, those charged with shaping national economies (including the major institutions providing external assistance) have been operating in terms of dynamic, disaggregated sectoral models which carry with them implicit if not explicit notions of optimum sectoral paths. If rendered explicit, those models would approximate that outlined here.

VIII

And, in fact, a redoubtable band of planning theorists and econometricians have been working their way toward such a disaggregated, dynamic model since the mid-1950's, spurred on by the challenge of providing a rigorous framework for policy in and toward developing nations where, palpably, many assumptions of classical equilibrium analysis do not apply.[43] From the special perspective of this paper two of their lines of approach have particular significance.

One line of approach is illustrated by Larry E. Westphal's *Planning Investments with Economies of Scale*. He introduces the possibility of economies of scale into a dynamic input-output model of the economy of South Korea and explores the optimum timing for two industrial plants which require a high proportion of total investment: a petrochemical complex and an integrated steel mill. Here the question of increasing returns is directly addressed. The central issue is when, in relation to assumed time-paths of domestic demand, the plants should be built, with prior reliance on imports and rapid movement into export markets for the period until domestic demand catches up with capacity, in order to exploit the advantages of increasing returns that go with full capacity utilization.

A second line of approach is incorporated in Hollis Chenery and Lance Taylor, "Development Patterns: Among Countries and Over Time," published in the *Review of Economics and Statistics*, November 1968. They break away from the tyranny of overaggregation (in the form of primary versus industrial sectors) and correlate the relative importance of various types of industries (in terms of share of GNP) with the rise of GNP per capita for a large group of contemporary nations. They group the industrial sectors in terms of "early," "middle," and "late" industries. As noted in Appendix B of the second edition of my *Stages of Economic Growth* ([Cambridge: At the University Press, 1971], pp. 230–233), these groupings roughly approximate the leading sectors for take-off, the drive to technological maturity, and high mass-consumption.

If further developed and related to each other, these two approaches could move us further toward a fully dynamic system. Specifically, the Chenery-Taylor approach requires further disaggregation so that the typical paths of industrial expansion are revealed in the detail required for, say, an investment planner in a developing nation. These would constitute a kind of planner's guide, like the ex post optimum sectoral paths considered in *The Process of Economic Growth* (see note 34). They would also represent a generalization of the sectoral time paths presented in Kuznets's *Secular Movements in Production and Prices*.

In fact, of course, the optimum sectoral path for any particular economy will not be identical with these ex post Chenery-Taylor averages. In David A. Kendrick's phrase, realistic model building "is more of an art than a science."[44] Certainly a realistic model for a particular economy over a particular period of time must be approximated sensitively in terms of its unique features. Nevertheless, a more disaggregated version of the Chenery-Taylor calculations would help.[45]

With Chenery-Taylor curves sufficiently disaggregated and adjusted for the unique circumstances of a particular economy and time period, the kind of sectoral and project analysis of investment represented by the work of Westphal and Kornai would have a firmer base than at present. In fact, a theoretical optimum pattern of industrial investment would flow directly from such curves, when interdependencies were taken into account, which, up to a point, present computer technology permits model builders to do.

In general, then, the imperatives of investment planning in developing nations have led to major advances in dynamic theory, which embrace some aspects of technological change, including significant aspects of the case of increasing returns. Important limitations, of course, remain. For example, the existing pool of technology is taken as given. These models do not deal with the dynamic interplay of science and technology. The quality of entrepreneurship is either not dealt with or embraced in interesting but rather abstract and over-aggregated calculations of absorptive capacity. Partly because they lack a refined Chenery-Taylor sectoral map, they do not make clear the role of leading sectors in growth; and the spreading effects that go with a fast-moving leading sector complex are inadequately measured in present multisectoral models—for example, what I call lateral spreading effects are not taken into account. But, in the long history of economic thought, the planning econometricians are beginning to make a serious dent on problems long set aside or swept under the rug by empty devices of formal elegance.

IX

In the end, of course, a dynamic disaggregated sectoral model on a national basis must be linked to neo-Keynesian income analysis and to the imperatives of balance-of-payments equilibrium.[46] The imperatives of avoiding inflation and controlling the foreign balance impose constraints on the planner. In a dynamic developing nation he must establish priorities in sectoral investment, foregoing or postponing desirable low-priority outlays to avoid inflation, with a given consumption function. He may have to constrain imports below the level he would like and allocate more resources to the generation of exports. If there is substantial unemployment or partial unemployment, he faces a challenge: to expand outlays (hopefully, productive labor-intensive investment) in ways compatible with the stability of the foreign balance.

In this familiar terrain of economic analysis and policy, I would underline only one point which flows from the mode of analysis developed here. It is conventional in contemporary income analysis to focus on the overall level of investment. In multiplier-accelerator analyses of business cycles, for example, the upper turning point comes about because the rate of increase in total output tapers off when full employment is approached, reducing the level of investment, and/or there is a tendency to slide down the curve of the marginal efficiency of capital, as total investment expands, or for the marginal efficiency of capital curve to shift inward. In Kaldor's analysis of increasing returns, for example, it is the volume of investment which determines those increases in efficiency included within his definition of the case.

In fact, neither the path of business fluctuations nor the path of growth (including the course of productivity in the economy) can be understood without reference to the composition of investment. Historically, business cycles have each been marked by definable leading sectors, often also leading sectors in growth (e.g., cotton textiles, railroads, etc.), but sometimes supporting sectors, requiring expansion for balance in the system, whose profitability is signaled by relative price movements (e.g., the opening up of new agricultural areas, housing, etc.). The downturns can only be understood in terms of an expected decline in profitability in those leading sectors: costs rise as relatively full employment approaches; while increased capacity, brought about by prior investment in the leading sectors, also reduces the expected profitability of further investment in those particular directions. Similarly, the scale of investment at a particular period of time (as well as its composition) is often determined by the attractiveness of investment in certain key sectors, as determined by new technologies or the possibility of absorbing efficiently into the economy already existing technologies. The possibility of major technological change can determine the direction and, even, the scale of investment. In Britain and continental Europe, for example, the proportion of income invested rose during the railway age; and in Europe of the 1950's, the scale as well as the pattern of investment was affected by the arrival of levels of per capita income which permitted the technologies associated with high mass-consumption to be absorbed efficiently in the automobile and related industries.

Thus, the exercise of even the most familiar and most widely accepted elements of Keynesian income analysis requires a degree of disaggregation and a degree of explicit attention to the interplay between the sectors and the aggregates which is not yet conventional.

x

To return to my central theme, Ayres anticipated well the current phase of disabuse with static equilibrium analysis of prices and production. He was also correct in arguing that the flow of technological change be brought toward the center of the stage in any modern economic theory worthy of the name.

But it is not sufficient to inveigh against static equilibrium analysis and to list in a sadistic or masochistic spirit the formidable array of unrealistic assumptions required for its logical exposition. The complications which must be introduced to render economic analysis realistic are considerable, but not insurmountable; and, without excessive strain, the complex process which lies behind the flow of technology into a modern economic system can be rendered substantially endogenous, if we are prepared to widen the frame within which we view the economy. A dynamic post-Walrasian general theory of production and prices is not an impossible dream, if we are prepared to sacrifice margins of elegance for essential elements of realism. Indeed, as I have noted, economic planners and planning theorists, as well as economic historians, have been able to make considerable sense of a world of changing production functions and increasing returns without abandoning important segments of conventional price and production theory. But we could do better. In the current debate on the future of economics it would be well to break through Marshall's painful frustration and, together, with our various insights and tools, address directly "the high theme of economic progress."

As I wrote on another occasion:

> It follows from this notion of sectoral patterns that there is, in theory, an optimum balanced sectoral map which an economy would follow in dynamic equilibrium, and an optimum balanced pattern of investment.
>
> But in real life economies do not work out their destinies by following neat balanced equilibrium paths. These paths are distorted by imperfections in the private investment process, by the policies of governments, and by the impact of wars. They reflect business-cycles and trend-periods. Nevertheless, the economic

history of growing societies takes a part of its rude shape from the effort of societies to approximate the optimum sectoral paths . . . They seek an equilibrium never attained.[47]

This dynamic disaggregated mode of analysis, linked to modern income and balance-of-payments analysis, is, I believe, the correct road to Allyn Young's "moving equilibrium," to Kornai's "broader synthesis," and to Kaldor's "different conceptual framework." It is also an appropriate response to Clarence Ayres's insistence that economic theory cease to be Hamlet without the Prince.

NOTES

In the preparation of this essay I was given valuable bibliographical or other guidance by Wendell Gordon, Nicholas Kaldor, David Kendrick, Simon Kuznets, Emmette Redford, and Robert Solow.

1. Alfred Marshall, *Principles of Economics* (London: Macmillan and Co., 1930), p. 461.

2. C. E. Ayres, *Toward a Reasonable Society* (Austin: University of Texas Press, 1961), pp. 27–28.

3. In the case of Ayres, a part of the difficulty was his strong and complex emotional reaction to modern science and scientists, a theme which dominates *Science: The False Messiah* (Indianapolis: Bobbs-Merrill Co., 1927). In his conclusion (p. 294) he asserts that "machine technology was not derived from science, but crept upon us after a fashion of its own." He also denies a link between necessity and invention with this aphorism: "Inventions are provided not to suit the needs of civilization but according to the development of science and invention" (p. 295). It is not difficult to see how these propositions, taken together, led Ayres to deal with the flow of technology as an autonomous phenomenon not lucidly linked to either science or incentives set up by the working of the economic system. Later he referred to science and technology as "inseparable," but he did not pursue this theme (*Toward a Reasonable Society*, p. 7).

4. This point is developed fully in the author's *How It All Began: Origins of the Modern Economy* (New York: McGraw-Hill Book Co., 1975).

5. Dwight H. Perkins, "Government as an Obstacle to Industrialization: The Case of Nineteenth Century China," *Journal of Economic History* 27 (December 1967): 485.

6. C. E. Ayres, *The Theory of Economic Progress*, 2nd ed. (New York: Schocken Books, 1962), pp. xvi–xvii.

7. For a subtle discussion of this weakness in Smith's analysis, see R. Koebner, "Adam Smith and the Industrial Revolution," *Economic History Review*, 2nd ser., 11, no. 3 (1959): 381–391. The quoted sentence is from p. 382.

8. See Adam Smith, "Effects of the Progress of Improvement upon the Real Price of Manufactures," chap. 11 in *Wealth of Nations*, bk. 1 (London: George Routledge and Sons, 1890).

9. Alfred Marshall, *Principles of Economics*, 8th ed. (London: Macmillan and Co., 1930), p. 461.

10. As I noted in *The Process of Economic Growth* (2nd ed., [Oxford: Clarendon Press, 1960], p. 6), Marshall also dealt with the problem of increasing returns in Appendix J, pars. 8 and 10, in *Money, Credit, and Commerce* (1923; reprint ed., Clifton, N.J.: Augustus M. Kelley, Publishers, 1975). These paragraphs are entitled, significantly: "Hindrances to the isolation for separate study of tendencies of Increasing Return to capital and labour in the production of a country's exports" and "Diagrams representing the case of Exceptional Supply, in which the exports of a country show strong general tendencies to Increasing Return, are deprived of practical interest by the inapplicability of the Statical Method to such tendencies." Marshall was impressed by the wide range of forces that might affect the long-period course of output and price. In both Appendix H and his treatment of the case of Exceptional Supply, he referred to the impact on demand of prior dramatic lowering of supply curves—i.e., of consumption habits built up over time by the nature and cheapness of supplies available. He noted, for example, the price inelasticity of British demand for cotton during the American Civil War, which in part could be attributed to the previous decline in price and growth in the habit of cotton using it induced. More generally, long-period analysis troubled him because demand and supply became interdependent and historical developments were not fully reversible. Equilibrium could not, therefore, be exhibited in terms of a static analysis.

11. Marshall, *Principles of Economics*, pp. 378–379.

12. Ibid., p. 460.

13. Ibid.

14. Allyn Young, "Increasing Returns and Economic Progress," *Economic Journal* 38 (December 1928): 527–542. A. C. Pigou dealt with the case of increasing returns extensively in his *The Economics of Welfare* (1920). His interest was primarily in how this case disrupted

the rules of general equilibrium, related to monopoly, and bore on tax policy. It was this study which led to J. H. Clapham's "Of Empty Boxes," (*Economic Journal* 32 [September 1922]: 305–314). Clapham's target was Pigou's use of the concept of increasing and diminishing returns industries. His attack set off a first-class controversy, fruitful in a number of directions—notably Piero Sraffa's fathering of the modern theory of imperfect (or monopolistic) competition ("The Law of Returns under Competitive Conditions," *Economic Journal* 36 [December 1926]: 535–550). But the relation of technology to the price system, as considered here, was not much advanced.

Among the participants in the "Empty Boxes" debate, D. H. Robertson sedulously kept the unresolved issue of increasing returns alive. See, for example, his "Those Empty Boxes" (*Economic Journal* 34 [March 1924]: 16–31) and his later observations in *Lectures on Economic Principles* (London: Staples Press, 1957), especially pp. 116–121. I record in the Introduction to *The Process of Economic Growth* (p. 6) Robertson's salutary warning to me about the pitfalls of the Marshallian long period as I began work on that book in 1949.

It should also be noted that G. T. Jones, in an original and creative study, tried to give rigor to the notion of increasing returns and to measure its operation in a selected group of British and American industries over the period 1850–1910 (*Increasing Return*, ed. Colin Clark [Cambridge: At the University Press, 1933]). But, following Marshall, Jones excluded the "epoch-making discoveries (e.g., the steam engine, the electric motor, the internal combustion engine) . . . Such discoveries are the creators of new industries rather than economies reaped from the growth of the old" (p. 15).

15. Young, "Increasing Returns and Economic Progress," p. 533.

16. Ibid., p. 535.

17. Ibid., p. 534, n. 2.

18. Ibid., p. 534.

19. Ibid., p. 535.

20. For a further discussion and criticism of multiplier-accelerator analysis, see the author's *Process of Economic Growth*, pp. 92–96.

21. Richard M. Goodwin, "Secular and Cyclical Aspects of the Multiplier and the Accelerator," chap. 5 in *Income, Employment, and Public Policy: Essays in Honor of Alvin H. Hansen* (New York: W. W. Norton and Co., 1948), pp. 124–132; quotation on p. 129.

22. For a more thorough exploration of Harrod's limiting assumptions, see the author's *Process of Economic Growth*, pp. 86–91. J. E. Meade's *A Neo-Classical Theory of Economic Growth* (London: Allen

and Unwin, 1961) is developed under similar inhibiting assumptions, explicitly excluding "economies of large-scale production, external economies, market forms other than the perfectly competitive, and so on" (p. v). It should be noted that Harrod's formulation triggered a lively exploration of the conditions required for the long-run neutrality of innovations and the long-run approximate stability of the shares of labor and capital in the distribution of income (see, notably, Charles Kennedy, "Induced Bias in Innovation and the Theory of Distribution," *Economic Journal* 74 [September 1964]: 541–547; Paul A. Samuelson, "A Theory of Induced Innovation Along Kennedy-Weisacker Lines," *Review of Economics and Statistics* 47 [November 1965]: 343–356; Charles Kennedy, "Samuelson on Induced Innovation," and Paul A. Samuelson's "Rejoinder," *Review of Economics and Statistics* 48 [November 1966: 442–444, 444–448]).

The Kennedy-Samuelson exchange does, in a highly abstract way, relate a part of the process of innovation to the market process. But, in the special perspective of this essay, it suffers three weaknesses. First, innovation emerges, once again, as a diffuse incremental process, with no serious attention devoted to the relations among science, invention, and innovation, except for Samuelson's observation in "A Theory of Induced Innovation" (pp. 353 and 355) that, after some major breakthrough, creative scientists have an instinct as to where the next promising line of inventive activity lies. Second, the character of invention and innovation is dealt with only as it relates to a capital- or labor-saving bias, leaving, as in other analyses of this type, a critical unexamined role for "exogenous technical changes." Third, the theoretical conditions for approximate long-run stability in distributive shares in a technically advancing economy with the supply of capital increasing faster than the supply of labor are explored with no empirical reference to the process by which that (very rough) stability has been achieved. In fact, the trend in distributive shares has varied—for example, in Britain between, say, the periods 1873–1896 and 1896–1914 (see the author's *British Economy of the Nineteenth Century* [Oxford: Clarendon Press, 1948], chap. 4, "Investment and Real Wages, 1873–86," and the Appendix, "Mr. Kalecki on the Distribution of Income, 1880–1913").

While recognizing the theoretical validity of the issues examined in the Kennedy-Samuelson exchange, I would suggest that the relation between patterns of investment and innovation, on the one hand, and distributive shares, on the other, are more likely to be illuminated by a study of how these relationships have unfolded by sectors through time than by a specification of the conditions for their aggregate stability—among other reasons because of the substantial role played by the relative prices of foodstuffs in income distribution, a factor which does not figure in the highly aggregated Kennedy-Samuelson formulations. Only a much more disaggregated and more dynamic model (of the kind laid out in secs. 4–7 of my essay), embracing opportunities and pressures for invention and innovation arising from the income elasticity of demand and diminishing returns in the input sectors of the economy, is capable of rendering invention a truly induced phenomenon. The assumption of a higher rate of increase in capital than labor in a two-factor single or dual commodity model does not suffice, either for that purpose or for a realistic explanation of distributive shares.

23. Paul A. Samuelson, *Economics*, 7th ed., (New York: McGraw-Hill Book Co., 1967).

24. Janos Kornai, *Anti-Equilibrium* (Amsterdam-London: North-Holland Publishing Co., 1971), p. 373.

25. Nicholas Kaldor, "The Irrelevance of Equilibrium Economics," *Economic Journal* 82 (December 1972): 1237–1255.

26. Ibid., p. 1240.

27. Ibid., p. 1246.

28. Ibid., p. 1255.

29. Ibid., p. 1249.

30. The way of looking at science, invention, and innovation outlined here is more fully developed in the author's *Process of Economic Growth*, especially chaps. 2 and 3.

31. A curve of this kind is implicit in the analysis of Thomas S. Kuhn, *The Structure of Scientific Revolutions* (Chicago: University of Chicago Press, 1962 and 1970). For a sustained debate on Kuhn's propositions and his response, see Imre Lakatos and Alan Musgrave, eds., *Criticism and the Growth of Knowledge* (Cambridge: At the University Press, 1970). For formulation of a similar sequence, see the author's *Process of Economic Growth*, pp. 62–63, including the relevant footnotes, where the difficulty of defining the economic yield from fundamental science is discussed.

32. See, notably, Jacob Schmookler, *Invention and Economic Growth* (Cambridge, Mass.: Harvard University Press, 1966). For earlier discussions of invention as an economically induced phenomenon, see A. P. Usher, *History of Mechanical Inventions* (New York: McGraw-Hill Book Co., 1929); S. C. Gilfillan, *The Sociology of Invention* (Chicago: Follett Publishing Co., 1935); R. S. Sayers, "The

Springs of Technical Progress in Britain, 1919–1939," *Economic Journal* 60, no. 238 (June 1950): 275–291, especially p. 282; and T. S. Ashton, *The Industrial Revolution, 1760–1830* (London: Oxford University Press, 1948), pp. 91–92. J. Schumpeter's indecisive discussion of this question should also be noted (*Business Cycles* [New York: McGraw-Hill Book Co., 1939], 1: 85, n.). Schumpeter allows not only for the existence of inventions and innovations induced by necessity but also for inventions not related to any particular requirement or not related to the requirement met by the particular innovation that incorporates them. Schumpeter states: "It might be thought that innovation can never be anything else but an effort to cope with a given economic situation. In a sense this is true. For a given innovation to become possible, there must always be some 'objective needs' to be satisfied and certain 'objective conditions'; but they rarely, if ever, uniquely determine what kind of innovation will satisfy them, and as a rule they can be satisfied in many different ways. Most important of all, they may remain unsatisfied for an indefinite time, which shows that they are not in themselves sufficient to produce an innovation." The issue is discussed in the author's *Process of Economic Growth*, pp. 83–86.

33. Nathan Rosenberg has discussed this point thoughtfully—and the limits it set on Schmookler's basic thesis—in "Science, Invention, and Economic Growth," *Economic Journal* 84, no. 333 (March 1974): 90–108.

34. W. W. Rostow, *How It All Began*, chap. 4.

35. Jacob Schmookler, *Invention and Economic Growth*, p. 200.

36. I. D. Burnet, "An Interpretation of Take-Off," *Economic Record* (September 1972): 424–428. The quotation is from p. 424 and the figure from p. 425.

37. Ibid., p. 425.

38. Simon Kuznets, *Secular Movements in Production and Prices* (Boston and New York: Houghton Mifflin Co., 1930), pp. 4–5. Also, Rostow, *Process of Economic Growth*, pp. 80–103. Kuznets did not relate his study to the theoretical literature on increasing returns. *The Process of Economic Growth* is presented as "an effort to explore a method for permitting the introduction of (Marshallian) long-period factors into economic analysis," including increasing returns (pp. 5–8).

39. In developing this system at greater length in *The Process of Economic Growth* (chap. 4), formal difficulties with the concept of an ex ante optimum pattern are examined, stemming from the impossi-

bility of predicting precisely the content of new inventions and shifts in the social and political framework of the economy (pp. 97–98). The concept of an ex post equilibrium is also introduced and illustrated, and its usefulness discussed (pp. 98–103). For present limited purposes this distinction between ex ante and ex post is not necessary, for we are assuming the stock of science and inventions as given, as well as the political and social framework of the economy, notably as it affects public policy and the quality of entrepreneurship by sectors.

40. Kuznets, *Secular Movements in Production and Prices*, especially pp. 11–35.

41. See, for example, Kuznets's calculations of the changing ratio of value added to the cost of raw materials in a number of industries, ibid., pp. 41–49.

42. Robertson, *Lectures on Economic Principles*, pp. 116–117.

43. The literature in this field is well summarized in the Selected Bibliography set out in Larry E. Westphal, *Planning Investments with Economies of Scale* (Amsterdam-London: North-Holland Publishing Co., 1971, pp. 365–370). See also references attached to David A. Kendrick's chap. 8, "Systems Problems in Economic Development," in *Economics of Engineering and Social Systems*, ed. J. M. English (New York: Wiley, 1972), pp. 323–324. To these listings should be added the work of Janos Kornai, notably *Mathematical Planning of Structural Decisions* (1967) and *Anti-Equilibrium* (1971), both published by North-Holland Publishing Co., Amsterdam-London. In particular, Kornai's analysis of the planning implications of increasing returns in a particular industry (man-made fibers) (*Mathematical Planning*, pp. 99–107) belongs in the same family of studies as Westphal's analysis referred to above.

44. David A. Kendrick, "Systems Problems in Economic Development," p. 216.

45. It should be noted that the shape of disaggregated Chenery-Taylor curves is not merely a function of GNP per capita levels (and the income elasticity of demand for consumers goods): like Kuznets's secular trend production curves, the Chenery-Taylor curves also reflect factors on the supply side (including increasing returns) which, in time, yield retardation in particular sectors, as new technologies are introduced into an economy and progressively exploited.

46. For a discussion of this model in relation to the possibilities of inflation and unemployment, see the author's *Process of Economic Growth*, especially pp. 86–96, and chap. 5, "Growth and Business

Cycles." Development planning models have, from the beginning, been sensitive to the foreign balance, given the critical role of imports of capital equipment and the implicit or explicit interest of the analysts in the level of foreign aid.

47. W. W. Rostow, *Politics and the Stages of Growth* (Cambridge: At the University Press, 1971), p. 19.

Limits to Growth:
Biospheric or Institutional?

JOSEPH J. SPENGLER

> In this state of temporary suspension of the critical faculty, we
> find it very easy to believe that science will provide. Our oil may
> be exhausted: science will find another way; our population may
> multiply like flies: science will provide food. Science will pre-
> vent war after the formula of Alfred Nobel by making it too
> dangerous to risk.—Ayres, *Science: The False Messiah*, p. 253

Many themes run through the work of Clarence Ayres, themes rang-
ing from the shortcomings of science, far more stressed in his early
than in his later work, to the defects of the capitalist economy.[1]
He found received economics subject to criticism on a number of
grounds, among them its emphasis upon price and the market, its
theory of human behavior, its conception of capital, and its failure to
explain how the economy functioned—a failure traceable to imperfect
analysis of pecuniary, allocative, and other economic institutions and
structures.[2] While he looked upon "growth" and "abundance" as
components of the set of goals of an industrial society, he did not
subordinate this set to "growth" as became common in the 1950's
and 1960's, when "the goal of economic growth ... achieved the
status of a secular religion."[3]

Ayres sought to explain the behavior of a society and its economy
in terms of that society's institutions.[4] He was a continuator, along
with Walton Hamilton and Wesley Clair Mitchell, of a tradition and
approach implicit in Marx and later authenticated by Thorstein Veblen, undergirded by the social philosophy of John Dewey, and com-
plemented by the work of John R. Commons. Of particular concern to
Ayres was the ascendancy and persistence of cultural fixity in society,
together with the circumstances making for the replacement of cultural stasis by cultural change—a concern to whose understanding
W. F. Ogburn and P. A. Sorokin, among others, contributed notably.[5]
In its emphasis upon the importance of institutional structures
Ayres's analysis is remindful of that of Plato and of Marx, who found
in structure a limit to growth; it is remindful also of D'Arcy W.
Thompson's discussion of the restriction of growth by form.[6]

My discussion will deal mainly with an issue that runs through much of Ayres's work, an issue of much greater import today than at the time Ayres's views were taking shape, namely, whether in the long run the limits to growth lie outside man or within him. In the shorter run, of course, these limits may lie alternatively within man in the sense of his concerns, acquired capacities, collective undertakings, and so forth, and outside him in the form of physical barriers which become temporarily limitational. At different times in man's history one or the other of these two sets of constraints has been stressed by commentators, at least temporarily. In the long run, however, one or the other should become essentially ascendant. Before turning to this issue, however, note may be taken of Ayres's treatment of economic theory.

AYRES ON THEORY

While Ayres was correct in emphasizing that the price system was imbedded in a matrix of institutions that condition the performance of the price system and the market,[7] his critique would have proved more effective had he broken up the market and dealt with it in parts, as might an operations theorist. His attack, despite his criticisms of noncompetitive behavior, had too much the appearance of a barrage attack.[8] For example, had he taken into account the limitedness and/ or exhaustibility of natural resources and the consequent degree to which sole reliance upon the price system makes for mal-allocation of these resources over time and hence among current uses, he might have been more persuasive. He might even have drawn attention to two conditions essential to the optimal functioning of the price system as an assembler and communicator of intelligence and as an allocator of actual and potential inputs—conditions usually missing. (1) The price system may carry a number of messages from among which responders must select those which are critical and then respond thereto. Responders may fail to do this because some of their response thresholds are too elevated and insensitive, with the result that response is confined to less important or insignificant stimuli. (2) The time horizons of biosphere-oriented prices may be quite out of line with the time spans of the biospheric processes to which these prices refer.

We may illustrate what has been said. (1) The world of information, of which the price system is but one of several or more conveyers, may generate signals, feedbacks, and so forth, in such a way that the potential responder is swamped, confused, and hence made incapable of interpreting adequately the flow of signals. (2) The function of future prices, as Gustav Cassel might have put it, is that of providing us with information regarding the future and making possible decisions in the present that optimize the stream of events associated with the process of transforming a temporally Continuing Future into a temporally Continuing Present. In reality, however, the time range of future prices and pricing does not map well upon sets of processes which may be of long as well as of varying duration, with the result that future pricing often tends to distort the significance of the future for the present. Moreover, this distortion may be further accentuated by pervasive uncertainty and by the degree to which ideology and a Boehm-Bawerkian emphasis upon the Present makes for disparity between the Future as viewed in the Present and the Future when it becomes Present.

The energy crisis is a case in point. The price system gave a distorted and misleading view of the future and thus desensitized the mass of population, together with its alleged leaders, to responding intelligently to nonprice signals. Partly responsible, of course, is what may be called Gresham's Law of Information; for, according to this law, Unwarrantedly Optimistic Information always drives out Warrantedly Unfavorable Information. This law continues to operate and hence to accentuate Future-Worsening Forces, probably in so great a measure that, over the long run, the contribution of assets by present to future generations may prove negative on balance instead of as highly positive as one might infer from present generations' continuing bequest of human, tangible, and intangible assets to future generations. Perhaps periodic Kiplingesque "Recessionals" are in order if this balance is to be kept positive.

With regard to Ayres's conception of institutional economics, it may be noted that he viewed the content and dynamics of institutions and institutional economics as part of a kind of moving and expanding stream which included Deweyism, empiricism, Darwinism, and related forces. It was the momentum of this stream rather than the efforts of particular individuals that carried it along. "Institutionalism appears clearly as a single intellectual massif, and as such a significant part of the whole intellectual landscape of our time."[9] "It is the altogetherness of this process that is most significant."[10] It thus resembles the momentum of the stream of forces underlying economic growth in recent decades. In the early thirties there was also a heritage of improvement in the air, and this facilitated the acceptance of both Keynesian and institutional views[11] even as did concern at weaknesses in the contemporary economy.[12]

Ayres's institutionalism was loosely structured and hence failed to incorporate and integrate components both of received price and related theory and of institutional theory. The economic analyst who would stress institutions may pursue one or the other of two courses of action. He may try to convert economics into an essentially behavioral science, or he may include institutions in his economic models and thus make them map more closely upon that portion of economic reality which is under analysis. The former approach is not very useful in that it entails throwing away much of the apparatus of economic analysis. The latter approach retains this apparatus and strengthens it as required.

What has been said may be illustrated. Let us write

$$B_i = f\,(s_i,\, p_b,\, p_s,\, e_i)$$

where B_i denotes the economically oriented behavior of individuals composing a population, and s_i denotes the stimuli (mainly prices of inputs and outputs, negative prices or implicit costs, taxes, income changes) directly incident upon individuals in the form of penalties and rewards, to changes in which individuals respond in the short run though subject to constraints issuing out of p_b, p_s, and e_i. Here p_b denotes physical parameters of state and p_s social or institutional parameters of state; e_i is a residual environmental category, some components of which (e.g., expectations and stock of money) affect B_i. Microeconomics deals mainly with s_i, in which the potential rate of change is usually high, whereas macroeconomics deals mainly with relevant components of e_i, which, even when subject to change in the short run, are sensed only generally rather than specifically and in ways not so clearly perceivable and interpretable by each individual as when he experiences changes in s_i. The impact of p_b and p_s is not easily perceived and assessed, nor are components of p_b and p_s subject to much change in the short run. Yet accomplishment of such changes in the long run may greatly affect s_i and e_i and hence B_i.

Institutionalists stress the importance of p_s, of man's societal institutions, but not, as a rule, the importance of p_b, believing its significance to be subject to governance through p_s. Moreover, institutionalists tend to underrate the importance of s_i, especially prices, whereas economic analysts in the orthodox tradition tend to underrate the importance of p_s and constraints originating in p_b and perhaps to overestimate the manipulatability of components of e_i.

CHANGE: ITS COURSE BEFORE 1800

I turn now to the course of change before 1800. In an age when the belief is widespread that "progressive change is king" it is not easy to imagine that at one time it was otherwise—especially when this belief is reinforced by the high rate of scientific and technological progress characteristic of recent decades, sometimes described as a knowledge explosion (albeit but a pale replica of the self-congratulatory print explosion which came in its wake). Yet, as Ayres was aware and as Robert A. Nisbet has pointed out, "Change is, however, *not* 'natural,' *not* normal, much less ubiquitous and constant. Fixity is . . . if we look at actual social behavior, in place and in time, we find over and over that persistence in time is far the more common condition of things . . . fixity, not change, is the required point of departure for the study of *not merely social order but social change.*"[13] Even the Renaissance, usually pictured as a golden age of salutary change, has many earmarks of a myth created in the nineteenth century, when a general philosophy of progress was ascendant.[14]

The first eighteen centuries of the Christian Era witnessed what was an almost imperceptible increase in man's numbers and the level of his material lot, with reverses sweeping away many if not all of the gains associated with temporary upsurges. In the first millenium after Christ in Europe, an ecclesiastical age unmarked by material progress,[15] population in Europe, as in the world as a whole, increased only in the neighborhood of 0.3 percent per decade. Over the next 750 years, Europe's population grew more rapidly and irregularly but at an overall rate of about 1.6 percent per decade and hence somewhat faster than the world's population, though at a rate less than one-tenth of that to be experienced in 1750–1950.[16] Product per capita, at a minimum level in post–Roman Europe around A.D. 900–1000, grew something like 1.6 percent per decade over the whole period 1000–1850 compared with 14–24 percent per decade in the following century.[17] In England and Wales (where classical political economy acquired its pristine form), product per capita grew about 1.9 percent per decade between 1695–1715 and 1765–1785 and 6.2 percent per decade over the ensuing forty years; the comparable rate in the United Kingdom between 1920–1924 and 1963–1967 was 16.9 percent.[18]

Over a long time, therefore—despite the sense some medieval and Renaissance authors had and reported of salutary change after A.D. 1000, of the quickening of the forces of change after the Age of Discovery, and of the shift of the center of European power from the

Mediterranean to the Atlantic—the European economy had the appearance of being nearly stagnant. Progressive change, albeit slow, was not wholly absent, however. Indeed, per capita incomes in the preindustrial stage of Europe's developed countries had risen by 1700–1800 to something like two to four times those achieved in the world's underdeveloped countries as of the 1950's.[19]

VISTAS OF THE FUTURE IN THE EIGHTEENTH AND NINETEENTH CENTURIES

By 1700 conditions had become satisfactory enough for many to shift their concern from a soporific transcendental future to a temporally more exciting mundane one. Their horizons were not, however, those of the bulk of the inhabitants of "pain" economies, convincingly described by the author of the *Panchatantra* over two millennia before learned sociologists began to write about the "culture of poverty." For, as he observed, "Until a mortal's belly-pot / is full, he does not care a jot" for music, wit, virtue, wisdom, scholarly fame, and so forth.[20]

Early exponents of the theory of progress turned to the contents of the minds of men and sought therein, in some measure as Ayres was to do later, the source of the forces retarding the improvement of man's lot.[21] These theoreticians, dating from the late seventeenth century (if not earlier), became lyrical in the following century and asserted that man's lot would continue to improve.[22] For, even as the present was better than the past, so would the future be better than the present, provided that false doctrines and institutions based thereupon were done away with.[23] Moreover, things might be set right at little cost, for Nature was inherently good and man, essentially the product of his environment—that is, of nature and the institutions surrounding him—could easily be reshaped in accord with the laws of nature by reorganizing his institutions.[24] Since constraints on the forces of salutary change were thus of man's own devising and were embedded in his inertia-oriented cultural heritage, he had only to make this heritage dynamic.

Events in the nineteenth century seemed to bear out the optimistic expectations of eighteenth century optimists. Forces of growth hitherto inoperative or ignored increased in strength with the result that, in time, nonconventional inputs were accounting for between half and four-fifths of the increase in Net National Product per head.[25]

Drunken with success, Western man began to assume that output would grow exponentially.[26] "At the rate of progress since 1800," in 1904 wrote Henry Adams, one of the nineteenth century's keenest observers, "every American who lived into the year 2000 would know how to control unlimited power. He would think in complexities unimaginable to an earlier mind. He would deal with problems altogether beyond the range of earlier society. To him the nineteenth century would stand on the same plane with the fourth. . . . Perhaps even he might go back, in 1964, to sit with Gibbon on the steps of Ara Coeli."[27] A year later Adams suggested that by 1938, the centenary of Adams and his lifelong friend, John Hay, "they would find a world that sensitive and timid natures could regard without a shudder."[28] A year later began the Second Modern Peloponnesian War.

PHYSICAL LIMITS TO GROWTH

Late eighteenth- and early nineteenth-century economists and students of man's natural history were only qualifiedly optimistic about man's future. They were aware of past improvements in man's material condition and of the role of institutions. But they also recognized the finitude of the physical environments of communities of men as well as limits to man's capacity to surmount these limits—a finitude expressed today in the concept "spaceship earth" and manifest in shortages of critical components of man's physical environment as well as in his awareness of the economic impact of increasing entropy.[29] They may therefore be described as in the tradition of Tertullian (A.D. 160?–230?). Tertullian observed that, while cultivation, trade, numbers, and so forth, had increased, "teeming population" had become "burdensome to the world, which can hardly supply us its elements" and meet man's ever more keen wants. "In very deed, pestilence, and famine, and wars, and earthquakes have to be regarded as a remedy for nations, as the means of pruning the luxuriousness of the human race."[30]

Even in eighteenth century England and earlier, population growth had checked man's efforts to improve his lot. "It is fair to say," writes Phyllis Deane of England, "that before the second half of the eighteenth century people had no reason to *expect* growth" and so even pamphleteers and observers supposed.[31] "When population rose in pre-industrial England, product per head fell: and if, for some reason . . . output rose, population was not slow in following and eventually levelling out the original gain in incomes per head. Alternately raised by prosperity and depressed by disease, population was ultimately contained within relatively narrow limits by static or slowly growing food supplies."[32] Not until the latter part of the eighteenth century was national product outstripping population and hope emerging that "the spectre of Malthusian stagnation" might be exorcised.[33] Indeed, the pace of growth as a whole was under the governance of the growth of landed products, the pace of which was set by natural rather than by stepped-up nonagricultural processes.

It remained for Thomas Robert Malthus and William Stanley Jevons to put the problem in theoretical context. Malthus, living as he did at a time when land was the source of most of man's needs, stressed the limitedness of the supply of accessible arable land. He drew attention to the contribution of population growth to the accentuation of the pressure of man's aggregate demand for landed products upon the limited source of these products. For then, unlike today in advanced countries, increase in demand for land-intensive products originated in relatively greater measure with increase in population than with increase in average consumption.[34] Malthus thus lay a basis for the classical anticipation of a stationary state, as subsequently sketched by Ricardo and developed by John Stuart Mill, a state in which the common man could realize comforts provided that he brought it into being early rather than late by controlling his numbers.[35]

Jevons, writing in a mineral age when coal reigned as the "great emperor" of western Europe,[36] pointed out that, unlike land—essentially a nondepletable resource—coal was a depletable resource, the cost of whose extraction would increase as its sources became less accessible. Whence the eventual exhaustion of economically accessible stocks and the consequent contraction of the basis of industrial power in the late nineteenth century would exercise a paralyzing effect upon such economies as England's.[37]

Jevons presented Western man with a more difficult problem than had Malthus: the need to find alternative sources of energy. Malthus could be and was somewhat sanguine. He pointed to the need for institutions suited to induce man both to regulate his numbers and to give expression to "that great *vis medicatrix republicae*, the desire of bettering our condition and the fear of making it worse."[38] Then, while the structure of society "in its great features" would probably remain unchanged, the ratio of laborers to proprietors would decline and the condition of both would greatly improve. Presumably the probable changes occasioned by progress in physical science would not materially affect the social structure.[39]

Change in technology, defined as "organized skill" and as essentially cultural in character, was the source of change and growth, of continuing "development." Moreover, Ayres virtually endorsed the idea that "the actual technological process is progressive" and exponential.[40] There "is no basis for setting any absolute limit to the rate or magnitude of technological advance."[41]

Ayres both resembles and differs from expositors of steady state behavior. At times he seemed to take it for granted that technological progress would give rise to exponential growth. Exponents of steady-state behavior, on the contrary, must postulate that technological progress, or increasing returns to scale, or these two forces in combination, are present in sufficient measure to insure exponential growth in output per man and a natural rate of growth equal to the sum of the rate of population growth and the rate of technological progress (equals rate of growth of output per man).[42]

Technological progress was not assured, however; it could flourish only if conditions were propitious.[43] Indeed, "technological and ceremonial behavior . . . stand as in the most literal sense obverse and reverse of each other. . . . As constructs—organized behavior systems —they are nevertheless distinct and opposed. . . . the ceremonial behavior system is opposed to technological activity in this sense, that whereas technology is of its own character developmental the ceremonial function is static, resistant to and inhibitory of change."[44] "The history of the human race is that of a perpetual opposition of these forces, the dynamic force of technology continually making for change, and the static force of ceremony—status, mores, and legendary belief—opposing change."[45]

Ayres made use of his thesis to account for the origin of the industrial revolution in Europe and the rapidity with which the Soviet Union caught up with the West. He thought that the industrial revolution originated in Europe rather than elsewhere because ceremonial patterns existing in Europe on the eve of the industrial revolution were too weak to halt the movement when new tools were combined to set it going. What took place illustrates a basic principle of economic development, namely, that "the technological revolution spreads in inverse proportion to institutional resistance."[46] Revolutionists, as in the Soviet Union, simply extirpated retardative indigenous culture and introduced a massive educational effort, including literacy, so essential to "take-off."[47]

Writing in 1967, however, Ayres expressed the belief that retardative institutional traditions had lost much if not all of their strength.
No longer did they change very slowly. Not only had modern technology changed the physical environment of mankind. The "power to
do" had also been accompanied by the "power to know," with the result that the "traditional institutionalizing process" had "been short-
circuited" and "the traditional institutions of Western society" were
coming apart. The task resulting was that of devising "efficient organizational expedients and instrumentalities to do better," to perform more effectively functions formerly performed by institutions
now become obsolete.[48]

Ayres overlooks or underestimates the costs of change—both the
aggregative and the distributive costs. In this he is not alone, for it has
been customary until recently to play down negative externalities
and inequitable distributive effects and to exaggerate the capacity
of engineers to foresee and dissipate bad effects. Indeed, one may say
that the engineers are desperately striving to give new form to the old
dream of perpetual motion, by virtually asserting that "technology"
will solve all the problems which it generates, compatibly "with the
betterment of man's lot and dignity."[49]

While Ayres dealt with the problem which Malthus posed by virtually dismissing it, he did not really consider that posed by Jevons.
"All our experience of problem-solving points toward the probability
that the population problem can and will be solved." Ayres counts
upon the development of effective means of contraception but neg-
lects the more difficult problem, that of establishing adequate motives
to induce man to make use of the means.[50] "Granted that the achievement of abundance is contingent in the end upon the solution of the
population problem—this contingency does not mean that universal
abundance is forever unattainable."[51] Elsewhere Ayres observed that
there was "no positive guarantee" that the population would continue
to grow "throughout the definite future, but neither is there any con-
clusive evidence that it will cease to do so."[52]

Ayres seems to ignore the limitedness of the supplies of arable
land relative to growing populations, though he indicates that the
"geographical configuration" of localities may act as "a limiting
factor" unless cumulating technical contrivances can extend these
limits.[53] He also calls attention to the fact that man has been increasing the fraction of the biosphere which is subservient to his purposes while overlooking the shrinkage of the stock of depletable resources. "Resources are not fixed by the 'niggardliness of nature.'
They are defined by the state of the industrial arts," and "come into

being . . . as the result of new scientific discoveries and technological processes." The term "limited resources," it is said, conjures up "the whole climate of opinion of the eighteenth century and thus implies their fixity."[54] The "economic superiority of Western society over the rest of the world" was not attributable "to the unexampled richness of our natural resources." For what the "natural resources of any society are conceived to be is determined by the technology of society." Ultimately it is "altogether a matter of what men do and what men know."[55]

Ayres thus underestimated the significance of the changing structure of the natural resource base of the economy, of the growing importance of depletable resources whose diminution might not in the long run prove surmountable through the substitution of abundant for scarce elements and increasing economy in the use of the latter. Development proceeds at the expense of low entropy, the inflow of which into the economy rises, with the result that the basis for opportunity among future generations is diminished. "Man's existence is now irrevocably tied to the use of exosomatic instruments and hence to the use of natural resources. . . . the maximum of life quantity requires the minimum rate of natural resources depletion. By using these resources too quickly, man throws away that part of solar energy that will be reaching the earth for a long time after he has departed."[56] Over the long run, limits to change and growth lie mainly within man's physical environment. These limits find expression in retardation of growth and in change in the composition of aggregate output due to the uneven incidence of change in the rate of growth of inputs. Some institutions conduce to more rapid growth than do others, but they cannot make for greater aggregate growth in the long run unless they augment the utilizability of the physical environment—and then they are likely to increase growth and change in the near future at the expense of the more remote future. Provision of physical and human capital for future generations, now very great, cannot in the long run wholly counterbalance a negative dowry of augmented high entropy.

SUMMARY

Two aspects of Ayres's work call for summary comment, his institutionalist approach and his assumptions regarding growth and change.

The contributions of Ayres and other institutionalists to economic analysis, despite their neglect of the analytical apparatus of received economics, has been significant and could be much greater. This was implied earlier in the section "Ayres on Theory." There it was suggested that a great deal of economic behavior, even though subject to the stimuli labeled s_i, is channeled or expressed through institutions included under p_s. These institutions frequently are suboptimal, poorly equipped with correction-producing feedbacks, and susceptible of great improvement. Moreover, what may be called the institutional structure of a modern economy is not adequately subject to rigorous competition and welfare-oriented selection; it could even become less so should the role of government, the concentration of economic power in the hands of a self-serving "managerial elite," and Balkanization of the economy and polity combine to transform society into that which Hobbes sought to avert.[57] Accordingly, since economic mechanisms (e.g., the price system) are embedded in institutional matrices which therefore condition economic behavior, an important concern of the economist needs to be the optimization of these matrices rather than flight to imaginary, institutionless worlds. This, of course, is coming to be recognized as the increasing burden of suboptimal institutional structures becomes apparent, along with the high costs of economic inflexibility, insulation against corrective feedbacks, and failure to maximize the role of s_i.[58] Of the institutionalists who have been interested in devising optimum institutional structures, J. R. Commons has been the outstanding exemplar.[59]

Devising satisfactory economic institutional structures is impossible, of course, when the deviser, institutionalist or otherwise, fails to make adequate use of economic theory. There are, as J. E. Meade points out, "a vast number of combinations derivable from a very limited number of alternative institutional conditions and modes of human behavior." As a result it is "impossible to devise a correct policy without much empirical inquiry into the nature of the surrounding conditions." However, while "the empirical researcher and policymaker are much more likely to ask the relevant questions," employment of simple economic models "inculcates a way of looking at things which helps greatly in reaching a sensible final decision." "But in the formulation of economic policy, when one is considering any particular decision, it is of basic importance to consider the whole range of economic implications and not merely the effect of the policy in one special part of the field."[60] It is to ends such as this that economic theory must contribute if institutionalist undertakings are likely to succeed.

Institutionalists have been guilty, along with most orthodox economists, of neglecting biospheric constraints on the current and the prospective state of human existence.[61] As I noted earlier, many economists were sensible of these constraints prior to the nineteenth century, but in the latter part of that century an emerging faith in science dulled this sensibility; and, in the twentieth century, deification of this faith, together with the analytical needs of model builders, virtually dissipated awareness of actual and/or prospective constraints on development issuing from the nonaugmentability of the stock of some biospheric elements and the gradual dissipation of the stock of others as economic entropy increased.[62] Presently, of course, awareness of these two trends is increasing as growth of population, together with rising direct and indirect per capita consumption of biospheric elements, steadily augments man's requirement of these elements—an awareness of such factors as the economy-shrinking impact of the Arab oil embargo, increases in public efforts to regulate land use, the growth of cities (e.g., Petaluma, California), immigration into national, regional, and local communities, and so on. This awareness, moreover, is finding effective theoretical and ethical expression —expression that is undermining the growthmania endorsed until recently by governments as well as by land speculators and other searchers after unearned increments.[63]

Neglect of biospheric limits can lead to misinterpretation of the requirements of international stability. For example, Ayres, finding the cause of war in underconsumption and hence in struggle for foreign markets, observed that the two crusades "against want and against war, in fact, are one."[64] Accordingly, termination of the "present cycle of wars" was "contingent upon the correction of the unbalance between industrial capacity and the distribution of purchasing power for which the capitalist system is responsible."[65] Ayres was confident, however, that "science and the efficiency of the machine" would prevail and give rise to an economy of abundance.[66] Ayres thus overlooked the degree to which the unequal distribution of critical natural resources over the face of the earth can give rise to international conflict.

Awareness of the increasing shortage of easily accessible space, together with resource dissipation and other forms of increasing economic entropy, is certain to grow as what may be called the struggle for low entropy produces (a) international and interregional struggle and (b) income for current and temporally near generations at the expense of generations somewhat removed in time. Increasing entropy within advanced industrial nations will press them to draw on the low entropy—on energy sources, minerals, and so forth—of less industrial nations and thereby probably constrain the long-run potential of the latter at the same time that these nations are becoming more aware of international income differences.[67] Failure to give adequate weight to these factors somewhat weakened Ayres's analysis of the prerequisites of international peace and security as also did his neglect of the enervating and softening influence of opulence.[68]

NOTES

1. My comments on Ayres's work are based mainly on *The Problem of Economic Order* (New York: Farrar and Rinehart, 1938); *The Theory of Economic Progress* (Chapel Hill: University of North Carolina Press, 1944; and 2nd ed., New York: Schocken Books, 1962, with Foreword); *The Divine Right of Capital* (Boston: Houghton Mifflin Co., 1946); *The Industrial Economy: Its Technological Basis and Institutional Destiny* (Boston: Houghton Mifflin Co., 1952); and *Toward a Reasonable Society* (Austin: University of Texas Press, 1961). See the following articles in the *American Economic Review*: "The Basis of Economic Statesmanship," 23 (June 1933): 200–216; "Addendum to *The Theory of Economic Progress*," 35 (December 1945): 937–942; "The Impact of the Great Depression on Economic Thinking," 36 (May 1946): 112–125; "The Co-ordinates of Institutionalism," 41 (May 1951): supplement, 47–55; "The Role of Technology in Economic Theory," 43 (May 1953): 279–287; with K. E. Boulding et al., "A New Look at Institutionalism," 47 (May 1957): 13–27.

See also the following essays: "The Principles of Economic Strategy," *Southern Economic Journal* 5 (April 1939): 460–470; "Capitalism in Retrospect," *Southern Economic Journal* 9 (April 1943): 293–301; "The Theory of Institutional Adjustment," in *Institutional Adjustment*, ed. Carey C. Thompson (Austin: University of Texas Press, 1967), pp. 1–18; "The Legacy of Thorstein Veblen," in *Institutional Economics: Veblen, Commons and Mitchell Reconsidered*, by Joseph Dorfman et al. (Berkeley: University of California Press, 1964). See also *Science: The False Messiah* (Indianapolis: Bobbs-Merrill Co., 1927).

2. See especially, Ayres, *The Industrial Economy*, chaps. 1, 2, 5, 13, 14; *The Theory of Economic Progress* and Foreword; *The Divine Right of Capital*; "The Role of Technology"; "The Basis of Economic Statesmanship"; and comments on K. E. Boulding's "A New Look at Institutionalism," pp. 1–12 and 26–27.

3. Angus Maddison, *Class Structure and Economic Growth: India*

and Pakistan Since the Moghuls (New York: W. W. Norton and Co., 1971), p. 11.

4. E.g., see Ayres, *The Industrial Economy*, chaps. 1, 4, 16; and *The Problem of Economic Order*.

5. E.g., see W. F. Ogburn, *Social Change* (New York: McGraw-Hill Book Co., 1922); P. A. Sorokin's critique of *Recent Social Trends*, ed. W. F. Ogburn, in *Journal of Political Economy* 41 (1933): 194–210; Ogburn's reply, ibid., pp. 210–221; and Sorokin's rejoinder, ibid., pp. 400–404. See also my "Theories of Socio-Economic Growth," in *Problems in the Study of Economic Growth*, ed. Simon Kuznets (New York: National Bureau of Economic Research, 1949), pp. 47–116.

6. For ancient views see E. A. Havelock, *The Liberal Temper in Greek Politics* (London: Jonathan Cape, 1957), pp. 34–35. On Greek views of progress, see also, ibid., p. 176 and chap. 3; and C. N. Cochrane, *Christianity and Classical Culture* (New York: Oxford University Press, 1944), pp. 242–245, 483–485. On growth and form see D'Arcy W. Thompson, *On Growth and Form* (Cambridge: At the University Press, 1917, 1942, 1961); and K. E. Boulding, "Toward a General Theory of Growth," *Canadian Journal of Economics and Political Science* 19 (August 1953): 326–340.

7. E.g., see M. Shubik, "A Curmudgeon's Guide to Microeconomics," *Journal of Economic Literature* 8 (June 1970): 405–434, especially 406–407, 414–415.

8. E.g., see Ayres, *The Industrial Economy*, chaps. 13–15.

9. Ayres, "The Co-ordinates of Institutionalism," p. 48.

10. Ayres, *The Industrial Economy*, chap. 16, p. 419.

11. Ayres, "The Co-ordinates of Institutionalism"; also, "The Impact of the Great Depression on Economic Thinking."

12. Ayres, "The Principles of Economic Strategy" and "Capitalism in Retrospect." "Capitalism . . . is collapsing precisely because of the maldistribution of income for which it is responsible" (*The Theory of Economic Progress*, 2nd ed., Foreword, p. 280, also pp. 292–293).

13. Robert A. Nisbet, *Social Change and History* (New York: Oxford University Press, 1969), pp. 270–271.

14. Robert A. Nisbet, "The Myth of the Renaissance," *Comparative Studies in Society and History* 15 (September 1973): 473–492.

15. J. C. Russell, "The Ecclesiastical Age. A Demographic Interpretation of the Period 200–900 A.D.," *Review of Religion* 5 (January 1941): 137–147.

16. E.g., see Simon Kuznets, *Modern Economic Growth: Rate, Structure, and Spread* (New Haven: Yale University Press, 1966),

chap. 2; and *Economic Growth of Nations* (Cambridge: Harvard University Press, Belknap Press, 1971), pp. 24–27, 68, 94–95, 153.

17. Kuznets, *Economic Growth of Nations*, p. 94, note; also pp. 11–14.

18. Ibid., p. 11.

19. Simon Kuznets, *Economic Growth and Structure* (New York: W. W. Norton and Co., 1965), pp. 176–185; Phyllis Deane, *The First Industrial Revolution* (Cambridge: At the University Press, 1965), pp. 5–11.

20. See my *Indian Economic Thought: A Preface to Its History* (Durham: Duke University Press, 1971), pp. 42–46; quotation on p. 45. Cf. S. N. Patten on "pain" economies, in *Essays in Economic Theory*, ed. R. G. Tugwell (New York: Alfred A. Knopf, 1924).

21. See R. Braibanti and Joseph J. Spengler, eds., *Tradition, Values, and Socio-Economic Development* (Durham: Duke University Press, 1961), chap. 1, especially pp. 4–8. Ayres observes that "the dynamic force making for social change . . . is rather the changing thought-patterns of the whole community." While he and his associates are here dealing with consumer interests, Ayres's argument has wider application (Ayres, *The Theory of Economic Progress*, 1st ed., pp. 297–298, note).

22. E.g., see Nisbet, *Social Change and History*, chap. 3; my *French Predecessors of Malthus* (New York: Octagon Books, 1965), passim; and G. H. Hildebrand (with F. J. Teggert), ed., *The Idea of Progress* (Berkeley: University of California Press, 1949).

23. Carl L. Becker, *The Heavenly City of the Eighteenth-Century Philosophers* (New Haven: Yale University Press, 1932), pp. 118, 122.

24. Ibid., pp. 137, 139.

25. Kuznets, *Economic Growth*, pp. 86–97, especially p. 93.

26. As early as 1877 Lewis Morgan implied that man was progressing exponentially (see Hornell Hart, "Technological Acceleration and the Atomic Bomb," *American Sociological Review* 11 [June 1946]: 277–293, especially 280). Hart found most technological and related trends to be logistic in form.

27. Henry Adams, *The Education of Henry Adams* (New York: Random House, Modern Library, 1931), pp. 496–497.

28. Ibid., p. 505.

29. N. Georgescu-Roegen, *The Entropy Law and the Economic Process* (Cambridge: Harvard University Press, 1971). See also Herman E. Daly, ed., *Toward a Steady-State Economy* (San Francisco: W. H. Freeman and Co., 1973); and Mancur Olson, ed., "The No-Growth Society," *Daedalus* 102 (Fall 1973).

30. Tertullian, *De anima* (ca. A.D. 210) 30, cited by J. S. Slotkin, ed., *Readings in Early Anthropology* (Chicago: Wenner-Gren Foundation, 1965), pp. 15–16.

31. Deane, *The First Industrial Revolution*, p. 11.

32. Ibid., p. 12.

33. Ibid., p. 222; also, pp. 12, 250–251.

34. Malthus noted, however, that redistribution of England's monetary income would further orient the composition of aggregate demand toward agricultural products inelastic in supply (Thomas Robert Malthus, *An Essay on the Principle of Population*, bk. 3, 6th ed. [1826; reprint ed., London: Ward, Lock and Co., 1890], chap. 5).

35. L. Robbins, "On a Certain Ambiguity in the Conception of Stationary Equilibrium," *Economic Journal* 40 (1930): 159–180. Ayres found the concept of "stationary state" to be misleading (Ayres, *The Theory of Economic Progress*, 1st ed., p. 103; *The Industrial Economy*, p. 248).

36. So wrote Henry Adams in 1901 (*The Education of Henry Adams*, p. 415). "Coal is King," Ayres wrote in 1927 (*Science: The False Messiah*, p. 82).

37. See William Stanley Jevons, *The Coal Question* (London: Macmillan and Co., 1865, 1866, 1906).

38. Malthus, *Principle of Population*, bk. 4, chap. 14, p. 539.

39. Ibid. He noted that the "views of physical science are daily enlarging, so as scarcely to be bounded by the most distant horizon" (p. 543).

40. Ayres, *The Theory of Economic Progress*, 1st ed., pp. 105, 119–121, 247, 248; also pp. 155–156, note; quotation on p. 120. In his foreword to a second printing of this book eighteen years later Ayres described its theme as "that human progress consists in finding out how to do things, finding out how to do more things, and finding out about how to do all things better" (p. v). See also, Ayres, "The Role of Technology in Economic Theory"; and *Toward a Reasonable Society*, pp. 29–30, 277–278.

41. Ayres, *Toward a Reasonable Society*, p. 242; also, p. 275. Writing in 1962 Ayres set down as the first principle of economic development that "the process of economic development is indivisible and irresistible" (*The Theory of Economic Progress*, 2nd ed., p. xviii).

42. R. M. Solow, *Growth Theory: An Exposition* (New York: Oxford University Press, 1970), pp. 33–38; J. E. Meade, *The Growing Economy* (Chicago: Aldine Publishing Co., 1968), chap. 7, especially pp. 103–105.

43. Ayres, *Toward a Reasonable Society*, pp. 277–279; *The Theory*

of Economic Progress, 1st ed., chap. 7, pp. 121, 154, 177, 202, 289.

44. Ayres, *The Theory of Economic Progress*, 1st ed., pp. 173, 174; also, pp. 182, 188.

45. Ibid., p. 176. In his foreword to this book eighteen years later Ayres observed: "Two forces seem to be present in all ages: one progressive dynamic, productive of cumulative change, the other counter-progressive, static, inhibitory of change" (p. vi). He goes on to say that "what happens to any society is determined jointly by the forward urging of its technology and the backward pressure of its ceremonial system. . . . people move when they have the technical means of doing so, if they are not prevented by recognized authority, moral law, and emotional attachments" (p. ix).

46. Ayres, *The Theory of Economic Progress*, 1st ed., pp. xviii–xx, chaps. 6–7. See also *The Industrial Economy*, chap. 3. Joan Robinson finds merit in Ayres's thesis (see her *Economic Philosophy* [Chicago: Aldine Publishing Co., 1962], pp. 109–113, 116).

47. Ayres, *The Theory of Economic Progress*, 1st ed., pp. xx–xxiii. Supply of funds from abroad was not essential, as the early growth of the American economy showed (ibid., p. xxii).

48. Ayres, "The Theory of Institutional Adjustment," pp. 15–17. In 1962 Ayres stated that "the process of economic development is indivisible and irresistible" (*The Theory of Economic Progress*, 2nd ed., p. xviii; see also, *The Industrial Economy*, chap. 16). For Ayres's views on functionalism see *Toward a Reasonable Society*, pp. 20, 47, 64, 75, 125, and 132–133.

49. Charles Susskind, *Understanding Technology* (Baltimore: Johns Hopkins University Press, 1973), p. 132.

50. Ayres, *Toward a Reasonable Society*, pp. 241–245, quotation on p. 244; *The Industrial Economy*, pp. 417–418.

51. Ayres, *Toward a Reasonable Society*, p. 244; see also, *The Industrial Economy*, pp. 404–407.

52. Ayres, *The Theory of Economic Progress*, 1st ed., pp. 243–244.

53. Ibid., pp. 130–133.

54. Ibid., p. 84; also, pp. 113, 120; also, Ayres, "A New Look at Institutionalism," pp. 26–27.

55. Ayres, *The Industrial Economy*, p. 85.

56. Georgescu-Roegen, *The Entropy Law*, pp. 20–21.

57. See my "Return to Hobbes?" *South Atlantic Quarterly* 68 (Autumn 1969): 443–453.

58. E.g., see Shubik, "A Curmudgeon's Guide to Microeconomics," pp. 405–434; Georgescu-Roegen, *The Entropy Law*, pp. 316–347, and

Analytical Economics (Cambridge: Harvard University Press, 1966), pp. 108–110, 113, 114, 117–118, 124, 360–362.

59. John R. Commons, *Institutional Economics* (New York: Macmillan Co., 1934), and other works.

60. J. E. Meade, *The Stationary Economy* (Chicago: Aldine Publishing Co., 1965), pp. 7–8.

61. On Veblen see my "Veblen on Population and Resources," *Social Science Quarterly* 53 (March 1972): 861–878.

62. On the biosphere see P. R. Ehrlich, J. P. Holdren, and R. W. Holm, eds., *Man and the Ecosphere* (San Francisco: W. H. Freeman and Co., 1971). All the articles included were originally published in *Scientific American*. See also the September 1970 number "The Biosphere."

63. E.g., see Daly, ed., *Toward a Steady-State Economy*; and Olson, ed., "The No-Growth Society."

64. Ayres, *The Theory of Economic Progress*, 1st ed., pp. 280, 281, 292–293; quotation on p. 280.

65. Ibid., p. 293.

66. Ibid., p. 294.

67. "The expansion of industrial nations, far from leaving the poorer countries unaffected, worsens their situation in certain respects. It also widens the gulf that impedes international collaboration, collaboration that is essential, not for sentimental reasons, but because economic growth itself (including population growth) creates acute global problems even in the short run" (see Goran Ohlin, "The Golden Rule in Modern Economic Theory," *Skandinaviska Banken Quarterly Review*, no. 2 [1971], pp. 33–36; quotation on p. 36).

68. Ayres, *Toward a Reasonable Society*, chap. 13; also, *The Theory of Economic Progress*, 1st ed., pp. 290–295.

Science's Feet of Clay

GORDON TULLOCK

Clarence Ayres wrote two books on science: *Science: The False Messiah* and *Huxley*.[1] At the literal level, there is a profound contradiction between these two books. Further, I do not think that this contradiction can be regarded simply as a product of the passage of a few years between the two books and hence a change of mind of the author. At a deeper level, however, the two books represent the same psychological attitude.

The contradiction in the literal sense, however, is clear. *Science: The False Messiah* is an attack upon science. The first of the "Theses to be Nailed to the Laboratory Door"[2] which make up Ayres's final chapter is, "that the truth of science is established only by belief, after the manner of all folk-lores" (p. 294). *Huxley*, on the other hand, is the celebration of a triumphant scientific career and the establishment of a new scientific theory. On a somewhat lower level of contradiction, Ayres in general is a believer in science as something to be applied, and the theory of evolution has never been applied. Indeed, in a strict sense, it has never actually even been proven.

Further contradictions in the literal text of the two books (even within individual books) will be mentioned later in this essay: the psychological similarities must now be discussed. Having read *Science: The False Messiah* first, I was not at all surprised to discover what Ayres said in *Huxley*. The attitude of mind and general approach to society is the same in both. Ayres, in *Science: The False Messiah*, attacks an entrenched establishment; *Huxley* celebrates the overthrow of another entrenched establishment and the great accomplishments of one of the warriors who achieved that overthrow. Ayres apparently identifies himself with Huxley and would like to feel (although he realizes that the evidence is against him) that his attack upon economic orthodoxy was as successful as Huxley's.

There are a number of similarities between Huxley and Ayres which may have led to this identification. First, both are clearly excellent writers with a fine grasp of controversial techniques. Second, neither invented the system that they proselytize. Huxley took his basic ideas from Darwin and Ayres took his from the German historical school, and more particularly its American reincarnation, the institutionalists. Third, each had the special talents needed for progress in his particular field. Ayres was a brilliant social critic and Huxley was an extraordinarily good technical biologist.

The great difference between the two, and the reason that Huxley's life is a triumphant one while Ayres fought a brilliant rearguard action covering the gradual retreat of the institutionalists, is simply the quality of the ideas they espoused. Darwinism was a new and rather simple scientific idea that could be presented with great logical rigor, and its opponent, the established biological position, was a diffuse and not particularly coherent body of factual matter with occasional bits and pieces of theory. Further, at least in the opinion of this writer (of which more below), the Darwinian theory of natural selection was correct, and the prevailing orthodoxy now called "the theory of special creation" was incorrect.

Ayres, on the other hand, was a reactionary figure (although it is not clear he realized this). The German historical school grew up as a reaction to the success of the classical economists. In essence, they celebrated the pre-Adam Smith mercantilist economy and the philosophical, political, and religious ideas that went with it. They were attempting to set back scientific progress. Economics is surely not a simple system, but it is fairly rigorous and, in a scientific sense, simple in that it is deducible from a fairly limited set of assumptions. Institutionalism, on the other hand, like pre-Darwinian biology, is a diffuse collection of factual statements pieced together with a few odd bits of theory. Again, like pre-Darwinian biology, a good deal of this theory is unconscious and not fully recognized by its users.

Last but not least, I presume it is obvious by now that I believe that the foundations of modern economics are basically sound and that the Prussian historical school (institutionalist variant) is basically erroneous. It is, in my opinion, the difference between the doctrines preached by Huxley and Ayres which accounts for their quite different success. Huxley was what Ayres wanted to be. In fact, Ayres's career resembles more closely that of another brilliant controversialist, Bishop Samuel Wilberforce, the man who asked Huxley whether he was descended from the monkeys on his father's or his mother's side.

But whatever Ayres's position in the development or retrogression of economics, the subject of these two books is science, and here his brilliance as a social critic gave him the necessary tools for significant contribution. Of the two books, *Science: The False Messiah* is clearly much more important. *Huxley* is one of a number of biographies and, in my opinion, is not particularly outstanding. Perhaps its easy readability may mean that it would have much more impact than the more scholarly studies of Huxley, but basically it is a work of secondary importance. I will discuss it below only insofar as it relates to *The False Messiah*.

Ayres's view of science is, as the second half of his title indicates, a heterodox one. The book is an attack on one of our more important sacred subjects. The attack is made offensive to the orthodox by the brilliance of Ayres's style and his tendency to find similes which must be particularly painful to the true believer.

Although the book is well designed to unsettle the average believer in science, this is not a significant criticism of a work clearly intended to undermine an existing orthodoxy. The more significant criticism would be that Ayres has nothing positive to put in place of the dogma which he attacks. It is not absolutely certain that he realized this. There are several places in the book where he seems to be claiming that he had established a new and correct theory. I believe, however, that this is an incorrect reading. In my opinion (and I must admit this is a bit controversial), he doubted the possibility of science in the sense of a well-articulated, general body of theory which has been reasonably well tested empirically. Hence, when he refers to his own work as having made a positive contribution, he is not alleging that it is, in our way of thinking, scientific. A sort of misty *Weltanschauung* was all that Ayres thought was possible, and that is all I believe that he was claiming for his own work. If this is' what he claimed, then there is no doubt he is correct. He does give a rather misty and imprecise view of a general feeling about the real world and the role of science in it. This is not an exalted view, but we will turn to the matter again later.

So far as I can see, his criticism of science has had substantially no impact on the world. In some areas the orthodoxy has changed and is now more in accord with Ayres's position. But this, I think, is largely the result of exogenous factors rather than his critique. This is in no sense a criticism of Ayres. I myself have had the misfortune to write a book on the social organization of science,[3] and as far as I can see it has had no impact on science. Scientists in general are narrow specialists in something or other and have only vague and poorly articulated ideas about the whole scientific apparatus. This is just as true of those scientists who write books and articles on the nature of science as it is of the others. They are unlikely to read critiques from outsiders, and, if they do, they are unlikely to apply the reasoning and techniques of validation which they apply within the narrow field of science where they are experts. Under the circumstances, it is extremely difficult to have any impact. Ayres failed and, so far, I have failed.

Ayres's general view of the state of the world was a pessimistic one. This is particularly impressive in *Science: The False Messiah*, which was, of course, produced in the 1920's—in some ways the most prosperous and progressive era in modern times. But he regarded many aspects of society as signs of decline, even though they superficially seemed desirable: "Sophistication and enlightened unbelief were general in Athens, in Rome, in pre-revolutionary France; and those civilizations lamentably fell" (p. 18).

In a way, Ayres's dissatisfaction with the era in which he lived and predictions of disaster were based on its individualism. As a good follower of the German historical school, he liked integrated societies, large, closely built families, tradition, and so forth. He actually begins his chapter entitled "Dissolution" with the following passage: "FOR SALE—Suburban: Choice five and six room bungalows; electric lights, gas stoves, steam heat; breakfast nook in kitchen; tiled bathrooms; garages with heat if desired; close to elevated and proposed subway extensions; moderate first payment and monthly instalments.

"With these sinister words every issue of every daily paper announces the break-up of the fundamental institutions of western civilization" (p. 99).

From Ayres's standpoint, this *was* the breakup of the fundamental institutions, although most of us would have regarded it as movement forward. Further, it should be pointed out that his position has much philosophical support. Tradition, large integrated families, people who tend to live in much the same place and in much the same way throughout their lives have all been praised by many philosophers and students of society. Confucius as well as Ayres favored the kind of life praised on the pages immediately following the passage above.

> To these people, the family meant something more extensive
> than a father and a mother and two children. It meant the parents
> of the father, if living; the mother of the mother, if widowed
> and without a son; any sisters of the father who remained un
> married; the children at intervals of fifteen months to a number
> seldom less than five or more than fifteen. This tribal group lived
> together under the same roof, though perhaps in different wings,
> for at least two reasons: the activities of the homestead were
> capable of absorbing them all, and there was no outside influence
> to separate them. (P. 102)

The contrast between the society that Ayres liked and what he saw around him has much to do with his basic pessimism. Once again, this pessimism is not necessarily unique to him. Indeed, in a way the commune movement which flourished a few years ago and which now seems to be dying out was an effort to artificially recapture the values that he saw disappearing in his time.

With regard to the substance of Ayres's criticism of science, he has two general themes and then a very large number of criticisms of particular aspects of science. The two general themes are, respectively, that science is not really very important—indeed, it is a sort of parasite on the development of technology; and, second, that scientific knowledge is not of any order of authority. In the quotation above, he referred to it as being similar to a "folk-lore." This last point is not equivalent to the modern philosopher of science's view that science, at any point in time, does not fit the real world perfectly and merely approximates more and more closely over time. Indeed, there is little in Ayres's book to indicate that he believes we can learn about the real world in any highly specific and definite way. This is, in my opinion, the weakest and least developed part of his critique, but I regard it as very natural coming from a follower of the German historical school.

Since he had this view of the prospects for knowledge about the world, it is perhaps reasonable that he did write little about it. I have already quoted his statement about science being essentially folklore, and I could have found many other generally vaguer similar statements scattered through the book. At one point he says, "The heresies may also be untrue. They have no more truth in them than their corresponding articles of faith. But they may also have no less; and that should be enough to give them temporary currency" (p. 14). That he is talking about his own book as the heresy is fairly clear from the context. It would be hard to carry skepticism about the possibility of objective and detailed knowledge further.

At one point, this skepticism takes a quite modern form and, indeed, shows signs of anticipating Kuhn's paradigm theory.[4] "The facts are what they are; and rather more so: there are always more facts which do not fit the theories, and about which we do not hear so much—until a new theory has been invented into which those erring facts do fit. No fact ever obliges anyone to invent a theory, or to believe one theory and not another. People believe theories and legends and all sorts of folklore for other reasons" (p. 25). He does not, however, develop this theme, and I think we can take it as a minor part of his thought. Basically, he is simply skeptical about the possibility of scientific knowledge.

His general skepticism about the possibility of determining the truth is almost the only thing that restricts his enthusiasm for the view that science essentially is applied. "Yet it remains as true as anything can be in this not very intelligible world that however pure may be the motives of an individual scientist of anything resembling pecuniary interest, the purpose of science as a whole is to be applied" (p. 170). In fact, he goes much further than that. His position is not really that applied science is more important than pure science, but that even applied science is really a sort of by-product of the development of machinery: ". . . the prime mover in our recent developments is not that galaxy of noble truths which we call science, but the thoroughly mundane and immensely potent driving force of mechanical technology. Science is the handsome Doctor Jekyll; machinery is Mr. Hyde—powerful and rather sinister" (p. 19). Although Ayres does not deny the possibility of pure science,[5] he definitely plays it down. And even in the applied field, science plays a subsidiary role: ". . . science itself [is] a symptom of a larger and deeper process. . . . the driving force behind science is machine technology . . ." (p. 113).

Although all of this bears some resemblance to the Marxist belief that all science is applied, I think it does not represent the Marxist influence. Indeed, he is vastly more radical than a Marxist. A Marxist talks of science as something which is directed and guided by the economic universe, but Ayres is not even convinced that the economic universe itself is subject to scientific rules. Further, his skepticism about the actual truth of science makes him doubt its real social value.

At one point he discusses other people's views of society in which the simile of science as a driver of the chariot of progress is implied. He then says, "Chariots have been known to carry flies as well as drivers. Doubtless science has arrived simultaneously with the rest of the cargo but in what capacity?" (p. 207). His own answer to this question is shown neatly in the last two sentences of the paragraph in which it occurs: "The fly buzzes and the chariot rolls on. This is what science teaches about the control of society by science" (p. 208).

These two grand themes—the importance of mechanical progress and skepticism about the truth of science—are ones with which I have no great sympathy. It is true that I think the role of applied science has been massively underestimated by previous writers and I am delighted to find Ayres on my side. But it seems to me he goes too far. Further, it seems to me that his exaggeration of the role of applied science comes from his genuine skepticism about the possibility of having scientific knowledge at all.

Since my summary of his work to this point is basically critical, it is a pleasure to be able to turn to things with which I agree. In the framework of the general ideas I have sketched above, Ayres has embedded a very large collection of specific comments on various aspects of science and the philosophy of science. Here one can not only enjoy the excellence of his literary and controversial style but also agree with his conclusions. Further, in many cases he uses his analysis of science to make quite pointed comments about society as a whole.

Both of these aspects of his work are well illustrated in his discussion of the effect of science on religion. The two chapters on the subject are typically titled "The Reform of Superstition" and "Science Betrays Religion." The first of these chapters is essentially a very acute bit of social criticism of the reformist Protestant churches of his day. When I say that it is social criticism, I have to be a little careful because it is not really clear that he objects to what is happening. Although I do not wish to criticize his exposition in this chapter, I do think that perhaps Veblen's tendency to use irony partially to conceal his own position may have affected Ayres here. Ayres has no doubt that the adaptations to science which the Protestant religion has made will lead to the decline of the power and influence of Protestant churches. On the other hand, I think it is fairly clear that he regards that as desirable. For example, toward the end of his chapter "The Reform of Superstition," he says, "Fundamentalists—worse luck!— are not beset with doubts. . . . there still remain to them an established church and a consecrated dogma" (pp. 183–184). This I think indicates his real value position, even though the rest of the chapter, which describes the decline of the church resulting from the abandonment of establishment and dogma, might be taken as critical. In essence, he is saying that the reformist Protestant churches have chosen an inappropriate tactic, granted the ends he believes they actually hold. Their decline is not something which he personally finds painful.

His discussion of the reformist churches is largely in terms of their giving up "superstition" and, hence, the loss of authority.

> They may have rejected the miracle of transubstantiation because it seemed unreasonable to suppose that the holy wafer can be transmuted into the actual flesh of Christ by the ministrations of a "dirty priest," as they not infrequently put it; and they may have accepted the miracle of the transformation of water into wine at the marriage feast at Cana because it seemed reasonable to believe that such a thing could be accomplished by the Son of God. But having once accepted such a test they were once and for all on different ground from the "Universal Church." As time passed, and more became known, or scientifically believed, concerning the constitution of liquids such as wine and water, the

possibility of water changing into wine became more and more difficult—upon the basis of reasonability. To be reasonable, one must believe in science. To be theologically reasonable, one must true the miracles with science. (Pp. 179–180)

Thus the initial surrender to science eventually would mean the gradual abandonment of the entirety of religious dogma. Interdenominationalism was thought by Ayres to be equally dangerous since it deprived churches of the power of excommunication.

All of this was produced over forty years ago. Surely Ayres, if he could see the present powerless state of the Protestant churches, would regard it as a triumphant demonstration that the corrosion has done its work.

The chapter "Science Betrays Religion" deals with another phenomenon which is less common now than it was in the 1920's. Scientists sometimes like to pretend they are both Christians and good scientists and that, indeed, their scientific discoveries somehow validate the Christian religion. There is, of course, no direct conflict between science and some vague sort of deism, but there is a great deal of conflict between science and the specific words of the Bible or any other sacred book. Ayres deals with this problem very neatly: "Nevertheless those masters of modern subtlety who conceive that it is a triumph of understanding to interpret the indeterminancy of the electron as a manifestation of the Creative Will of the Almighty might perhaps do better if they would cultivate Huxley's passion for clearness and answer bluntly whether they believe the Hebrew demonology or not."[6] In a way the contest between religion and science is an important theme in *Huxley* and, in particular, in the chapter in which this quotation occurs. Nevertheless, on a general level the briefer treatment of the same subject in *Science: The False Messiah* is better.

On a somewhat related subject, Ayres demonstrates his skillful and controversial style in disposing of the antivivisectionist movement in one paragraph. It begins, "An anti-vivisectionist is a person who prefers that his neighbors' children shall die rather than that his own fine feelings should be offended by the thought of the suffering of experimental animals in laboratories."[7] The paragraph ends with a proposal for a Paretian solution: "Perhaps a satisfactory resolution of the difficulty would be a division of the population into two groups. One would undertake to develop fine feelings and would agree to forego the science of medicine; . . . The other would permit themselves to become callous and brutal, sacrificing guinea pigs on the altar of science without a quiver and would content themselves with endeavoring to preserve their own children and their neighbors' from sickness and death as slight spiritual compensation for their brutality toward the guinea pigs."[8]

Another area where Ayres saw through the existing literature to the underlying truth has to do with the moral position of scientists. Scientists, of course, are not particularly wicked men, but they are also not any more virtuous than the rest of us. You would never deduce this from reading the standard scientific accounts of their activity. Ayres's principal victim in this field was *Microbe Hunters* by Paul de Kruif, which was, at the time, probably the most widely circulated scientific popularization. De Kruif had, for example, praised Spallanzani for very, very carefully checking his own results, thus demonstrating his "real devotion to the truth!" (p. 254). Ayres then goes on:

> What he fails to mention is the strange behavior of bookkeepers who, having added a column of figures upward and found the sum, actually—so great is their devotion to the truth!—add the same figures downward in the quaint hope of detecting themselves in error. Of course, to be fair to the rest of the human race, we are bound to note that if the bookkeeper made a mistake his employer's accountant would almost certainly run it down, with disastrous results for the bookkeeper. But if we are to make that allowance, we are also bound in justice to the bookkeepers of the world to raise the question whether any one else might ever have checked up the demonstrations of the noble Spallanzani. It is impossible to deny that such is the case. We need not feel any less kindly towards the great scientist on that account; but we are bound to note that he had as great a personal stake in being careful as a man can ever have in anything: if his demonstrations had been inaccurate, and if any of his numerous opponents in the world of science had found it out—as some of them were sure to do—that would have been the end of Spallanzani.
> (P. 255)

When I wrote *The Organization of Inquiry*, I was not aware of this passage and hence devoted a good deal more words to making the same point with a great deal less grace.

In another area, Ayres demonstrates that de Kruif gives great praise to a scientist for behaving with simple, ordinary honesty. It had to do with Paul Ehrlich's discovery of the 606 treatments for syphilis which led to his Nobel prize. This discovery was, in fact, a rather accidental by-product of Ehrlich's main work, and Ehrlich himself always said that this was so. It is, indeed, doubtful that he could have gotten away with any other story, granted the publications that he had produced based on his main line of research. Ayres neatly deflates de Kruif's exaggerated praise of Ehrlich's modesty.[9]

The reader of the present day is apt to be impressed particularly by another discussion in the same chapter I have been quoting.

> . . . many enormous sums of money have been given to establish research foundations of all kinds for the study and cure of cancer; so much so indeed that it is a saying among biologists that to get a free education or to prosecute a problem you have only to show your keen interest in cancer and all the rest is added unto you. . . . But no honest man who knows the facts can deny that, measured in terms of present knowledge and treatment of this disease itself, the results achieved are incommensurate, widely incommensurate, and ridiculously incommensurate with the aggregate of effort expended. (Pp. 261–262)

This situation has, of course, continued from the time Ayres wrote to the present. At the moment there are a few encouraging signs, but it is still true that an immense research effort in this area has so far borne little or no fruit. Planning research or adjusting research to the most important problems does not necessarily lead to good results.

Ayres was a professor of economics. It will not have escaped the reader that in general I think he was not a very good economist. My criticism, however, is more of the school in which he worked than of his own personal abilities. I am reminded of Gibbon's statement about Belisarius: "His vices were those of his age, his virtues were his own."

Neither of these books is about economics, but both have various economic asides in them. In general, I think these are distinctly inferior; but I am happy to be able to point to at least one example of very good economics. At one point Ayres says, "The fact is, academic people are reformers. There is no economist who does not dream of stabilizing currency and arresting the tidal flow of business cycles . . ." (p. 206). Ayres was a good monetarist long before Milton Friedman. This was, of course, the orthodoxy of his day.[10] But Ayres was so unorthodox in many things that he at least showed very good taste in choosing what bit of orthodoxy he should endorse.

I could go on listing more areas where Ayres made penetrating and, in my opinion, correct observations about science. It seems to me better, however, to recommend that the reader peruse the books for himself. In general, they contain much brilliant and well-expressed social criticism of the scientific community embedded in a matrix which, in my opinion, is incorrect. Ayres's problem was his basic philosophy. In reading his material, one can hardly avoid being impressed with his intelligence and ability to penetrate through the screen of received opinion. One also can hardly avoid regretting that he did not use these same abilities in the choice of his basic position.

NOTES

1. C. E. Ayres, *Science: The False Messiah* (Indianapolis: Bobbs-Merrill Co., 1927); Clarence Ayres, *Huxley* (New York: W. W. Norton and Co., 1932).

2. Ayres, *Science: The False Messiah*, p. 294. Hereafter all page numbers appearing in parentheses after a quotation refer to *Science: The False Messiah*.

3. Gordon Tullock, *The Organization of Inquiry* (Durham, N.C.: Duke University Press, 1965).

4. Thomas S. Kuhn, *The Structure of Scientific Revolutions* (Chicago: University of Chicago Press, 1962).

5. Ayres, *Science: The False Messiah*, especially pp. 35–36, 52.

6. Ayres, *Huxley*, pp. 198–199.

7. Ibid., p. 150.

8. Ibid., p. 151.

9. As a matter of fact, Ehrlich had even more grounds for being modest, although there was no reason for either he or Ayres to know this. It is now believed that the treatment was not only of no positive benefit to syphilis sufferers, but probably in most cases caused harm. Since it was many years after Ayres wrote that this was discovered, we can hardly criticize.

10. J. Ronnie Davis, *The New Economics and the Old Economists* (Ames: Iowa State University Press, 1972).

Ayres's Views on Moral Relativism

ALFRED F. CHALK

The assumption that normative propositions lie outside the purview of science has been one of the more important methodological by-products of the empiricist movement. Indeed, most social scientists in the Western world accept this assumption in what might be called axiomatic fashion. Thus introductory textbooks in economics typically inform the student that any statement about what "should" be the case is extrascientific, for science is ostensibly concerned exclusively with analytic propositions concerning what "is" or "will be" the case. This is customarily done in the form of a few brief assertions, and little, if any, effort is made to explain *why* it is true.

In short, the orthodox contemporary view is that values are somehow unique to the individual, and for this reason no scientific judgment can be made concerning the relative merits of different values. Science is not only precluded from judging the behavior of individuals, but it is likewise incapable of passing judgment on the values of any culture. This latter doctrine, widely referred to as cultural relativism, is apparently accepted by a substantial majority of social scientists, and it has been supported in an especially vigorous manner within the discipline of anthropology.

Having done his doctoral work in philosophy, Clarence Ayres developed an early interest in methodological issues, and he repeatedly challenged the relativist views which have permeated the literature of the social sciences and philosophy for more than a century. In doing so he drew heavily on the work of John Dewey and laid special stress on the ends-means problem as it relates to the theory of valuation. In essence, what Ayres argued was that the traditional moral relativism which has been associated with the empiricist movement led to a kind of impasse in moral theory. One of Ayres's chief protagonists, Frank H. Knight, frequently told his students an important half-truth to the effect that the purpose of education is to raise rather than to solve problems. Judged by this criterion, the remarks in this brief essay will suggest that, at the very least, Ayres deserves credit for raising some of the "right" questions with regard to moral relativism in general and cultural relativism in particular. Although no defense of Ayres's specific policy prescriptions will be made, the following comments are intended to support his general thesis that, *in principle*, relativism is an inadequate method of approaching socioeconomic problems.

A few brief historical notes my serve to clarify some of the central issues, because most of the modern arguments for moral relativism are based upon the empiricist epistemology developed by Locke and Hume. Starting with the premise that the basis for virtually all knowledge is experiential, Locke and his followers stress the decisive importance of sensations impinging on the mind. For these early empiricists the mind thus plays an essentially passive role in the learning process compared with the more active role attributed to the mind by earlier rationalists. Not only does Locke observe that the external stimuli of experience produce varied responses among different individuals, but also on the basis of this fact he concludes that only the individual can correctly judge whether a given action would give him pleasure or pain.

In other words, it is the perennial problem of the limitations of human knowledge that is posed by Locke's epistemology. Since individuals respond differently to given environmental stimuli, it behooves government to permit a wide range of choice by consumers and producers. As Locke emphasizes, the earlier rationalists had debated interminably about "whether the *summum bonum* consisted in riches, or bodily delights, or virtue, or contemplation, and they might have as reasonably disputed whether the best relish were to be found in apples, plums, or nuts."[1] Anticipating Jeremy Bentham, he continues by observing that "the greatest happiness consists in having those things which produce the greatest pleasure, and in the absence of those which cause any disturbance, and pain. Now these, to different men, are different things."[2] If there were any doubt about his relativism, it would be removed by his assertion that "things are good or evil only in relation to pleasure or pain" and his subsequent comment: "What is it moves desire? I answer, happiness, and that alone."[3] Our moral precepts, therefore, are presumably derived from the "sensations" of pleasure and pain, and these sensations differ so greatly among men that the traditional rationalist efforts to establish universal standards for behavior should be abandoned.

It was the renowned skeptic David Hume who worked out most of the logical implications of Locke's empiricism. With respect to moral theory, Hume insists that reason has almost nothing to do with the formation of value judgments. On the contrary, he argues that all judgments about what is good or bad are made solely on the basis of *sentiments*, which in turn are determined by what he calls "habits of the mind" implanted by *nature*. Parenthetically, this is metaphysical reasoning with a vengeance, and it is quite ironic that it should be found in the works of the most distinguished empiricist of the eighteenth century. In any event, for Hume emotion rather than reason becomes the determining factor in the field of values. Expressed in his words, the "ultimate ends of human actions can never be accounted for by reason, but recommend themselves entirely to the sentiments and affections of mankind, without any dependence on the intellectual faculties."[4] What Hume says, in effect, is that what "ought" to be the case cannot be derived from any statement about what "is" the case.

In such fashion was the broad foundation for moral relativism laid by the early British empiricists. Not only was this point of view destined to become the dominant one in philosophy, but also, within less than a century after Hume, the relativist thesis became just as widely accepted in the social sciences. Although such early classical economists as Adam Smith and James Mill continued to adopt the traditional rationalist position that normative problems can be resolved within the framework of science,[5] later classicals openly adopted the views enunciated by the empiricists. Despite his general utilitarian sympathies, for example, J. S. Mill repeatedly asserted that, from a methodological point of view, it is essential to exclude all value judgments from purely scientific investigations. In book six of the *Logic* he explicitly states that the ends of human activity "are not propositions of science."[6] This basic argument is also developed in his *Essays*, wherein Mill states that "political economy is a science and not an art," and as such it is "conversant with laws of nature, not with maxims of conduct, and teaches us how things take place of themselves, not in what manner it is advisable for us to shape them, in order to attain some particular end."[7] Since the time of J. S. Mill most orthodox economists have accepted the methodological proposition that ends must be treated as given data for analytical purposes, and the science of economics is thus restricted to the study of alternative means of achieving *given* goals. This can be confirmed by even a cursory examination of the works of such prominent economists as Alfred Marshall, Lionel Robbins, and Frank Knight.

Some scholars have suggested that the widespread acceptance of moral relativism can be traced to the fact that it was one facet of a broad outlook introduced by empiricism, which provided much of the intellectual foundation for the liberal revolution. Specifically, moral relativism was only part of what has been described as a "tentative" approach to knowledge that was characteristic of the empiricist epistemology. British empiricism thus constituted a rebellion against the certainties which had characterized the rationalist philosophy from Plato to Descartes. With a few exceptions—for example, his belief in the existence of God and the truths of mathematics—Locke abandoned the time-honored rationalist conviction that man can possess absolute truth. Most students of intellectual history agree that this general temper of mind lent strong support to such emerging liberal institutions as political democracy, religious freedom, freedom of the press, laissez faire, and so forth.

Despite its widespread acceptance, however, the methodological principle of moral relativism has made numerous scholars "uncomfortable," primarily because the end product of this principle has been moral anarchy. Even those who accept the relativist view often admit to a certain uneasiness with this position and bemoan their inability to develop a satisfactory alternative to the prevailing view among contemporary social scientists and philosophers. In philosophy, for example, some modern self-styled empiricists occasionally acknowledge that the skepticism inherited from Hume has led to something which closely resembles intellectual chaos. Thus the distinguished philosopher Bertrand Russell admits that "one awkward consequence" of the skepticism derived from Hume is "that it paralyzes every effort to prove one line of action better than another," and in further pursuit of this theme he makes the following comments, which border on despair: "It is therefore important to discover whether there is any answer to Hume within the framework of a philosophy that is wholly or mainly empirical. If not, there is no intellectual difference between sanity and insanity. The lunatic who believes that he is a poached egg is to be condemned solely on the ground that he is in a minority . . . This is a desperate point of view, and it must be hoped that there is some way of escaping from it."[8]

Similar misgivings about relativism in moral theory were expressed by Ayres more than a generation ago. Possibly because of his interest in anthropology, he focused attention primarily on the concept of cultural relativism, the origins of which can be traced in large measure to the pioneering work of W. G. Sumner. The relativity of mores having been firmly established in cultural anthropology, Ayres observes that this principle "seems to extend to every sort of social behavior, including all values whatsoever, and to result in a sort of intellectual nihilism which . . . entangles our present ideas in all sorts of contradictions."[9] If all judgments about what is good or bad are merely relative to the customs of a given community, then the comments of any social scientist concerning the merits or demerits of a given policy are "qualitatively indistinguishable from the myth-making of savage society."[10] Like Russell, therefore, Ayres feels a desperate need to find a satisfactory alternative to the moral nihilism which characterizes so much of the literature of modern social science.

If relativistic moral theory has led to such a frustrating impasse, the question might be raised whether the only escape is a retreat to philosophic rationalism. In other words, is the only alternative to relativism a revival of absolutism? Clarence Ayres most certainly would have answered in the negative, for he neither accepted the traditional skepticism of empiricism with its attendant moral anarchy nor the opposite rationalist belief in the existence of final or absolute truth. More specifically, his general approach to this methodological problem was based upon at least two fundamental considerations: (1) his support of Dewey's so called ends-means continuum as a substitute for the customary type of ends-means dichotomy, and (2) his insistence that present confusion concerning the proper role of value judgments can be resolved only if we cease to derive our values from predominantly metaphysical sources. These two facets of his thought will be reviewed briefly in the hope that they may clarify some of the issues currently under discussion among students of moral theory.

As mentioned previously, Ayres repeatedly acknowledged his indebtedness to the instrumentalist philosophy of John Dewey, and this influence is nowhere more evident than in Ayres's analysis of the ends-means relationship. For many centuries, and especially since the rise of empiricism, it has been fashionable to speak of ends and means as though they were "distinct orders of phenomena."[11] In effect, all human experience has been bifurcated into a kind of dualism of ends and means. But Ayres emphasizes that, although we quite properly "distinguish the particular means by which a given end is to be arrived at," the end is "not on that account the 'end and aim' of all existence but is itself the means to something else."[12] In the real world, as Dewey and others have emphasized, we are faced with a kind of ends-means continuum in which the roles of ends and means are being more or less continuously reversed. What is now regarded as an end, once it is achieved, frequently comes to be viewed as a means for achieving some new end. Briefly, nothing should be regarded as either an end or a means in any permanent sense.

The traditional ends-means dichotomy was apparently utilized by early empiricists for the purpose of circumscribing a prescribed area of inquiry within which statements could be made that were free of valuations. One could then assign an area of "neutrality" to statements about the means of achieving *given* ends. Such a procedure, however, involves the tacit assumption that no value is attached to means except those of a purely instrumental nature. Unfortunately, as several students of methodology have noted, such an assumption is in fact a gross oversimplification of what occurs in everyday life.[13]

This oversimplification results in part from the demonstrable fact that people often *do* attach "direct," as well as instrumental, value to what are customarily called means. An excellent example is found in the frequent assertion of economists that the end of economic activity is consumption, whereas production is "merely" a means of achieving this end. Such an assumption concerning the independence of means and ends has been the foundation of much of modern welfare economics. As one critic observes, however, the fact is "that neither the conditions in which production is carried on, nor the relationships generated by exchange are purely instrumental. They are *human* conditions and *human* relations which are valued as much as, and in some cases more strongly than, the end of consumption."[14]

Expressed in a slightly different manner, what is being questioned is described by Ayres as the "metaphysical principle of the primacy of ends."[15] An integral part of Ayres's analysis of the value problem involves the mutual interaction of means and ends and the associated concept of the ends-means continuum. Thus the achievement of any end is no longer regarded as a kind of "consummatory" psychological state but instead is viewed as part of a continuing process in which "every operation is the end of some earlier means, and the means to some later end."[16]

The second broad characteristic of Ayres's approach to the methodological problems of moral relativism is found in his effort to avoid the metaphysical underpinnings of traditional value theory.[17] This can be illustrated most readily by describing briefly a few of the more important distinguishing features of his theory of value, which he probably regarded as his most important contribution to social science methodology. As often happens when more or less novel ideas are presented in a discipline, his theory of value has been severely criticized, and not infrequently misrepresented, in the professional literature. In any event, the purpose of the following remarks is neither to defend nor criticize the substance of his value theory, but rather to show that Ayres believed the hitherto metaphysical character of the value problem could be largely eliminated if a concerted effort were made to derive values from *this* world through the use of rational procedures rather than to import values from ceremonial, nonrational sources.

Fundamental to Ayres's theory of value is his widely discussed dichotomy of technology and institutions. He views all social behavior as either technological (rational) or institutional (ceremonial) in nature. Technology ostensibly provides the inherently dynamic force causing cultural change, whereas institutional behavior plays an essentially inhibitory role with respect to such change. Both technological and ceremonial types of behavior are present in all societies, although the influence of technology is relatively more important in modern industrial societies than in primitive ones.

The term "technology" as used by Ayres has reference to what he labels "the sum of human skills" and "also the sum of human tools."[18] In this context human tools include not only physical tools but in addition all the intellectual tools used in the sciences and the arts. A mathematician, for example, who exercises his skill "just thinking" is nevertheless utilizing an array of tools, that is, mathematical symbols, which are essential to all creative work in mathematics. More specifically, the "coincidence of tool and act (skill) is what defines the technological behavior function."[19] Accordingly, Ayres believes one of the most common errors made in discussions of the technological process is the assumption "that technology has to do only with things," for such a conception disregards "all the basic facts: the fact that technology is not 'things' but a form of human behavior; the immense range of tool behavior, extending as it does not only to all forms of artisanship but to the highest reaches of intellectual exploration and artistic creation; and finally to the concertedness of all these activities."[20]

Although the term *technology* as used by Ayres embraces both tools and human skills, it is nevertheless true that tools receive special emphasis in his analysis of the role of technology. This is accomplished through his use of the so-called tool-combination principle. Briefly, according to this principle all inventions are properly viewed as "combinations of previously existing devices."[21] Drawing on the work of such scholars as S. C. Gilfillan,[22] Ayres says the "heroic" theory of invention, which attributed virtually exclusive responsibility for technical innovation to the efforts of extraordinarily gifted people, is now regarded as inaccurate, for the evidence suggests that a new invention is "usually itself the end-product of a long series of inventions."[23] Moreover, this is held to be true of scientific discoveries as well as mechanical inventions.[24] Indeed, even innovations in the arts are explained in much the same manner. In sum, all such innovations are viewed as resulting in large measure from a combination of preexisting tools. For Ayres, therefore, technological change is explained not only by the skills people possess but also by a kind of inherent developmental logic associated with the use of tools in all innovative activities in the arts and sciences.

Partly because of the tool-combination principle mentioned above, Ayres asserts that technology is by its very nature a dynamic force responsible for social and economic change. Moreover, invention and discovery create new types of activities for which established institutions are usually ill adapted. The advent of the automobile, to take a simple example, forced the creation of new institutions to deal with a variety of problems which emerged as a result of this new technology. Ayres cautions, however, that there is nothing teleological about technological change, for no law of nature decrees it will continue indefinitely into the future.

At this juncture mention must be made of a different type of behavior which constitutes the other part of Ayres's dichotomy. This is what he defines as institutional behavior, which is distinguished by the fact that it inhibits technological progress. Such a characteristic stems from the fact that it is based primarily upon nonrational considerations of ceremonial adequacy, mores, and so forth. These institutional elements are typically linked strongly to the past and therefore tend to be static in nature. Thus institutional behavior in some primitive cultures was so deeply imbedded that it successfully resisted almost all technological change for many centuries, and even today the relative influence of institutional and technological behavior varies greatly in different societies.

Having placed all human behavior into two categories, technological and institutional, it is not surprising that Ayres views the former as the source of all value—that is, virtually everything that is "good" for man ostensibly results from technological behavior, which in Ayres's language means tool-using behavior. It would be difficult to exaggerate the importance which he attributes to tool-using activities, as evidenced by the following comments:

> Mankind is a tool-using species. All that man has done and thought and felt has been achieved by the use of tools. The continuity of civilization is the continuity of tools. All the arts, all the sciences, and the whole elaboration of organized activity by which "the great society," as Graham Wallas called it, has come to be, together owe their existence and derive their substance from the continuity which links the surrealist's pigments to the clays with which the Aurignacian caves were daubed, and in terms of which the cyclotron is but a continuation of Neanderthal experiments in chipping flint.[25]

On the basis of such statements as those quoted above, Ayres concludes that "value is a synonym for continuity, and the continuity of which it is a synonym is technological continuity."[26] In other words, he specifically identifies technological development with "progress."[27] This point of view has puzzled many readers, partly because it has been customary to regard tools and machines as "mere" means to achieve some end. Furthermore, as Ayres acknowledges, the concept of progress has been in disrepute among many social scientists because it presumably implies a "movement toward a preconceived 'end' or consummatory state."[28] But surely there is no compelling reason why this transcendental approach to the idea of progress must be accepted. We speak of progress in mathematics, medical care, and so forth, without such metaphysical connotations being present, and similarly we should be capable of referring to social progress without assuming a movement toward some preconceived end. Expressed somewhat differently, progress implies "direction," but this does not necessarily imply some type of ultimate end. Using Ayres's analogy, the series of cardinal numbers "is directional, since the numbers continually grow larger as we count," but it "would be ridiculous to say that in counting we are striving to approximate infinity, or that counting is meaningless except as infinity is preconceived to be its end."[29]

Ayres would say that the basic methodological problem in such situations as those mentioned above relates to the mistaken use of the customary ends-means dichotomy, and Paul Streeten, another critic of the orthodox ends-means model, has addressed himself to a very similar problem which arises within the framework of traditional welfare economics. Paretian optimum conditions, according to Streeten, involve the use of a kind of "puzzle-solving" model in which recommended means to achieve an optimum condition become a "merely technical matter."[30] But if a more empirical approach is taken, wherein it is recognized that means and ends are in fact interdependent variables, it becomes more meaningful to speak of *improvements* than of *optima*. Relating this to the ends-means dichotomy, Streeten makes the following pertinent observations: "Nobody really knows what an optimum economic system is like, but many can make wise proposals for betterment. The fallacy of the means-end pattern of thinking lies in the belief that 'improvement' always logically implies an 'optimum' or 'ideal.' It may, if we judge the change with reference to a given ideal . . . But improvement need not imply 'optimum' . . ."[31]

In similar fashion, Ayres argues that one can speak of progress without implying the existence of some metaphysical "ultimate" end. In broader terms, this issue may help to explain why moral relativism has been so widely accepted. Many relativists have apparently assumed that any attempt to evaluate the merits of alternative ends on a rational basis must be based upon some presumed "ultimate" value, which is then rejected forthwith on the grounds that of necessity it would be metaphysical in nature. Joseph A. Schumpeter, for example, maintains that the acceptance of one value judgment either entails the acceptance of an indefinite number of additional value judgments and therefore raises the problem of an infinite regress, or it dictates the acceptance of some ultimate or absolute value which can then be used as the basis for judging all other values. This is the fundamental reason, according to Schumpeter, why science can never pass judgment on the validity of any normative statement.[32]

Ayres, of course, follows Dewey in vigorously denying any need to resort to some absolute value in order to apply rational analytical tools in judging the merits of an end or goal. When he argues that the "locus" of value is to be found in technology, I interpret him to mean that it is the continuity of the tool-using function which makes possible all human progress. But this continuity does not entail the use of scientific tools which are assumed to be valid in any absolute sense. In this respect Ayres unquestionably adopts the tentative approach to knowledge so characteristic of the empiricist tradition, for he is quite unprepared to engage in what Dewey called the "quest for certainty." Expressed somewhat differently, Ayres does not believe a rejection of moral relativism need logically necessitate a return to the opposite extreme of rationalist absolutism. While it is true that the scientific community no longer believes it will attain absolute truth, it can and does "approach the approximate" truth, which is far removed from the kind of intellectual anarchy that characterizes extreme moral relativism.

In the final analysis, however, one of the more important, if not the most important, methodological issue that must be faced relates to the *source* of our values. If one insists on deriving his values from other-worldly sources, then a kind of metaphysical impasse is reached immediately, and any attempt to apply rational criteria in judging the merits of such values is automatically foredoomed. A prominent biologist, Conway Zirkle, expressed this fact in a manner which Ayres would doubtless have found quite acceptable: "If our standards come from directives handed down from Olympus, and if our ethical ideals are based upon our acceptance of these directives, then our course of action is clear. We must adapt ourselves to the commandments and live according to them as well as we can. If, on the other hand, our standards are derived from the past accomplishments and aspirations of our own species, we should find them useful and accept them gratefully, but with a recognition of their human origin and human imperfections."[33]

If this general approach were adopted, some rationally based conclusions could be made concerning the relative superiority or inferiority of certain cultures. To take an extreme case for illustrative purposes, some years ago a primitive tribe, the Xetás, was discovered in southeastern Brazil, and this group is said to be a "remnant of the Stone Age." These people are reported to have no agriculture, and they do not know how to work pottery or metal. Hunger is a commonplace experience, and their level of understanding is so limited that they have a grossly false picture of the world and the universe.[34] Now, a doctrinaire cultural relativist, such as the famous anthropologist M. J. Herskovits, would nevertheless insist that one cannot demonstrate on any rational basis that the values of this tribe are inferior to those found in the more "advanced" cultures. Referring to this relativist judgment, Eliseo Vivas expresses his frustration by observing that "one wonders what makes men espouse a doctrine, come hell or high water, when it is self-evident that our lives are better than those of the Xetás in almost every conceivable respect."[35] Ayres would maintain that the position adopted by Herskovits can be defended only if one accepts at the outset some other-worldly source of value. Members of the tribe, for example, might believe their existence is appropriate and "just" because God was long ago displeased with the behavior of their ancestors and modern generations are being punished for the sins of their forefathers.

At this point it may be worthwhile to recall that such cultural relativists as Herskovits acknowledge the superiority of Western technology compared with that of primitive tribes. But Ayres, Vivas, and other critics stress the fact that such superior technology does not emerge from a vacuum; it presupposes science, which in turn requires for its growth the acceptance of certain virtues, such as freedom of inquiry and self-discipline.[36] If the relativist anthropologist is to acknowledge the technological superiority of the West, he "should either grant the superiority of these values or give us a fully reasoned argument as to why he does not need to recognize these virtues as superior to other virtues the nonliterate possesses."[37]

While extreme cases involving comparisons of advanced and primitive cultures are sometimes useful in discussions of problems of principle, it should be noted in passing that, from what might be called an operational point of view, normative issues are often much more complex than those referred to in the case of the Xetás. For example, broad normative conclusions concerning the relative merits of different subcultures in the Western world would not only be much more difficult but also often impossible to justify, even within the philosophical framework of instrumentalism. This stems from the basic problem broached by Locke almost three centuries ago, the limitations of human knowledge. Differences between these subcultures are in most instances comparatively small, and their effects on what Ayres calls the "tool-using" activities of man are frequently so elusive as to preclude any conclusions being made with a high degree of confidence in their validity. Unfortunately, policy pronouncements made by Ayres and other instrumentalists all too frequently leave the impression that rational analysis could somehow solve a broad range of very complex normative problems, the solutions for which clearly defy our present limited knowledge.[38] An exaggerated conception of the power of reason to resolve moral issues is at least as dangerous in its implications as the modern retreat from reason that has been associated with relativism.

Quite aside from any theoretical weaknesses associated with the doctrine of cultural relativism, a few concluding remarks may be in order concerning one of the more serious practical consequences of this doctrine. It is a commonplace observation that many forces, including technology, are tending to draw our contemporary world closer together, but it is unfortunate that moral relativism, which has gained such widespread acceptance in the West, makes any resolution of cultural differences extremely difficult, if not impossible. Surely it is apparent that if the validity of a society's values is assumed to be determined exclusively by the mores and "sentiments" of the community, then, as Ayres observes, "The most we can say to people who hold other values than our own—such as the people of the Soviet Union—is: you hold certain things to be the true values of human life, and we hold different values; and we shall just have to see who is stronger."[39]

This same thesis has been developed by Professor Vivas, who also considers the effects of cultural relativism to be harmful. By stressing the distinctive rather than the common traits people have, the relativist doctrine tends to reinforce nationalism. While the posture of relativism may have been somewhat appropriate in the past, when one of its apparent objectives was to protect primitive peoples against the "ravages of those who would save their souls at the cost of their identity and dignity," what these people often need today is "protection from their own blind and fanatical nationalism."[40] In sum, any "doctrine that, however indirectly and however subtly, prevents the peoples of the world from coming together, from mediating their differences—which is to say, from reaching beyond their boundaries in terms of moral judgments—is today an obviously pernicious doctrine."[41]

In a broad sense, the comments offered above have been designed to suggest that one facet of the empiricist tradition is in need of careful reexamination. Borrowing the terminology used by James Malin, the hypercritical characteristics of Western culture have produced a "man-afraid-of-his-mind."[42] The result of this has been a debilitating intellectual paralysis in the sphere of moral theory, and in my judgment it is to Ayres's credit that he insisted on the need to apply rational analysis to normative problems. Whether the specific solutions he offered are eventually accepted or rejected is not of paramount importance. As stated at the outset, the important consideration is that he asked many of the "right" questions.

NOTES

1. John Locke, *Essay Concerning Human Understanding*, ed. P. H. Nidditch (Oxford: Oxford University Press, 1975), p. 269.

2. Ibid.

3. Ibid., p. 258.

4. David Hume, *Enquiries*, ed. L. A. Selby-Bigge (Oxford: Oxford University Press, 1946), p. 293.

5. Smith, of course, adopted this position on the basis of the influence of rationalist natural-law theory, whereas James Mill was a doctrinaire utilitarian who never recognized any vital distinction between the scientific validity of normative and analytic propositions.

6. J. S. Mill, *On the Logic of the Moral Sciences*, ed. H. M. Magid (New York: Bobbs-Merrill Co., 1965), p. 140.

7. J. S. Mill, *Essays on Some Unsettled Questions of Political Economy* (London: John W. Parker, 1948), pp. 124–125.

8. Bertrand Russell, *A History of Western Philosophy* (New York: Simon and Schuster, 1945), p. 673.

9. C. E. Ayres, *The Theory of Economic Progress* (Chapel Hill: University of North Carolina Press, 1944), p. 208.

10. Ibid., p. 209.

11. Ibid., p. 224.

12. Ibid.

13. For an excellent analysis of this and other problems related to

the use of the traditional ends-means schema, see Paul Streeten, "Programs and Prognoses," *Quarterly Journal of Economics* 68 (August 1954): 364–368.

14. Ibid., p. 365.

15. Ayres, *The Theory of Economic Progress*, p. 224.

16. C. E. Ayres, *The Industrial Economy* (Boston: Houghton Mifflin Co., 1952), p. 307.

17. The term *value* as used in this context refers to the meaning attributed to it in philosophy rather than in economics, for philosophical value is a normative term, whereas in economics it only refers to a rate of exchange.

18. Ayres, *The Industrial Economy*, p. 52.

19. Ibid. See also, Ayres, *The Theory of Economic Progress*, p. 108, for a similar statement.

20. Ayres, *The Industrial Economy*, pp. 311–312.

21. Ayres, *The Theory of Economic Progress*, p. 112.

22. S. C. Gilfillan, *The Sociology of Invention* (Cambridge: M.I.T. Press, 1970).

23. Ayres, *The Theory of Economic Progress*, p. 112.

24. Ibid., p. 113.

25. Ibid., p. 222.

26. Ibid., p. 221.

27. Ibid., pp. 105–124.

28. Ibid., p. 122.

29. Ibid., p. 123.

30. Streeten, "Programs and Prognoses," p. 367.

31. Ibid., pp. 367–368.

32. Joseph A. Schumpeter, *History of Economic Analysis* (New York: Oxford University Press, 1954), pp. 805–806.

33. Conway Zirkle, "Human Evolution and Relativism," in *Relativism and the Study of Man*, ed. Schoeck, Helmut, and James W. Wiggins (Princeton: D. Van Nostrand Co., 1961), p. 28.

34. Eliseo Vivas, "Reiterations and Second Thoughts on Cultural Relativism," in ibid., p. 54.

35. Ibid.

36. Vivas (ibid., p. 65) makes these points quite effectively in his attack on cultural relativism.

37. Ibid.

38. For a discussion of the dangers inherent in this approach, see Russell, *A History of Western Philosophy*, pp. 825–828.

39. Ayres, *The Industrial Economy*, pp. 299–300.

40. Vivas, "Reiterations and Second Thoughts on Cultural Relativism," pp. 66–67.

41. Ibid., p. 67.

42. James Malin, "Adventure into the Unknown: Relativist 'Man-Afraid-of-His-Mind,'" in *Relativism and the Study of Man*, ed. Schoeck et al., p. 194.

Methods and Morals in Economics: The Ayres-Knight Discussion

JAMES M. BUCHANAN

INTRODUCTION

I base this essay on the 1935 discussion between C. E. Ayres and Frank Knight, the discussion which Ayres entitled "Moral Confusion in Economics" and which Knight characteristically modified to read "Intellectual Confusion on Morals and Economics."[1] An initial reaction is one of vivid contrast between the economist's intellectual world of 1935 and that of the 1970's. Ayres and Knight, leading members of the profession, explicitly concerned themselves with fundamental philosophical issues that emerge naturally from the discipline. By comparison, how many economists in the 1970's debate similar issues or, more critically, so much as recognize that they exist? Surely the basic problems have not been resolved, despite the developments, good and bad, that have resulted from the Robbins, the Robinson-Chamberlin, and the Keynesian "revolutions." These issues have only taken different form, as effected by forty years of additional history.

In this paper, I propose to present the 1935 Ayres-Knight discussion in modern dress, so to speak. I shall argue that developments in economics since 1935 have been such as to bring their positions more closely into agreement, although both continue to be sharply divergent from mainstream economic methodology. Both of these scholars should have become increasingly disturbed at the growing mathematization of economic theory, quite independently of the uses to which this might have been put. By "mathematization" here I refer to the conceptualization of economics as a branch of applied mathematics. Both scholars should have been equally if not more disturbed by the emergence of the dominating professional emphasis on empirical testing of hypotheses themselves grounded in idealized theoretical constructions, as if the interaction of human beings in society is fully equivalent to the interaction of chemical elements. Ayres might have been at least ambivalent with respect to developments in theoretical welfare economics, properly characterized as "theories of market failure." This might have been matched by Knight's ambivalence toward developments in public choice theory, which could be dubbed "theories of government failure." Both Ayres and Knight would have continued to emphasize the limits to the explanatory potential of purely economic models of man, and both might have maintained their interests in exploring the moral-ethical requirements for social order, requirements that must be met before effective economic interaction begins.

THEORY OF SOCIAL ORDER

As we read the 1935 discussion between Clarence Ayres and Frank Knight, their differences emerge; their points of agreement tend to be obscured because these were mutually acknowledged by the participants. This is perhaps most clearly demonstrated by Knight's silence on Ayres's insistence that the function of economics is to offer a theory of social order, of social interaction. "Of course," Knight would have responded here, and students at the University of Chicago, before and after 1935, placed this at the core of Knight's teaching. Modern (post-1935) developments make this elementary methodological principle worthy of reemphasis. By saying that economics offers or should offer a theory of social order, we must, by direct implication, say that economics is not exclusively or even primarily a "theory of choice."[2] Yet the thrust of post-1935 development, influenced perhaps too strongly by Robbins's *Nature and Significance of Economic Science*,[3] has surely been toward the latter rather than the former. Once we accept the Robbins formulation of the "economic problem," we are, almost necessarily, forced into a choice-theoretic framework, and the tools of applied mathematics suggest themselves immediately. Economics comes to be conceptualized as a varied set of exercises, all of which involve the maximization of some appropriately selected objective function subject to the appropriately defined constraints, with, of course, the dual minimization problems always offering alternative avenues toward solutions. Formally, the problem faced by the isolated Robinson Crusoe is no different from that facing the political community of persons. Once a utility function is specified and his constraints defined, the economist observer can tell Crusoe just what his "efficient" pattern of behavior must be. Once a "social welfare function" is specified and the constraints are known, the same observer can tell the benevolent despot just how the whole economy must be "efficiently" organized and operated. The role of the economist shifts readily and almost imperceptibly from that of disinterested "engineer" to that of normative counselor, proffering his own judgmental advice as to ends as well as means, if indeed these can ever be separated in fact.

There is a subtle, but vitally important, distinction between this choice-theoretic approach and that which is properly attributable to the theorist of social interaction. In the latter, Robinson Crusoe economics continues to occupy a place, but never to the conceptual or imagined purpose of proffering advice and counsel. We seek to understand Crusoe's isolated behavior as a first and preliminary conceptual stage in understanding the emergent interrelationships among men as they meet in socioeconomic processes. The focus of attention is upon "that which tends to emerge" from the behavioral interaction, and this is not conceptualized as a "solution" to any applied maximization problem faced by some representation or idealization of the whole community of participants. Economists, as specialists, describe characteristics of these results, but it is the structural-procedural aspects that command attention, never the results, as such. To introduce a simple example from the Crusoe-Friday world, the economist is unconcerned as to whether the established trading ratio between coconuts and fish settles at 5:1, 1:1, or 1:5. He does not view the exchange process as an "analogue computing device" that makes "choices" for the idealized community. His concern is devoted to the demonstration that in idealized conditions of exchange the trading process insures an equality among the internal trading ratios for all participants.

I am not suggesting here that either Frank Knight or Clarence Ayres fully articulated and consistently held the second position that I have outlined. Through his insistence on the central role of the equimarginal or "economic" principle, even in the multiperson setting, Knight's work is, of course, fully consistent with and can readily be interpreted as falling within the broad choice-theoretic framework. By his query, "Are we going on the rocks?" repeatedly made in his 1935 essay, Ayres implies that he viewed the social economy in a "ship of state" analogue, one which readily translates into "social welfare function" notation. Had he used a slightly different metaphor, he might have asked a more appropriate question for a theorist of social order. Had he said, "Is the island sinking?" he would have implied thereby a potential disintegration or breakdown in the institutional foundations of society within which human interaction takes place and from which outcomes emerge—but outcomes that are not purposefully directed by any single choosing agent. Nonetheless, I should argue that both men equally would view as essentially absurd modern attempts to "compute" equilibrium prices along with both the expressed hopes and fears that advanced computer technology can replace exchange processes or, more generally, can essentially remove human actors from society.

Homo Economicus

Since 1935, technological advances in computers and intellectual advances in mathematical statistics have combined to make the testing of hypotheses in economics less labor intensive and the results more credible. Predictably, economists have responded to this major shift in relative cost-benefit ratios, with the observed modern preoccupation with regression routines. This shift, alone, tends to corroborate Ayres's hypothesis that technology itself independently affects social process. Could the modern emphasis on empirical tests have emerged at all save for computer availability in each research setting?

The larger question, however, concerns the relevance or importance of this development for economics, as a discipline, and the possible distortions in understanding that may have been produced as a result. The opportunity cost of securing proficiency in econometrics is naïveté in basic economic theory itself, naïveté that is manifested in failures to recognize the necessary limits or qualifications with which the elementary propositions of the theory must be hedged. The practical effect is that such limits are ignored, with the result that *homo economicus* has come to occupy a more central role than it ever assumed in its putative neoclassical heyday. The basic set of hypotheses which are tested in modern regressions is derived directly from the assumption that men behave in terms of narrowly defined and objectively measurable self-interest. There are few, if any, alternative behavioral models behind modern empirical work, although there exist, of course, essentially behavioristic models without any analytical basis. Let us consider an example. Suppose that we organize an experiment by placing coins (nickels or dimes) on a sidewalk in a busy central city, and that we observe passersby with a view toward predicting pickup rates. The experiment is conducted and, let us suppose, the initial hypothesis of rational economic behavior is falsified. Men do not, as observed, respond to measured self-interest. But these results may also be "explained" by the fact that other motivations, such as time and trouble or "transactions costs," may more than outweigh the measured pecuniary returns. This being the case, however, what will the experimental results have shown? That *homo economicus* does not exist? That economic theory is tautological?

The elementary fact is, of course, that *homo economicus* does exist in the human psyche, along with many other men, and that behavior is a product of the continuing internal struggle among these. The task of economic theory is not that of predicting specific patterns of behavior; it is that of providing a structural understanding of the processes within which the divergent behavioral plans of persons are integrated and reconciled. Knowledge of the strength of the definable economic motivation may be important for making comparisons among institutional-organizational alternatives. But economic theory does not relinquish its explanatory role if its central predictive hypotheses fail to be corroborated empirically. *Homo economicus* need not reign supreme over other men, and his failure to do so does not signal his nonexistence. From this there emerges an implicit organizational norm. When alternatives are possible, social efficiency will be gained by channeling man's self-interest toward mutually compatible goals. This principle, the heart of eighteenth-century wisdom, remains untouched by modern empirical testing, yet the failure of modern economists is measured by their loss of the understanding of this precept.

This does not suggest that economists should desert their econometric playthings and become modern apologists for market capitalism, as Ayres seemed to classify neoclassical economic theorists. Nor does it suggest the more likely opposite, that they become the intellectual vanguard for further socialist experimentation. As Knight often remarked, economists should adopt the morals of the physical scientists even if they should shun the latter's methods. This morality must include a willingness to go beyond the limits of empiricism. In effect, modern economists opt out of their essential moral responsibility by their self-imposed limitation to data-determined inquiries. Ayres's strictures against the neoclassical purists of the 1920's and 1930's should be as nothing when compared to those which might be posed against the sterilities of the econometricians of the 1970's. The hard questions are not readily formulated in terms of testable hypotheses. But this offers no cause for not thinking about such questions, for not discussing them, for not searching for an appreciation and understanding. Empirical science provides solutions to problems posed, solutions which, once obtained, become "truth," to be followed by the invention of new problems and new solutions. "Moral science" (if I may be permitted to use an old-fashioned word in what seems to be its proper meaning) is concerned with age-old "problems," for which "solutions" are, almost by definition, inappropriate. We do not "solve" the "problem" of social order by producing a unique "solution," regardless of the sophistication of empirical techniques. There is no objective "truth" to be established here. The "problem" of social order is faced eternally by persons who realize that they must live together and that to do so they must impose *upon themselves* social rules, social institutions. Economics and economists cannot evade their responsibility in the continuing discourse over such rules and institutions by shifting attention to trivialities. To the extent that they do so, their functional roles can only be filled by the charlatans and the fools, whose presence about us requires no demonstration.

MARKET AND GOVERNMENTAL FAILURE

As noted, Ayres viewed the neoclassical economists of his time as imposing a conceptual model upon economic reality that was, first of all, fallacious, and, second, designed and used deliberately to provide an intellectual-moral defense of a particular form of social order, market capitalism or free enterprise. Viewed in modern perspective, Ayres was somewhat out of date, even in 1935, because the central body of neoclassical theory had already been turned on its head by Pigou, whose great influence seems now to be only remotely correlated with his ability. Ayres should have been ambivalent about the post-Pigovian developments in theoretical welfare economics. In so far as his strictures were laid against the imposition of a behavioral model which he held to be overly restrictive, Ayres could only have been upset by the theories of market failure that emerged from the marginal social product-marginal private product calculus of Pigou because this calculus embodied even more restrictive assumptions about human behavior than those which informed the neoclassical models of competitive order. On the other hand, because this theoretical welfare economics did produce market *failure* results, and as such did much to undermine the neoclassical defense of market organization, Ayres might have independently welcomed such developments. In this aspect of the debate, Knight seems clearly to have been corroborated by intellectual developments within economics itself. In a formal sense, pure economic theory is surely value neutral. The uses to which this theory is put need not be so, and the resort by modern economists to theories of market failure as a means of providing a putative intellectual-moral basis for socialist experimentation is fully comparable to the behavior of the laissez-faire proponents of earlier epochs.

Developments in the 1950's and 1960's have, however, offered something of a Hegelian antithesis. *Homo economicus* was introduced to assist in explaining man's behavior in decision roles outside of and beyond market exchange, including political or public choice decisions. Once this simple step was taken, the theorems of governmental or political failure emerged, at least on all fours with the market-failure theorems of post-Pigovian welfare economics. The synthesis, as and when it emerges, can only be represented in a value-free and strictly pragmatic stance. Economic theory can tell us little or nothing about alternative organizational forms, except on a case-by-case basis. Frank Knight would have welcomed some methodological consensus on this point. We cannot be so sure about Clarence Ayres, although some of his students have indeed expressed approval of the "modern institutionalism" that is descriptive of the work of an increasing number of scholars.

THE LIMITS OF SELF-INTEREST

Markets fail; governments fail. Demonstration of these propositions is straightforward once *homo economicus* is plugged into the model of interaction. Even in those aspects of economic intercourse that involve no externalities or spillover effects in the Pigovian sense, some limits must be imposed on the working of pure self-interest. Individuals must abide by behavioral standards which dictate adherence to law, respect for property and personal rights, and fulfillment of contractual agreements—standards which may not, in specific instances, be consistent with objectively measurable economic self-interest. Absent such standards as these, markets will fail even when there are no imperfections of the sort that have attracted the attention of the welfare theorists. And, of course, even when such standards prevail, markets fail once any of these more familiar imperfections are introduced, failure here being measured against the conceptual ideal. But political attempts at correcting market breakdown also founder on the rocks of measurable economic self-interest of the participants. No person is motivated to undertake the costs of organization that may be required to generate the "public good" that corrective reform represents. Elected and appointed politicians and bureaucrats are not different from other men. They are motivated at least in part by their own interest, not by some higher version of the "social good."

"Social order" requires general acceptance of a minimal set of moral standards. Well-defined laws of property and freedom of market exchange minimize the necessary scope and extension of such standards, but they by no means eliminate them. As individual property rights become confused, and as markets are replaced by or subverted with governmental interventions, the dependence of order on some extended range of moral responsibility increases. (So long as the individual confronts market *alternatives*, his dependence on the behavioral pattern of any single person or administrative unit is correspondingly reduced. If he confronts a single governmental or political alternative, his well-being is of necessity put at the mercy of the behavior of a single person or decision unit. In the limit, his dependence is complete.)

Markets do not, however, carry moral weight comparable with their organizational alternatives. Then and now, critics become disturbed at the inequalities that result even from the idealized workings of market processes. These objections, made by Clarence Ayres and other critics, do not really concern the division of the gains-from-trade generated by exchange, the realizable surplus that only markets make possible. At base, the objections are to the basic assignment of property rights among persons and families, the allocation of potential "tradeables" among persons *before* they enter market activity. But, somewhat surprisingly, market institutions themselves are held responsible for their failure to redress these initial imbalances among unequals. Markets are condemned for their failure to produce distributive justice, even if the injustice observed arises in premarket distribution rather than in any sharing of the gains. Comparable failure of the political apparatus to accomplish similar objectives does not seem to mitigate the continuing force of this morally based criticism of market orders.

Maintenance of a viable social order characterized by substantial individual liberty depends critically on the widespread acceptance of a common set of moral precepts. Such acceptance is by no means assured in our world of the 1970's. These precepts include respect for individual rights, once these are defined in law and/or customary standards of behavior, along with the recognition that the historically determined assignment or allocation of rights among persons may embody significant departures from assignments or allocations that might plausibly emerge from a "renegotiated social contract."[4] This recognition, in turn, should suggest that adjustments may be needed in the structure of rights, as such, rather than interferences in the social process through which assigned rights and titles are exchanged among persons. Moral energies should be diverted away from criticisms of markets, as such, and distributionally motivated, politically implemented attempts at redress of premarket injustices should be shunned. Distributional objectives should be furthered through instruments that operate directly on the underlying extramarket assignment of individuals' rights.

Historical evidence offers little grounds for optimism that the moral energies will be channeled as suggested. Market organization, which minimizes the dependence of man on the morality of his fellows, may continue to be subverted in the mistaken hope that inequalities can be erased. In the attempt, the realizable surplus made available to society only through the working of markets may be dissipated, and the grosser because less tractable inequalities of political power increased.

INSTITUTIONS, TECHNOLOGY, AND MORAL VALUES

Clarence Ayres might not have accepted these conclusions, but the insistence of Ayres and his institutionalist compatriots on the independent importance of institutions and of technology becomes germane to any current examination of the moral requirements for social order. Institutions and technology affect the behavior of men, including their acceptance of ethical-moral precepts. Major changes have occurred in the forty years since Ayres and Knight addressed these issues. The institutions of order—the family, the church, and the state—have undergone dramatic change, and the directions of effect on individual adherence to traditional moral standards seems clear.

The family's role in transmitting moral values, including a sense of respect and honor for the institution itself, has been undermined by the shift from the extended unit to the nuclear cell. Ayres might have intervened at this point to add, appropriately, that this changing role for the family is itself traceable to the dramatic changes in technology which moved us off the farms and into the great conurbations. Can urbanized man be expected to live by the moral precepts ideally characteristic of the sturdy yeoman farmer?

The decline of the church as an institution of order, and of orthodox religion as a shaper of the attitudes of men and women, has perhaps a more tenuous relationship with technology. But this decline is fact, and one that must be reckoned with in any attempt to assess moral requirements. "God Will Take Care of You"—this hymnal statement was meaningful to many more persons in 1935 than it is in the 1970's. Orthodox religion has, by now, almost abandoned its role in softening man's urge to moral wrath against the social structure in which he finds himself. If anything, the modern church has become itself subversive of existing and traditional moral standards, changing its color from an institution of order to one promotive of disorder and instability.

There has been an accompanying change in man's vision of "the state," the governmental-political process. In 1935, man did not know about the Stalinist purges; Hitler was only partway along toward his final solution; the postwar failures in socialist democracies were in the future; the debacles of Great Society programs, the weirdness of the Warren Court and of Watergate were more distant still. Despite the Great Depression, individuals in 1935 honored politics and politicians, and patriotism remained extant as a major motive force. There was widespread respect for "law," as such, and rare indeed were those who felt themselves morally capable of choosing individually determined norms of obedience.

Alongside this partial disintegration of those institutions which tended to establish and to maintain order and stability in society, with the predictable effects of such disintegration on individual adherence to traditional moral norms, the parallel role of the school must also be examined. Within the context of strong and stable institutions of family, church, and state, the school can appropriately combine a rational transmission of moral values with a critical and searching reexamination of these values. As the offsets are weakened, however, and as the internal mix within the school changes toward criticism and away from value transmittal, this institution becomes one of disorder and instability in modern society.

The institutional developments alone, independently of technology, would have placed increasing pressure on the sometimes fragile stability of social order. This pressure has been enhanced by technological change, which has exerted independent influence. The genuine revolution that has occurred in transportation and communication has helped in creating a highly mobile society, with the result that "locational loyalty," as a force making for moral value stability, has largely disappeared. Perhaps even more importantly, what has been, and what will be, the impact of television on individual attitudes and behavior in all sorts of social interaction, in the market place, in the voting booth, in the day-to-day adherence to ordinary standards of conduct, in manners? Will mass television so modify behavior patterns as to make adjustments in the institutional constraints, in legal order, necessary, or, if not necessary, desired? Can the basic norms of a free society be extended to cover this medium? Is "freedom of the press" automatically extendable here, or do we require a new definition?

CONCLUSION

These are not "economic" questions, as such, and few modern economists bother to ask them, much less attempt to provide answers. To their shame—for it is precisely these issues and these questions that would have occupied the minds of both Clarence Ayres and Frank Knight in the 1970's. These two would have, no doubt, continued to disagree sharply on both diagnosis and prescription, but, at the same time, both would have treated the piddling trivialities that occupy modern economists with the contempt that they deserve.

Retrospectively, we might say that both Ayres and Knight should have been admonished in 1935 by the Adam Smith statement: "There's a deal of ruin in a nation." Forty years later we live in a more affluent but still tolerably free society that has not suffered moral collapse. The optimistic critic would be tempted to apply much the same admonition to my own assessment. Despite the institutional and technological changes that have occurred, there may be major elements of stability in our society that I have tended to overlook in my discussion. Perhaps the excesses of the 1960's were aberrations from the more orderly development of a social order embodying affluence, justice, and freedom. Perhaps. But hoping will not make things so, and those of us who do sense the vulnerability of social order to what seem to us to be gradual but unmistakable changes in the moral bases of this order would be derelict in our own duty if we did not raise warning flags.

NOTES

1. C. E. Ayres, "Moral Confusion in Economics," *International Journal of Ethics* 45 (1934–1935): 170–199; Frank H. Knight, "Intellectual Confusion in Morals and Economics," *International Journal of Ethics* (January 1935): 200–220; C. E. Ayres, "Confusion Thrice

Confounded," *International Journal of Ethics* 45 (1934–1935): 356–358.

2. For an elaboration of my own position, see my paper, "Is Economics the Science of Choice?" in *Roads to Freedom: Essays in Honor of F. A. Hayek*, ed. E. Streisser (London: Routledge and Kegan Paul, 1969), pp. 47–64.

3. Lionel Robbins, *The Nature and Significance of Economic Science* (London: Macmillan and Co., 1932).

4. For a further discussion of this point, see my paper, "Before Public Choice," in *Explorations in the Theory of Anarchy*, ed. Gordon Tullock (Blacksburg: Center for Study of Public Choice, 1973); also, my book, *The Limits of Liberty: Between Anarchy and Leviathan* (Chicago: University of Chicago Press, 1975).

Clarence Ayres's
Economics and Sociology

TALCOTT PARSONS

By far the most important personal contact I had with Clarence Ayres was when I was an undergraduate at Amherst College, Class of 1924. In my junior year, I took a full-year course with him which was offered under the Department of Philosophy and had the title "The Moral Order." Since I later became a professional sociologist, it seems to me only fair to grant that this course constituted in a very important sense my introduction to sociology, which was not represented formally in the Amherst curriculum at that time—indeed, which has only come to be in very recent years. Most of the material from the reading list, which also figured in class discussions, would have been regarded as quite unorthodox from a philosophical point of view. I remember in particular reading excerpts from the not so unorthodox book of John Dewey, *Human Nature and Conduct*, from Thorstein Veblen's works, from Sumner's *Folkways*, and from Durkheim's *Elementary Forms of the Religious Life*. Since the last of these has become something of a specialty for me, I shudder to think how little I understood about what Durkheim was trying to do in those first readings from his work.

Ayres was unquestionably a stimulating teacher. He taught by the more or less Socratic method, inviting and guiding free and open class discussion. He continued to pose deeper and more difficult problems of human meaning and ethics to his class. One incident I remember in particular was when, apropos of the disappearance of a certain number of library books which had been reserved for members of this class, he suggested imposing on the class a pattern of collective responsibility: unless this surreptitious sequestering of reserved books should stop, the class as a whole should be penalized without any attempt to identify the individual culprits. This clearly posed a very fundamental moral problem which was put to me in dramatic form for the first time on this occasion.

With his informality as a Socratic-type teacher Ayres had an informality of dress which went rather far for the time. My memory may well play tricks, but I always remember him appearing in class in a worn and baggy corduroy suit—never the more conventional woolen suit which was much commoner among the professoriate at that time than it has since become.

My junior year was a very decisive one for me. I had had relatively clear intentions previous to that of going either into graduate work in biology or into medicine. I had become interested in biology in my freshman year and indeed had served as an assistant in the biology department. In my junior year, however, Ayres and another of my teachers, Walton H. Hamilton, who was in the Department of Economics, were the principal agents of my conversion to a concern with social science. Like college students of later generations, I was certainly attracted by, among other things, a mild political activism and by movements stemming from the Left. Many of us at Amherst at that time were enthusiasts for the Russian Revolution and for the rise of the British Labor Party, and we were firmly in the opposition to the current United States regime during the presidencies of Harding and Coolidge.

The great blowup occurred at Amherst at the end of my junior year, and both Ayres and Hamilton were among the faculty members who resigned from the college in protest at the dismissal of President Meiklejohn. I did, however, return in the fall to finish my degree course and underwent various vicissitudes in that year, since none of the courses I had elected for my putative senior year were in fact given. Every single instructor had left the college. I did, however, persist in my plans to become a social scientist. The following year, namely, 1924–25, I spent as a graduate student at the London School of Economics, and then I took up an American Exchange Fellowship at the University of Heidelberg in Germany.

Clarence Ayres and Walton Hamilton can reasonably be paired because of their common concern with what they and others of that generation called "institutional economics." This was the kind of economics I was first brought up on. Ayres, when he arrived at the University of Texas, transferred formally to the discipline of economics. Whereas, in a sense, Hamilton, when he joined the faculty of the Yale University Law School, transferred out of it into a certain kind of amalgam of social science and law. The problems posed by this tradition, however, exerted a particularly potent influence on my thinking for the first several years of my postcollege career. Before outlining the relevant intellectual history, however, it may be relevant to remark that, after having contracted to fulfill the requirements for a doctoral degree at Heidelberg, I returned to teach in the Department of Economics for a year at Amherst, but under conditions that had changed radically from the time that Ayres and Hamilton were important influences. My chairman was a new appointee who had arrived since I had graduated, named Richard Meriam, who had been trained at Harvard. During my two and more years in Europe, I had formed the ambition to make a special study of the relations between economic and sociological theory. This was in a framework which had crystallized about understanding of the work of Max Weber, who, though he died some years before my arrival in Heidelberg, was still the dominant intellectual influence in the social sciences there. I came to be interested above all in Weber's treatment of the significance of modern capitalism.

Meriam advised me that if I was to pursue this interest I should become much better versed in economic theory than I had so far been. And both on his advice and with his help in my placement, I went the following fall—namely, 1927—to Harvard in a curious amalgam of the status of a graduate student who was not a degree candidate and an instructor, the latter appointment insuring a modest but adequate living. It was at Harvard under such mentors as J. A. Schumpeter, F. W. Taussig, and Edwin F. Gay that I thought I really learned my orientation to economics.

This was a very different orientation from that which I had absorbed from Hamilton, and secondarily from Ayres. I say secondarily since, in the course I took with him, Ayres did not particularly stress economic problems.

The line of thought which I pursued relied heavily on the concept of analytical abstraction and the definition of economic theory as an analytically abstract discipline. This conception was particularly strengthened by the contact I had with Schumpeter, but again strengthened by making, during my early years, the acquaintance of the work of Vilfredo Pareto.

To make a long story short, after a considerable period of gestation I finally produced a large book which bore the title *The Structure of Social Action*. Of the intellectual influences to which I had been exposed since leaving Amherst, those at the London School of Economics were the closest to the Hamilton-Ayres point of view. Here, however, I found myself much less concerned with economic problems than with another range, notably those of anthropology as taught by Bronislaw Malinowski. At Heidelberg under Weber's posthumous influence I was plunged back into the problem of the nature of the relations between economic and noneconomic aspects of social phenomena, but in a very different frame of reference from that of American institutional economics. Indeed, Weber himself was far from unsympathetic to what in those days tended to be called "neoclassical" economic theory, but he made it one major reference of a far more comprehensive analysis of both comparative-historical phenomena

and the modern socioeconomic order which he called that of capitalism. I was thoroughly immersed in this kind of material because I
wrote my Heidelberg dissertation on the idea of capitalism in what, at
that time, was recent German literature dealing with the topic. Three
major figures in that dissertation were Karl Marx, Werner Sombart,
and Weber, of whom Weber was, to me, by far the most important.

In my early days at Harvard I was thus exposed to the influence of
economic theory as then taught at Harvard, and to Pareto, and, on my
own, to Emile Durkheim, to whose work I had originally been introduced by Ayres, but understanding of whom required far more study
than I devoted to it in my undergraduate days. After that I felt the
need to come to terms with the problems posed by the American
tradition of institutional economics. At the invitation of Professor F.
W. Taussig I wrote a long article which was published in two install-
ments in the *Quarterly Journal of Economics* in 1934 and 1935—of
which Taussig was then editor—under the title "Sociological Elements in Economic Thought." In this article, I reviewed a wide range
of different contributions to this problem area, including considerable
attention to institutional economics as I had learned it in the classes
of Hamilton and Ayres, notably to the work of Thorstein Veblen,
who was, I suppose, the most important single culture hero of that
movement.

By this time, I had decided on the main plan of the book entitled
The Structure of Social Action. The initial study attempted to attack
certain problems of the status of economic theory in the central British tradition by an analysis of the work of Alfred Marshall, who may
be regarded, more than any other, as the founder or the principal of
the twentieth century phase of Anglo-American economic theory. I
was then at work on comparable essays on contributions to the problem by Pareto, Durkheim, and Weber. My article "Sociological Elements in Economic Thought" was a kind of justification for the major
intellectual turn I had taken, away from the orientations in this field
to which I had been exposed as an undergraduate at Amherst.

I think, in retrospect, that I had two major theoretical objections
to the institutional point of view. The first was that, in the name of a
generalized radical empiricism, it denied the legitimacy of the analytical abstraction—a conception I found running through all of the principal authors whose work was treated in my study, and one that was
extremely pervasive outside that group, for example, in the *Philosophy of Science* of A. N. Whitehead. The second main objection was
the neglect of the cultural-normative factors in the larger picture
which transcended the economic perspective. This was particularly

conspicuous in the work of Durkheim and Weber but could also be discerned in that of Pareto. In a sense, this issue came to a certain kind of head in the strong emphasis which the institutional economists, including both Hamilton and Ayres, placed on technology as almost the institution *par excellence*. This was an emphasis which was extremely strong in that movement and has by no means disappeared from current discussion. But in my own view of institutions, I followed an alternative direction with respect to which property, authority, and other such categories took precedence over technology in the broader perspective.

I think my own record of theoretical development is sufficiently in the public domain so that I need not elaborate these matters further on the present occasion. I would like to close, however, with acknowledging that I received enormous stimulus from my two old Amherst teachers, namely Clarence Ayres and Walton Hamilton, and without their influence I would probably never have become a social scientist at all. I hope my apostasy from the views they represented has not totally disqualified me as an authentic representative of some of the relevant traditions of social science.

Clarence E. Ayres as a University Teacher

MARION J. LEVY, JR.

Clarence E. Ayres is not and will not be what many, including he himself, would consider to be a famous man, but he was a very successful man from a point of view about universities that is almost entirely neglected—he was a very great university teacher. To assess Ayres's role as a teacher one must first say something about what has happened to the university in general and to the American university in particular. The strongest case for Ayres's enormous success as a teacher lies in the fact that he managed to preserve what has always lain at the heart and core of a university. He actively, zestfully, and vigorously loved knowledge, especially in its teachable forms. It excited him. He understood without a trace of pedantry why the university library is always symbolically and actually *the* central building on any university campus—regardless of the library's physical location. He adapted and supplemented that intoxication with knowledge to fit in with changes in the university in general and the American university in particular without being involved in any of the witting or unwitting corruptions that have been associated with those developments.

In the generality of human history the university that we take so much for granted in the United States today is, like so many other things we take for granted, a set of unbelievably bizarre patterns. It is common today to look to the university as a device for doing any and all things with, to, and for our young at a certain period of their development. This attitude is not only bizarre in human history, it is also nonsensical even in terms of our own queer world. There are after all only three things for which the university setting has a comparative advantage. Those three things are: the preservation of knowledge, the transmission of knowledge, and the creation of new knowledge. The formation of character is not among them.

The characters of modern American university students have, of course, in all of their main outlines been formed long before they get anywhere close to the university environment, save for the few who are born to parents who happen to teach in it. The sharpest part of the learning curve for all children as far back as we know anything about the species—the part during which human animals learn to walk, to talk, to eat and to sleep, to control bodily functions and to interact with other human beings, the part on which everything else is based—is lived out almost entirely in some sort of family context, at least for the first three years or so of the animal's existence. It is almost certainly true that for most human beings basic character structure is laid down by the time the individual reaches the age of six or eight at the outside. Subsequent experiences after that may burnish the character and perhaps even slant it a bit in one direction or another, but short of traumatic experiences subsequent events tend to flesh out the structures already laid down. Clarence E. Ayres was well aware of these limitations as well as of these comparative advantages. He labored to make as much as possible of the material that came to him. He was no alchemist. He did not see himself as transmuting base metals or more than base metals into gold. He could and did add marvelous inlays and aid in the construction of remarkable forms. He did preserve, and he did create, but above all he taught.

There is another thing about the university. During most of the university's history the universities have had very little to do with the creation of new knowledge. Most of the history of universities has been concerned with the preservation of knowledge and the transmission of knowledge. Some new knowledge, of course, accumulated there, but that was on the whole accidental. Few societies developed the tradition of private scholarship as subtly or as fully as did the Chinese, but it is not until well into the nineteenth, if not the beginning of the twentieth century, that it became overwhelmingly probable that the great intellectual ornaments of humankind be associated with universities. It is sobering to reflect on the fact, though, that it is still not primarily the case with regard to that category of intellectuals who are generally regarded as artists.

In that long history of universities before we reach the stage of university development that can in some sense be called the age of the American university (much as sociology is known as the American science), only 1 or at the outside 2 percent of the age cohort went on to universities in one form or another. The university members viewed themselves as existing primarily to provide replacements for themselves. In this circumstance, if they ruined 50 percent of their students, it made little or no difference. The students generally came from extremely well-to-do homes and could be, as it were, wasted. Nowadays, university or higher education in some form or another touches, at least glancingly, 50 to 60 percent of all children born in the United States. Japan is in hot pursuit of the American ideal, and other countries regard their higher education shortcomings with a kind of diffidence lest they be regarded as nonmodernized if they don't move toward similar percentages. In a situation in which for one reason or another some form of higher education moves toward universality as an ideal if not as an actuality, a new and special form of university corruption stalks the world. This new form of corruption is in addition to and quite apart from the corruption that has led an increasing proportion of the faculty of the university to be interested in practically anything but teaching. We still require only a relatively small number of our students to replace ourselves. In the world in which we live, however, when we cock our teaching and our evaluations of American university students toward the ones most likely to replace ourselves—if that has an intellectually deforming influence, quite apart from character formation—we threaten not a small number of the young from relatively affluent backgrounds; we threaten a substantial portion of all of our young from all of our backgrounds.

Another thing needs saying about the American university, and it will probably apply reasonably well to the developing university world in general. Leaving geniuses to one side (for they can do anything by themselves in some sense), for the general run of students, excellent, bad, and indifferent, the undergraduate portion of the university education—and that is the one that is becoming universal—does only three things well, if indeed it does them well. The undergraduate college can and should provide a basis for general cultural-historical literacy, a basis for further specialization, and a basis for critical thinking.

The university setting can give the students the opportunity at least to acquire for themselves a general cultural-historical literacy about humankind. Do not knock those survey courses. Most of our students have little opportunity for good courses in world history, in the history of art, in the history of music, in the history of literature, until they get to the university. Despite all the guff associated with anthropology courses, for example, they stand in a special relationship to these matters, for properly considered anthropology is the comparative conscience of the university vis-à-vis the humanities, which have generally been developed with an overwhelmingly Judeo-Christian Greco-Roman ethnocentrism, and of the social sciences, which have developed with an overwhelming preoccupation for isolated aspects of highly modernized large-scale societies. Ruth Benedict's *Patterns of Culture,* however unfashionable today, is a broader shock to ethnocentrism for more people than travel.

The second thing that is done for university undergraduates—it is probably the thing that the American university does best—is to give them the basis for going on to further specialized work in one or two disciplines, either professional work in the narrow sense of the term or other academic developments in a broader sense. One of the marks *par excellence* of the American university undergraduate is that he or she thinks in terms of majors; they are not just college graduates, they are college graduates in economics, or physics, or dry fly-tying. Do not knock this either. We live and are going to continue to live in a world with ever further developing specialization, and increasingly that specialization rests on matters for which a generalized intellectual basis is critical. No amount of antielitism is going to change this.

The third thing that the American university can do well for undergraduates, but almost never does do well, is to teach them to think critically. That brings us back to Clarence E. Ayres. More than anyone I ever met, Ayres was geared to teaching the students under him to think critically without paralyzing them as individuals. Not only could one learn a great deal from Ayres without having to agree with him, but also no one ever got any brownie points simply for agreeing with him. In a world that increasingly placed a high value on consensus, his attitude was a marvelous question: "What is the last time you learned something from someone who agreed with you?"

However unjust it may be, I do not think Clarence E. Ayres is going to be remembered for his contributions to the frontiers of knowledge. What is even more unjust is that I do not think he will be remembered in detail for the impact he had on teaching, which I think was very great indeed and was the greater for the fact that the mark of his success lay in the fact that he was doing what needed to be done in terms of a system increasingly set up to minimize the doing of that very vital factor. He taught you always to question what you accepted most easily. Better irksome error than smug truth.

It is at least not much of an oversimplification to say that a very considerable part of Ayres's own substantive economic contribution took off from the various insights and possibilities flowing from Veblen's "instinct of workmanship." I think he certainly conceived it so, but I think he was wrong in one respect. What Ayres was really hooked on was Veblen's "idle curiosity," his "propensity to pry." One can after all become set in one's ways about theories stemming from the instinct of workmanship. But once one is high on curiosity, there is no complacency.

Clarence E. Ayres had his preparation and began his teaching before the day of the great specialist dawned. He belonged to that vanished set of enormously learned faculty members of omnivorous curiosity. Students never knew in his courses when an important point would be illustrated by a detailed, learned disquisition on how human beings learn to sail into the wind or how significant it was when ingenious individuals invented new "paradigms" for harnessing horses. He was a specialist in economics, all right, but he gave the impression that he had read everything and had read it solely because he loved reading, could never get enough of it, could hardly decide which book to read next for the greatest excitement. His desire for knowledge was insatiable. His eyes lit up when he saw books; a library was hog-heaven for him. And so he taught students that learning was very exciting indeed for the learner. He always seemed excited by the stuff he taught, including the tangents brought up by students' questions.

He exulted in an extraordinarily large vocabulary without being in the least a pedant. In a way far more characteristic of people in humanities courses than in social science courses, even in his day, he sent his students scurrying to the dictionary and left them with the feeling that words made a lot of difference and that they ought to make a lot more difference than they did to most people. In the midst of an economics course, only he was likely to ask a student, "What does Veblen mean by the phrase *Levitical cleanliness* here, and why did he use that phrase?"

In all this he started from a very heterodox position. He grew up in a world in which economists tended to be one of two stripes—either perfectly ordinary, orthodox, classical economists, or, if they had a terribly liberal or unusual streak about them, Marxists. Not so Ayres. His plunging-off point with students and for himself was Veblen. Veblen didn't look at anything the way either of those two established orthodoxies (however radical one of them was supposed to be) looked at things. To this very day Thorstein Veblen remains the one truly original self-invented person of American social science. Even a far more brilliantly puristic theorist like Paul Samuelson isn't that. The fact that Ayres started off from Veblen gave his students a special comparative perspective that very few other students were getting in the social sciences in those days. Both the more orthodox economists and the Marxists were equally annoyed, baffled, and upset by Veblen. All a student had to do to have his wits sharpened after his exposure to Veblen was to step outside and come in contact with others who had not and find out how enraged they were by the questions he raised. If Ayres didn't teach you to think critically directly, you hardly got far outside with the freight he burdened you with before others forced you to do just that.

There was in this a more substantive contribution: Ayres's students were prepared for the modern world of economics in a way that most were not, for Ayres pounded away at the lesson that he had learned so well from Veblen. That lesson is a simple one—the problem with technical, classical economics is not that it errs in its logic, is not even that it does not have a great deal to say; it is rather that, in the hands of all save the very able indeed, the particular parameters used by the teacher tend to be applied uncritically by the pupil. Even if the teacher is highly flexible and adaptable, the students frequently are not. At this very point in time most people still confuse two ideas: the one that holds that economic analysis is inherently conservative, and the other that holds more correctly that the parameters frequently used for economic analysis apply only to a very special set of cases— that those parameters have been supplied by individuals whose views today rightly or wrongly would be regarded as conservative ones. If you looked where Ayres taught you to look and continued to do so, you had to change much of the substance and detail of your analysis with the changes of the times. What Ayres taught you to do was to change with the times, and he didn't train you to be an economist; he educated you in thinking in economic terms about anything that came up, and he didn't confuse that with other ways of thinking or regard it as a substitute for other ways of thinking. And so he didn't educate you as his replacement, but as your own person.

Yes, there were the later famous who went through his hands, among them Talcott Parsons, Joseph Dorfman, Kingsley Davis, William J. Goode, C. Wright Mills—none of them maimed and chained to his way of thinking. Yes, you could learn from him without having to agree. We don't know who will remember any of these fifty years from now, let alone a hundred, but after he came to rest in Texas, where he had most of his impact, thousands of young people were touched by him—by what he stood for in the great university in that place at that time, even if they did not take his courses. He taught them to think; he made curiosity exciting for them as young adults as it had not been for them since childhood; and he didn't bind them to himself or to the university. Very unusual!

Notes on the Contributors

WILLIAM BREIT is professor of economics at the University of Virginia. He is coauthor with Kenneth G. Elzinga of *The Antitrust Penalties: A Study in Law and Economics*, coauthor with R. L. Ransom of *The Academic Scribblers: American Economists in Collision*, and coeditor with H. M. Hochman of *Readings in Microeconomics*. His publications have appeared in such professional journals as the *American Economic Review*, the *Journal of Law and Economics*, and the *Harvard Law Review*.

JAMES M. BUCHANAN is University Professor of Economics at Virginia Polytechnic Institute and State University and Director of the Center for Study of Public Choice. A past president of the Southern Economic Association, his research interests are in political economy, collective decision making, and public finance. His many publications include *Fiscal Theory and Political Economy*, with Gordon Tullock *The Calculus of Consent, Cost and Choice*, and *The Limits of Liberty: Between Anarchy and Leviathan*.

ALFRED F. CHALK is professor of economics at Texas A&M University. An authority on the philosophical foundations of economics, his publications have appeared in such journals as the *Journal of Political Economy*, the *Southern Economic Journal*, and the *History of Political Economy*.

A. W. COATS is head of the Department of Economic and Social History at the University of Nottingham. An expert on American economic thought, his publications have appeared in the *American Economic Review*, the *Economic History Review*, and the *Journal of Political Economy*. He edited *The Classical Economists and Economic Policy*.

WILLIAM PATTON CULBERTSON, JR., is associate professor of economics at Louisiana State University. His publications have appeared in the *American Economic Review* and the *Economic Inquiry*, and his fields of research are in the economics of "black markets" and international trade. In addition, Dr. Culbertson is a consultant to the Louisiana Department of Conservation and has served on the faculties of the University of Texas and the University of Virginia.

S. HERBERT FRANKEL, a recognized authority on the economic problems of multiracial societies, held the chair in the Economics of Underdeveloped Countries at Nuffield College, University of Oxford, until his retirement in 1971. He was chairman of the Commission of Enquiry into the Mining Industry of Southern Rhodesia in 1945 and a member of the East Africa Royal Commission, 1953–1955. Among his extensive publications are *The Economic Impact on Underdeveloped Societies* and *Investment and the Return to Equity Capital in the South African Gold Mining Industry, 1887–1965.*

JOHN KENNETH GALBRAITH, the author of the Foreword to this volume, was, until his recent retirement, Paul M. Warburg Professor of Economics at Harvard University. A past president of the American Economic Association, he served as United States Ambassador to India, 1961–1963. Professor Galbraith is the author of many publications, among which are *American Capitalism, The Affluent Society, The New Industrial State,* and *Economics and the Public Purpose.* In 1965 he was elected to the National Institute of Arts and Letters.

RONALD MAX HARTWELL is Professorial Fellow of Nuffield College and Reader in Recent Social and Economic History in the University of Oxford. A past editor of the *Economic History Review* and an authority on the industrial revolution, his publications include *The Industrial Revolution and Economic Growth.* In addition, he served as editor for the Pelican Classics edition of David Ricardo's *Principles of Political Economy and Taxation,* for which he contributed a detailed Introduction.

MARION J. LEVY, JR., is Musgrave Professor of Sociology and International Affairs at the Woodrow Wilson School, Princeton University. A recognized scholar on oriental cultures, his principal research has been a comparative analysis of social structure. The author of *Modernization and the Structure of Society,* his other books include *Levy's Nine Laws of Disillusionment of the True Liberal.*

TALCOTT PARSONS is professor emeritus of sociology at Harvard University and a past president of the American Sociological Association. Among the most influential social scientists of the twentieth century, Professor Parsons has written *The Structure of Social Action* and *The System of Modern Societies.*

WALT WHITMAN ROSTOW is professor of economics and history at the University of Texas at Austin. He was a Rhodes Scholar at Balliol College, University of Oxford, from 1936 to 1938, and Harmsworth Professor of American History at Oxford in 1946–1947. He has served on the faculty of the Massachusetts Institute of Technology and was counselor and chairman of the Policy Planning Council, State Department, under President John F. Kennedy, and Special Assistant to President Lyndon B. Johnson. Among his many publications are *The Process of Economic Growth*, *The Stages of Economic Growth*, and *How It All Began*.

JOSEPH J. SPENGLER was, before his recent retirement, James Biddle Duke Professor of Economics at Duke University. He is a past president of the American Economic Association and a distinguished scholar in demographic change and the history of economic thought. His most influential essays are collected in *Population Economics*.

GORDON TULLOCK is editor of the journal *Public Choice* and professor of economics at Virginia Polytechnic Institute and State University. One of the pioneers in the application of economic theory to politics and law, Professor Tullock has served on the Council of the American Political Science Association and is the author of many publications, including (with J. M. Buchanan) *The Calculus of Consent*, *Private Wants, Public Means*, and *The Logic of the Law*.

Clarence Edwin Ayres:
A Chronological Bibliography

1917.   "The Nature of the Relationship between Ethics and Economics." Ph.D. Dissertation, University of Chicago.

BOOKS

1927.   *Science: The False Messiah*. Indianapolis: Bobbs-Merrill Co.
1929.   *Holier Than Thou: The Way of the Righteous*. Indianapolis: Bobbs-Merrill Co.
1932.   *Huxley*. New York: W. W. Norton and Co.
1938.   *The Problem of Economic Order*. New York: Farrar and Rinehart.
1944.   *The Theory of Economic Progress*. Chapel Hill: University of North Carolina Press.
1946.   *The Divine Right of Capital*. Boston: Houghton Mifflin Co.
1952.   *The Industrial Economy: Its Technological Basis and Institutional Destiny*. Boston: Houghton Mifflin Co.
1961.   *Toward a Reasonable Society: The Values of Industrial Civilization*. Austin: University of Texas Press.
1962.   *The Theory of Economic Progress*. 2nd ed., with "Foreword—1962," pp. v–xxv. New York: Schocken Books.
1973.   "Prolegomenon to Institutionalism." Preface to the new edition of *Science: The False Messiah* and *Holier Than Thou: The Way of the Righteous*. New York: Augustus M. Kelley, pp. iii–xii. [The two volumes are bound together with pagination identical to the originals.]

ARTICLES AND REVIEWS

1916–1917.   "Poverty and Riches." *International Journal of Ethics* 27:531–532.
1917–1918.   "The New Era of Fruitfulness in Ethical Thinking." *International Journal of Ethics* 28:373–392.
1918.   "The Epistemological Significance of Social Psychology." *Journal of Philosophy, Psychology and Scientific Methods*, January 17, pp. 35–44.

1918.   "The Function and Problems of Economic Theory." *Journal of Political Economy* 26 (January): 69–90.

1921.   "Instinct and Capacity—I." *Journal of Philosophy*, October 13, pp. 561–565.

1921.   "Instinct and Capacity—II." *Journal of Philosophy*, October 27, pp. 600–606.

1922.   "A Parable of Politeness." *New Republic*, January 24, pp. 230–231.

1922.   Review of *Human Nature and Conduct*, by John Dewey. *Journal of Philosophy*, August 17, pp. 469–475.

1923.   "John Dewey: Naturalist." *New Republic*, April 4, pp. 158–160.

1923.   "Matter Enough!" *New Republic*, August 29, p. 26.

1923.   "The New Spiritualism." *New Republic*, July 11, pp. 184–185.

1923.   "Pragmatic Sentiments." *New Republic*, December 12, pp. 72–74.

1923.   "Sampler Psychology." *New Republic*, June 13, pp. 77–78.

1924.   "Behind Coolidge: Butler." *New Republic*, June 18, pp. 96–98.

1924.   "The Best Kept Secret." *New Republic*, July 23, pp. 249–250.

1924.   "The Drama of Intelligence." *New Republic*, November 19, p. 300.

1924.   "Education by Celebrity." *New Republic*, September 3, pp. 16–18.

1924.   "The Father of Schoolmasters." *New Republic*, October 29, p. 229.

1924.   "Freudianalysis." *New Republic*, December 17, pp. 98–99.

1924.   "A Halo for Coronet." *New Republic*, August 20, pp. 365–366.

1924.   "Hush! It's Butler!" *New Republic*, September 10, p. 48.

1924.   "Introducing Intelligence." *New Republic*, December 31, pp. 150–151.

1924.   "My Stick, Please." *New Republic*, November 26, p. 21.

1924.   "Nostr' Omo." *New Republic*, August 27, p. 391.

1924.   "Papini Finito." *New Republic*, August 6, pp. 303–304.

1924.   "A People's Houses." *New Republic*, December 10, pp. 7–8.

1924.   "Pro Bono Nordico." *New Republic*, October 15, pp. 181–182.

1924.   "The Scholar's Homily." *New Republic*, July 2, pp. 164–165.

1924.   "Scholz of Reed." *New Republic*, October 22, pp. 197–199.

1924.   "Selectivity and Amplification." *New Republic*, November
        12, p. 276.

1924.   "What Science Warrants." *New Republic*, December 24,
        pp. 123–124.

1925.   "The Cambridge Fallacy." *New Republic*, June 10, pp. 80–81.

1925.   "A Clinical Thermometer." *New Republic*, August 5, pp.
        298–299.

1925.   "The College of Money-Changing." *New Republic*, February
        4, pp. 250–252 and 280–283.

1925.   "The Compleat Conservative." *New Republic*, March 4,
        pp. 46–47.

1925.   "Demi-Mondaine Science." *New Republic*, February 25, pp.
        23–24.

1925.   "The Egyptian Theory." *New Republic*, March 25, p. 128.

1925.   "47 at Yale." *New Republic*, May 20, pp. 337–339.

1925.   "Grooming the Universe." *New Republic*, May 27, pp. 24–
        25.

1925.   "Gypsy Anthropology." *New Republic*, January 21, pp. 235–
        236.

1925.   "The Human Aspect of Science." *New Republic*, April 15,
        pp. 14–15.

1925.   "Idealism on Demand." *New Republic*, January 14, pp. 203–
        204.

1925.   "The Liquidation of Psychology." *New Republic*, April 29,
        pp. 270–271.

1925.   "Main Themes and Criticism." *New Republic*, May 6, pp.
        296–297.

1925.   "Mrs. Austin's Genius." *New Republic*, June 3, pp. 53–54.

1925.   "The Mystery of Religion." *New Republic*, January 7, pp.
        178–179.

1925.   "The New Higher Criticism." *New Republic*, December 9,
        pp. 85–86.

1925.   "On the Firing Line of Science." *New Republic*, October 28,
        pp. 260–261.

1925.   "Our Aesthetic Shame." *New Republic*, June 17, pp. 105–
        106.

1925.   "Our Changing Monogamy." *New Republic*, February 18,
        p. 343.

1925.   "Philosophy: And This Was All the Harvest." *New Republic*,
        February 4, p. 11.

1925.   "Philosophy Au Naturel." *New Republic*, March 25, pp.
        129–131.

1925.   "Psychology Comes of Age." *New Republic*, February 11, pp. 316–317.

1925.   "Reading for Effect." *New Republic*, August 26, pp. 23–25.

1925.   "Rolling Mark Hopkins's Log." *New Republic*, May 20, pp. 347–348.

1925.   "The Shall to Believe." *New Republic*, May 13, pp. 322–323.

1925.   "Truant House." *New Republic*, September 2, pp. 41–42.

1925.   "The Truth about Nature." *New Republic*, September 9, pp. 75–76.

1925.   "Watson Explains Watson." *New Republic*, July 8, pp. 185–186.

1926.   "Abroad in Christianity." *New Republic*, January 27, pp. 276–277.

1926.   "Dayton's Aftermath." *New Republic*, May 12, pp. 378–380.

1926.   "For Hammock Consumption Only." *New Republic*, September 1, pp. 49–50.

1926.   "The Great Modern Omniscience." *New Republic*, June 2, pp. 65–66.

1926.   "Men, Flies and Statistics." *New Republic*, January 13, pp. 223–224.

1926.   "The Ordeal of History." *New Republic*, November 10, pp. 330–331.

1926.   "What Professors Think." *New Republic*, August 4, pp. 312–313.

1926.   "When and If." *New Republic*, October 27, pp. 276–277.

1927.   "Back to Locke!" *New Republic*, July 27, pp. 247–249.

1927.   "The Facts of Life." *New Republic*, December 14, pp. 105–107.

1927.   "God, by Grace of Church." *New Republic*, May 4, pp. 307–308.

1927.   "Gog, Magog and Evolution." *New Republic*, September 7, p. 76.

1927.   "Huxley and Huxley." *New Republic*, June 29, pp. 155–156.

1927.   "An Intellectual Genius." *New Republic*, April 13, pp. 227–228.

1927.   "An Outmoded Classic." *New Republic*, July 6, p. 182.

1927.   "Personalism." *New Republic*, November 23, p. 24.

1927.   "Psychology Is Called to Order." *New Republic*, January 5, pp. 200–201.

1927.   "The Saga of Science." *New Republic*, August 3, pp. 286–287.

1927.   "Scientific Gossip." *New Republic*, November 30, pp. 52–53.

1927. "A Scientist Off Duty." *New Republic*, August 17, p. 338.

1928. "The Gospel According to Darwin." *New Republic*, March 7, pp. 100–101.

1928. "Mr. Russell Recapitulates." *New Republic*, January 18, pp. 250–251.

1928. "Pale, Sickly Thought." *Bookman* 68:681–683.

1928. "The Quixotic Saint." *New Republic*, January 11, pp. 219–220.

1928. "Science and Life." *Religious Education* 23 (February): 99–108.

1929. "A Critique of Pure Science." In *Essays in Philosophy by Seventeen Doctors of Philosophy in the University of Chicago*, edited by Thomas Vernor Smith and William Kelley Wright. Chicago: Open Court Publishing Co.

1929. "A Gad-Fly." *New Republic*, June 19, p. 132.

1929. "Henry Was Right." *Bookman* 69:84–87.

1929. "A Preface to Culture." *New Republic*, December 18, pp. 109–110.

1929. "Who Owns Middletown?" *New Republic*, August 21, pp. 8–10.

1929. "Why We Believe." *New Republic*, May 22, pp. 47–48.

1929–1930. "Philosophy and Genius." *International Journal of Ethics* 40:263–271.

1929–1930. Review of *The Quest for Certainty*, by John Dewey. *International Journal of Ethics* 40:425–433.

1930. "Domesticity." In *The New Generation: The Intimate Problems of Modern Parents and Children*, edited by V. F. Calverton and S. D. Schmalhausen. New York: Macaulay Co., pp. 365–401.

1931. "The Irony of Science." *Forum* 86 (September): 160–166.

1931. "The Lion and the Lamb." *Forum* 86 (August): 124–128.

1931. "Whither Bound?" In *Economic Behavior: An Institutional Approach*, by members of the Department of Economics, Washington Square College, New York University. Vol. 2, pp. 475–504, unsigned essay. Cambridge, Mass.: Houghton Mifflin Co., Riverside Press.

1933. "The Basis of Economic Statesmanship." *American Economic Review* 23 (June): 200–216.

1934. Review of *A History of the Economic Institutions of Modern Europe*, by Frederick L. Nussbaum. *Southwestern Social Science Quarterly* 15 (June): 84–85.

1934.   "Values: Ethical and Economic." *International Journal of Ethics* 45 (July): 452–454.

1934–1935.   "Confusion Thrice Confounded." *International Journal of Ethics* 45:356–358.

1934–1935.   "Moral Confusion in Economics." *International Journal of Ethics* 45:170–199.

1935.   "The Gospel of Technology." In *American Philosophy Today and Tomorrow*, edited by Horace Kallen and Sidney Hook, pp. 24–42. New York: Lee Furman.

1936.   "The Ethics of Competition," review of *Ethics of Competition*, by F. H. Knight. *International Journal of Ethics* 46 (April): 364–370.

1936.   "Fifty Years' Developments in Ideas of Human Nature and Motivation." *American Economic Review* 26 (March): 224–236.

1936.   *The New Republic Anthology 1915–1935*, edited by Groff Conklin. New York: Dodge Publishing Co. [Reprints a number of Ayres's *New Republic* essays.]

1936.   "The Organization of the Government's Consumer Services." Unpublished memorandum for the Consumers Division of the NRA. Washington, D.C., September.

1936.   Review of *The Frustration of Science*, by Sir Daniel Hall et al. *International Journal of Ethics* 46 (January): 241–242.

1937.   "Middletown Comes Clean." *Southern Review* 3:39–50.

1938.   "The Grand Tradition," review of *What Man Has Made of Man*, by Mortimer J. Adler. *New Republic*, February 16, p. 52.

1938–1939.   "Talking of Cities." *Southern Review* 4:227–234.

1939.   "America and the Next War." *Forum*, June 14, p. 149.

1939.   "Dewey and His 'Studies in Logical Theory.'" In *Books That Changed Our Minds*, edited by Malcolm Cowley and Bernard Smith, pp. 110–126. New York: Doubleday, Doran.

1939.   "Dewey: Master of the Commonplace." *New Republic*, January 18, pp. 303–306.

1939.   "Philosophic Garland," review of *Intelligence in the Modern World*, by John Dewey. *New Republic*, May 17, pp. 51–52.

1939.   "The Principles of Economic Strategy." *Southern Economic Journal* 5 (April): 460–470.

1940.   "The Wealth of Nations." *Southwestern Social Science Quarterly* 21 (June): 1–9.

1941. "The Economics of the Total State." *Southwestern Social Science Quarterly* 22 (September): 107–115.

1942. "Economic Value and the Scientific Synthesis." *American Journal of Economics and Sociology* 1 (July): 343–360.

1943. "Capitalism in Retrospect." *Southern Economic Journal* 9 (April): 293–301.

1943. "Economic Essentials of a Lasting Peace." *Southwestern Social Science Quarterly* 24 (June): 68–79.

1943. "The Path of Progress." *Southwest Review* 28 (Spring): 229–244.

1943. "The Significance of Economic Planning." In *The Development of Collective Enterprise*, edited by Seba Eldridge, pp. 460–481. Lawrence: University of Kansas Press.

1943. "Technology and Progress." *Antioch Review* 3 (Spring): 6–20.

1943. "The Twilight of the Price System." *Antioch Review* 3: 162–181.

1944. "Academic Freedom in Texas." *New Republic*, December 4, pp. 740–742.

1945. "Addendum to *The Theory of Economic Progress*." *American Economic Review* 35 (December): 937–942.

1945. "Ordeal of the Social Sciences: Reply to D. L. Miller." *Southwestern Social Science Quarterly* 25 (March): 247–257.

1945. "What's the Matter with Texas?" *New Republic*, September 3, pp. 275–277.

1946. "The Impact of the Great Depression on Economic Thinking." *American Economic Review* 36 (May): 112–125.

1946. Review of *Economic Mind in American Civilization*, vols. 1–2, 1606–1865, by Joseph Dorfman. *Yale Law Journal* 55 (June): 855–858.

1947. "Are Professors Dangerous?" *Southwest Review* 32 (Winter): 8–15.

1947. "Freedom Means Planning." *New Leader*, January 4.

1948. "The New Economics." *Southwest Review* 33 (Summer): 223–232.

1949. "Instrumental Economics." *New Republic*, October 17, pp. 18–20.

1949. "Piecemeal Revolution." *Southwestern Social Science Quarterly* 30 (June): 12–17.

1949. Review of *Economic Mind in American Civilization*, vol. 3, 1865–1918, by Joseph Dorfman. *Saturday Review of Literature*, April 23, p. 19.

1949.   "Twin Bases for a Limited Capitalism." *Antioch Review* 6:
        17–31.
1949.   "The Value Economy." In *Value: A Cooperative Inquiry*,
        edited by Ray Lepley. New York: Columbia University
        Press. [Also, criticisms and rejoinders by Ayres.]
1950.   "The Values of Social Scientists." *Journal of Social Issues*
        6, no. 4, pp. 17–20.
1950.   "What Should Teachers Swear?" *Southwest Review* 25
        (Autumn): 240–248.
1951.   "The Co-ordinates of Institutionalism." *American Economic
        Review* 41 (May): 47–55.
1951.   "Economic Pioneer." *Saturday Review of Literature*, July
        14, pp. 18–19.
1952.   "Creeping Socialism: A Worm's Eye View." *Southwest Re-
        view* 37 (Autumn): 280–288.
1952.   "The Integration of Industrial Society." In *The Cleavage in
        Our Culture: Studies in Scientific Humanism in Honor of
        Max Otto*, edited by Frederick Burkhardt, pp. 165–177.
        Boston: Beacon Press.
1953.   "Dynamic Theorists at Work." *Saturday Review*, September
        19, pp. 27–28.
1953.   "The Role of Technology in Economic Theory." *American
        Economic Review* 43 (May): 279–287.
1953.   "Technology and Progress." In *Antioch Review Anthology*,
        edited by Paul Bixler, pp. 349–362. Cleveland: World
        Publishing Co. [Reprint of Ayres's 1943 *Antioch Review*
        article.]
1954.   "Can Education Stay Secular?" *New Leader*, June 21, pp.
        21–23.
1955.   "The Core of Conservatism." *New Leader*, January 10,
        pp. 18–20.
1955.   "The Secular Faith of Horace Kallen." *New Leader*, May
        2, p. 28.
1955.   "The 'Security' Menace," review of *Government and Sci-
        ence*, by Don K. Price. *New Leader*, January 31, p. 28.
1956.   "The Classical Tradition Versus Economic Growth." *South-
        western Social Science Quarterly* 36 (March): 343–350.
1956.   "Reply to Professor Ferguson." *Southwestern Social Science
        Quarterly* 37 (September): 170.
1957.   "The Conflict of Values." *Colorado Quarterly* 6 (Autumn):
        178–187.

1957.   "Institutional Economics: Discussion." *American Economic Review* 47 (May): 26.

1957.   "The Pestilence of Moral Agnosticism." *Southwest Review* 42 (Spring): 116–125.

1958.   "Further Explorations in Monopolistic-Competitive Price Theory: Discussion." *American Economic Review* 48 (May): 486–488.

1958.   "Larger Forces of Learning." *Saturday Review*, July 5, pp. 12–13.

1958.   Review of *Economics and Social Reform*, by Abram L. Harris. *Ethics* 69, no. 1 (October): 64–67.

1958.   "Veblen's Theory of Instincts Reconsidered." In *Thorstein Veblen: A Critical Reappraisal*, edited by Douglas F. Dowd. Ithaca: Cornell University Press.

1959.   "Excellence in an Industrial Society." *Southwest Review* 44 (Spring): 139–149.

1959.   "The Industrial Way of Life." *Texas Quarterly* 2 (Summer): 1–19.

1959.   "The Peril of the Social Sciences." *Graduate Journal* 2 (Spring): 109–114.

1960.   "Economic History and Economic Development: Comments." In *Economic Growth: Rationale, Problems, Cases*, edited by Eastin Nelson, pp. 211–214. Austin: University of Texas Press.

1960.   "From a 'Classical' Liberal." *New Leader*, June 20, pp. 26–28.

1960.   "Hamilton: Impulse and Paradox." *New Leader*, March 7, pp. 17–18.

1960.   "Institutionalism and Economic Development." *Southwestern Social Science Quarterly* 41 (June): 45–62.

1961.   "Economic Progress and the American South." *Economic Development and Cultural Change* 9 (January): 197–199.

1961.   "Epistemological Problems of Economics." *Southern Economic Journal* 28 (October): 199–202.

1962.   "Reply." *Southern Economic Journal* 28 (April): 387.

1963.   "The Legacy of Thorstein Veblen." In *Institutional Economics: Veblen, Commons and Mitchell Reconsidered*, by Joseph Dorfman et al. Berkeley: University of California Press.

1963.   "Reason and Unreason." *Graduate Journal* 5 (Winter): 280–300.

1963.   Review of *Market Theory and the Price System*, by I. M.
         Kirzner. *American Economic Review* 53 (September): 755–
         756.
1964.   Contribution to the symposium "A Man, His Land, and His
         Work: Walter Prescott Webb." *Graduate Journal* 6 (Win-
         ter): 51–55.
1965.   "Individualism—or Something: A Plea for Verbal Plural-
         ism." In *Innocence and Power: Individualism in Twenti-
         eth Century America*, edited by Gordon H. Mills. Austin:
         University of Texas Press.
1965.   "Nature and Man: The Emergence of the Social Sciences."
         In the University of Denver Centennial Symposium, *The
         Responsible Individual and a Free Society in an Expand-
         ing Universe*. Published for the University of Denver by
         Big Mountain Press, Denver.
1966.   "Guaranteed Income: An Institutionalist View." In *The
         Guaranteed Income: Next Step in Economic Evolution?*
         edited by Robert Theobald, pp. 161–174. Garden City,
         New York: Doubleday and Co.
1966.   "Nature and Significance of Institutionalism." *Antioch Re-
         view* 26 (Spring): 70–90.
1966.   "Theory of Institutional Adjustment." *Texas Quarterly* 9
         (Spring): 125–136.
1967.   "Ideological Responsibility." *Journal of Economic Issues* 1
         (June): 3–11.
1967.   "The Theory of Institutional Adjustment." In *Institutional
         Adjustment*, edited by Carey C. Thompson. Austin: Uni-
         versity of Texas Press.
1968.   Foreword to *Economics of Dissent*, by Ben B. Seligman.
         Chicago: Quadrangle Books.
1968.   "The Price System and Public Policy." *Journal of Economic
         Issues* 2 (September): 342–344.
1968.   Review of *The Causes of the Industrial Revolution in Eng-
         land*, by R. M. Hartwell. *Journal of Economic Issues* 2
         (June): 252–254.
1968.   "Some Reflections on Regionalism." *Social Science Quar-
         terly* 49 (June): 33–35.
1969.   Review of *Thorstein Veblen: The Carleton College Seminar
         Essays*, edited by Carlton Qualey. *Journal of Economic
         History* 29 (June): 386–387.
1970.   "Beyond the Market Economy: Building Institutions That
         Work." *Social Science Quarterly* 50 (March): 1055–1057.

1970.   "Institutionalism and Economic Development." *Social Science Quarterly* 50 (March): 1037–1054. [Reprint of Ayres's article in *Southwestern Social Science Quarterly*, June 1960.]

1971.   "Notes and Communications." *Journal of Economic Issues* 5 (September): 96.

1971.   "The Place of the Market Economy in Institutional Thought." *Social Science Quarterly* 51 (March): 995–996.

1971.   Review of *The Challenge of World Poverty: A World Poverty Program in Outline*, by Gunnar Myrdal. *Political Science Quarterly* 86 (September): 549–550.

1972.   "Economics-Philosophical Background." In *Collier's Encyclopedia*, 8:540–541. [First published in the 1959 edition.]

Index

Absolutism, 29, 151, 156
Academic freedom, 15–18, 32
Adams, Henry, 121
Africa, economic development of, 63, 64–68
Aggregate demand, 101
Aggregated flows, 85
Aggregate income analysis, 83, 88
Agricultural land, 99, 124; marginal yield of, 96
Agriculture, 100
American Civil Liberties Union, 17
American economics, regional "schools" of, 25
Amherst College, 5, 175
Anti-Equilibrium (Kornai), 85
Antivivisectionist movement, 142–143
Ashton, T. S., 49
Association for Evolutionary Economics, 19, 24, 37
Atkins, Willard, 7–8
Autonomous investment, 84
Ayres, Clarence Edwin: academic freedom and, 15–18, 32; "Americanness" of, 23; appearance of, 4, 10; assessment of, 23–48; biographical data on, 3–22; children of, 7; comparison of, with Veblen, 24–26; death of, 20; economic concepts of, 30–43; economic criticism and, 33–35; as economic historian, 50–52; on economists, 46; editorship of, 6–7, 30; education of, 3, 4; faculty appointments of, 5, 8; on industrial revolution, 49–62; influences on, 10, 14, 23, 25–28, 30, 37, 45, 46, 50, 75; as institutionalist, 10, 23–25, 35–36, 43; institutional theory formulation and, 9, 12; intellectual interests of, 6–7, 10; marriages of, 5, 6; New Deal and, 10–11, 14–15, 30; optimism of, 31, 32, 46; personality of, 3–4, 6; pessimism of, 138; philosophical presuppositions of, 25–30, 37; political views of, 30; as "radical,"

16–18, 30; as rancher, 7; readings of, 49–50; research objectives of, 35, 36; retirement of, 19; social theory of, 75–76; status of, as economist, 33, 42; and *technology* definition, 29–30, 45; and University of Texas appointment, 8; as university teacher, 5, 10, 175, 181–186; on Viet Nam, 18–19; work habits of, 9–10. Works: *The Divine Right of Capital*, 22, 33, 39; *Holier Than Thou: The Way of the Righteous*, 8; *Huxley*, 8–9, 135, 136, 142; *The Industrial Economy: Its Technological Basis and Institutional Destiny*, 22, 35, 39, 50; *The Problem of Economic Order*, 12, 49–50, 57, 59; *Science: The False Messiah*, 8, 26, 106, 135, 136–145; *The Theory of Economic Progress*, 12–13, 33, 37, 39, 43, 50, 58, 64, 73, 78; *Toward a Reasonable Society*, 13, 29, 75
Ayres, Mrs. Clarence Edwin (Anna Bryan), 5; death of, 7
Ayres, Mrs. Clarence Edwin (Gwendolen Jane), 6, 9, 10
Ayres, Edith. *See* Copeland, Mrs. Morris
Ayres, Ernest, 3
Ayres, William S., 3
Ayres, Mrs. William S. (Emma Young), 3
Ayres-Knight discussion, 12, 163–174

Balance of payments, 103
Behavioral models, 118, 166–167, 169
Benedict, Ruth, *Patterns of Culture*, 183
Bentham, Jeremy, 148
Beveridge, William, *Full Employment in a Free Society*, 30
Biosphere, in growth limitation, 115–133
Black, Joseph, 92
Boehm-Bawerkian analysis, 117
Brady, Robert, 8
Bruner, Jerome S., 70